The Secret of New Heaven

In the teachings of ignorant scholarship and religion, mankind is serving fake gods and fighting like beasts against each other. There has been no studies nor religion until 1980.

The human being is not animal species nor the created thing from dirt. Everyone is the Son of God and a Noble Being.

A Korean found that human ego is the spirit of desire, Satan, and our original spirit was the Holy Spirit. So He cries out that the Holy Spirit under the slavery of Satan should resurrect after overcoming the Satan, self.

Things of self-centered are of Satan-centered and are products of it. Introducing, things of God-centered in this book.

When people understand the new words and our standpoint shift from Satan-centered to God-centered, the world will turn to the world of God.

Contents

Foreword..7

I The Era of Light & the Secret of the Universe....................10
    The Era of Brilliant Light is coming here   10
    Neo-humans would reveal the secret of the universe   35
    False Self-awareness & breaking fixed notions   39

II The New Era is Opened by the Hidden Manna 42
    The Secret of the hidden manna   42
    The Holy Dew Spirit and the Immortal world   48

III The Secret of the Victor & the Testimonies of saints 50
    The seven secrets of the Victor in the Bible   52
    The testimonies of Neo-humans   56

IV The Secret of the Five covenants & Other existence................80
    I will remove worldwide communism   85
    I will halt the monsoon rains in South Korea   91
    I will protect Korea from typhoons   92
    I will make Korean harvests abundant   94
    I will prevent wars in Korea   95

V The Secret of Number 5 & The Lost Tribe of Israelite 99
    The secret of Arirang   100
    The secret of the Hanryu   101
    The secret of the lost tribe of Dan   106
    The secret of the Rose of Sharon, Mugunghwa   129
    Gyeokamyourok, the master key of prophetic books   130

VI The Secret of the Pure Land of Utmost Happiness 135
- The secret of the Amrita Sutra — 135
- The hidden secrets of the Nirvana Sutra — 145

VII The Philosophy of Immortality by the Principle of Blood 164
- The principle of immortality and the secret of genetics — 166
- The principle of immortality by the spectrum of blood — 171
- The new view of the past, the present and the afterlife — 175
- The Hanmoum(One body) philosophy — 181
- The Law of Liberty and the secret of killing Satan — 187

VIII New Heaven & New Words 192
- The New Words by the Victor — 192
- New Songs in New Heaven — 287

Conclusion 312

Terminology 314

Read Hangul in an hour 324

The secret keys

1. Human's mind	15
2. Human's hometown	15
3. A UFO & a UFO rider	18
4. Sin and Self-awareness	22
5. New food of Neo-humans	25
6. Radiocarbon dating technology	33
7. Drawing New Heaven	39
8. The white stone and the promised land in the Bible	44
9. The root of human being	49
10. The fruit of life	50
11. Savior's name	51
12. The Victor in the Bible	52
13. The number five	54
14. The Savior's nation and chosen people	55
15. The number 144000	56
16. The true teacher, the Victor Savior	60
17. The fruit of life	61
18. The belief from God	64
19. New Jerusalem	73
20. Armageddon War	84
21. The creation of Hangeul	105
22. Death	170
23. Happiness and laughing	173
24. Healthy life	181
25. Bright philosophy of Neo-humans	185
26. Oxygen and H_2O	188
27. Satan and Ego	190
28. The Golden bell	193
29. New song & new heaven's lotus	287
30. The lost tribe, Dan	308
31. Zion	310

VI The Secret of the Pure Land of Utmost Happiness 135
    The secret of the Amrita Sutra   135
    The hidden secrets of the Nirvana Sutra   145

VII The Philosophy of Immortality by the Principle of Blood 164
    The principle of immortality and the secret of genetics   166
    The principle of immortality by the spectrum of blood   171
    The new view of the past, the present and the afterlife   175
    The Hanmoum(One body) philosophy   181
    The Law of Liberty and the secret of killing Satan   187

VIII New Heaven & New Words 192
    The New Words by the Victor   192
    New Songs in New Heaven   287

Conclusion 312

Terminology 314

Read Hangul in an hour 324

The secret keys

1. Human's mind — 15
2. Human's hometown — 15
3. A UFO & a UFO rider — 18
4. Sin and Self-awareness — 22
5. New food of Neo-humans — 25
6. Radiocarbon dating technology — 33
7. Drawing New Heaven — 39
8. The white stone and the promised land in the Bible — 44
9. The root of human being — 49
10. The fruit of life — 50
11. Savior's name — 51
12. The Victor in the Bible — 52
13. The number five — 54
14. The Savior's nation and chosen people — 55
15. The number 144000 — 56
16. The true teacher, the Victor Savior — 60
17. The fruit of life — 61
18. The belief from God — 64
19. New Jerusalem — 73
20. Armageddon War — 84
21. The creation of Hangeul — 105
22. Death — 170
23. Happiness and laughing — 173
24. Healthy life — 181
25. Bright philosophy of Neo-humans — 185
26. Oxygen and H_2O — 188
27. Satan and Ego — 190
28. The Golden bell — 193
29. New song & new heaven's lotus — 287
30. The lost tribe, Dan — 308
31. Zion — 310

Sermons

Dec 31, 1991	145
Aug 25, 2001	193
Feb 8, 2001	203
Oct 17, 1989	217
Mar 1, 2002	227
Oct 10, 2000	235
Oct 20, 2000	241
Feb 27, 2001	248
June 7, 2001	254
July 30, 2001	264
Sep 21, 2001	273
Nov 18, 2001	282

Hymns

Prophets and kings line up	281
Sinners captivated in Satan's prison for 6000 years	287
Please pour the grace of Fresh Water and the Holy Dew Spirit	288
When we see wild land bloom like roses	288
Hymn of the Savior	290
Come to the light of the Holy Spirit	290
The new wind	292
Neither pains nor death	292
The shining morning star	294
How to	294
Hymn of Jeongdoryeong	296
How long time we have been waiting	298
Fox in mountains have caves	298
All my physical worries	300
Hymn of Victory	300
The prayers	302
We are the offspring of Dan tribe, the son of Jacob, Israel	302
Our mommy the Olive Tree	304
Mugunghwa	306

Foreword

So far, there have been only human religions, which are the products of the thoughts of ignorant people who do not even know what God is. The religion of God is supposed to be formed by the reincarnated God and led by Him; it aims to attain immortality and to build heaven.

By the pouring of oil, the Bible is understandable; religions by humans which is not the element of understanding are proceeding out of all scriptures and the Bible. As a result, nobody knows heaven and the theory of salvation, and nobody has accomplished immortality on the earth so far. Only God, the basis of wisdom, can say science and religion, interpret the Bible, all scriptures, and prophetic books.

Now, I will introduce the words of God that came to Korea wearing a human's body. The God is the Savior, the seventh angel, who opened the seventh seal in the Bible. He is not only the God of alpha but also the God of omega. Plus He is the Maitreya Buddha in the Buddhist Books. The symbol of the Savior and the Maitreya Buddha is the *Sweet Dew*. The Savior is pouring out the *Sweet Dew* to save people in Korea now. Heaven was already built in Korea because wherever God resides is heaven according to the Bible.

Just like ordinary people have secrets, there are secrets in the universe. Also, God has hidden secrets to complete his project to change the mortal world into an immortal one by defeating its enemy, the spirit of death. I will tell you about the secrets of God in detail in this book.

Although the Bible says that God was almighty and created the world, people also believe so. There is a different explanation. In the book of *Gyeokamyourok* God neither created the world nor was almighty. The Korean prophetic book with 100 percent accuracy says that God, in the beginning, was weaker than Satan, causing the God of light to lose to Satan (the spirit of death).

As Satan overpowered God, the Saviour God hid the secrets of heaven in the Bible, the Buddhist scriptures, and the prophetic books. These secrets have passed down to this day through a few prophets and chosen people.

Now, it is the time to reveal the hidden secrets of heaven because a new era is approaching. What one must keep in mind is that God hid His circumstances of the beginning and His strategies to recover the lost heaven; a foretold says the hero will come and uncover the hidden to explain clearly in a man of Korean, the chosen people.

The *Victor Savior* has already revealed the top secrets of heaven, the hero of all scriptures for 40 years. 韓流 *Hanryu* (the Korean wave which is generating across the world) is ringing a golden bell to announce a new era. Due to the advent of the *Victor God*, humanity's long-cherished wishes will come true; the culture of immortality will take root.

The Author, Ariel Han, has researched for 20 years about new Korean religions as a researcher of faiths and prophecies and as a journalist of KTN; He has experienced the culture of immortality that is generating in Korea. Ariel Han has studied Korean new religions by examining the Bible, the Buddhist scriptures, and the prophetic books of the world. While his studying, he found that all predictions in the Bible, the Buddhist scriptures, and the predictive books have come to reality in the Victory Altar in *Sosa* (meaning the white stone) Korea. Ariel felt a heavy responsibility to send the message of God as a journalist. So he made up his mind to publish this book.

Co-author Angela Kim, a school teacher, has studied Korean new religions for 20 years. She found that the words of the Savior are the truth, which all humans should learn and experience to attain perfect happiness and eternal life. Hence Angela felt a vital assignment to announce the fact as a person who knew the truth early. So she writes this book.

This book will be good news to the people of the world because a new era when people will be reborn as *Neo-humans* is approaching. The blood of humans is that of the *Trinity*. So everybody is one tree of the *Trinity*. Therefore, she is campaigning to make all humans be one and announcing the everlasting culture of *Neo-humans* to the world. While she writes this book, she highlights crucial things that are inscribed in detail in Key points throughout the book. So you will see some contents multiple times.

Chapter I
The Era of Light & the Secret of the Universe

The Era of Brilliant Light is coming here

The era of light is approaching soon. There are two kinds of light. One is straight. It goes 300,000 km per second. However, the light that I will speak of in this book is not the worldly light but the light transcending self-awareness(ego), which saves people from death. The shining goes in spiral form, and its penetrating power is so strong that it can pass through any material; its name is Neutron-light.

Sunlight and electricity light is the light of dark spirit and the energy of *yin-yang*. The light cannot penetrate obstacles. When the sun shines on the east side of the earth, it is night on the west of the planet because the sunlight cannot go through the earth. So there is night and day on the planet. The light cannot go through things; there are shadows behind objects.

Initially, humans were Neutron-light itself, which is God. So they could fly freely at their will and change their shape as they wanted. However, the Neutron-light was captivated by the spirit of Darkness (*yin-yang* which is the spirit of male and female and is the spirit of death). So the Neutron-light came to be divided into female and male and be confined to all things such as humans, stars, and so on.

Among them, humans are the houses of God, so they emit light. All things live on the aura that comes from humans. It is the Life of God in all things that have perished since the captivity 6000 years ago.

Fortunately, God who is the prime ancestor of humans overcame the spirit of death and appeared in Korea as the almighty Savior of brilliant light to redeem people.

Due to the advent of the Victor, humans came to have new hope. The hope is being reborn as the *Holy Spirit* and returning to human's original form, the Neutron-light. That is, humanity is facing the era when he is reborn as the *Holy Spirit*, living happily and enjoying eternal life in the body of light.

To get immortality, people should have a new philosophy and listen to the new words of life and the new secrets of New Heaven from Korea.

Joel 2: 28-30 of the Bible says, "Even on my servants, both men and women, I will pour out my Spirit in those days. I will show wonders in the heavens and on the earth, blood and fire and billows of smoke." The wonders of heavens and earth take the shape of the *Holy Dew Spirit*.

Neo-humans are crowding to the *Holy Dew Spirit* because by receiving it; their blood is turned immortal. The immortal blood forms immortal cells; the immortal cells form immortal bodies. Finally, these people's bodies will change into the immortal that emit eternal light.

Let's confirm predictions in the scriptures.

The advent of the *Sweet Dew* (the *Holy Dew Spirit*) means that the predictions of the Bible, the Buddhist scriptures, and the prophetic of Korea come true.

1. The Sweet Dew Water which is predicted in the Buddhist scriptures

The *Bomoon* part(普門編) of the *Dharma Flower Sutra* says in Chinese " 澍甘露法雨 滅除煩惱焰 . "

Interpretation: The rain of *Dharma* eradicates Humans' agonies and desires. Everybody can reach *nirvana* by receiving the light of the *Reincarnate Maitreya Buddha*. Chapter 4:60 of the part the nature of the *Maitreya Buddha* of the *Great Nirvana Sutra* volume 9 interprets, "If the light of great *nirvana* permeates into the pore of people, although people do not try to reach *nirvana*, they can reach it." The *Great Nirvana Sutra* calls this great *nirvana* (nirvana with living bodies).

Pic 1-1. Sweet Dew (甘露) Photos in the Great Nirvana Sutra

If people eat the *Sweet Dew* (the *Holy Dew Spirit*), they will not die.

Chapter 4:2 of the part of nature of the *Reincarnate Maitreya Buddha* of the Great Nirvana Sutra volume 5 has, "dying means the collapsing of bodies and finishing life-span. However, death is not here. That is, this is the *Sweet Dew*（甘露）. The *Sweet Dew* is true nirvana."

The *Reincarnate Maitreya Buddha* is the man who accomplished this good deed. Like you looked at the pictures above, the light of Great Nirvana looks like dew. So, most of the Buddhist scriptures expressed the brightness of Great Nirvana as the Sweet Dew（甘露）.

Therefore, the Great Nirvana is the *Sweet Dew*.

2. The hidden manna in the Bible

When the *Holy Dew Spirit* appears, death perishes on the earth. The hidden manna is the symbol that heralds the era of the new heaven and New Jerusalem.

Isaiah 26:19 says, "But your dead will live; their bodies will rise. You who dwell in the dust wake up and shout for joy. Your dew is like the dew of the morning; the earth will give birth to her dead." (Refer to the picture of the descending of the *Sweet Dew* Photo-1)

3. The Essence of the Sweet Dew predicted in Gyeokamyourok（格菴遺錄）, a Korean prophetic book with 100 percent accuracy.

If people eat the Sweet Dew, they will not die. The part of the song of the *Sweet Dew* of *Gyeokamyourok* sings "Where is the *elixir*, which *Qinshihuangdi* of a Qin dynasty and *Emperor Wu* of Han dynasty（秦皇漢武）sought? The *Sweet Dew* is like seven-rainbow-colored cloud and morning mist. It is the *Sweet Dew*（海印）. The three kinds of abundant grace which are fire, rain, and dew are the *Sweet Dew*."

The book predicts that *Sweet Dew* is an elixir that has been passed down as a legend, it is an immortal medicine. The *Sweet Dew* falls though it is on a sunny day; it is like sweet cloud and sweet dew, which makes people neither grow old nor die.

The next page introduces the extraction from the first part of *Gyeokamyourok*.

Pic 1-2. Gyeokamyourok (格菴遺錄) a Korean prophetic book

The essence of the Sweet Dew is the Reincarnate Maitreya Buddha, the Lord, and *Jeongdoryeong* (正道靈), the hero who speaks in the right way.

Sipseungga (十勝歌, a song in the *Gyeoamyourok*) describes the essence of the Sweet Dew as follows.

"The predicted great hero in *The Great Hidden Scriptures* (八萬高麗大藏經) is *Jeongdoryeong*, who pours down the Sweet Dew. *Jeongdoryeong* is *Sipseung* (十勝). The Counselor (prophet) of the Bible is the *Sipseung*, *Sipseung* is the Victor God. The western prophet in the Bible is the *Sipseung*. In spite the names of the

Savior of Confucianism, Buddhism, and Christianity are different, the man who carries the secret to unite all religions at the end of times is the *Sipseung*. That is, the Reincarnate Maitreya Buddha (彌勒佛) is the *Victor God* (十勝). *Jeongdoryeong* is the *Victor God* (十勝). The *Lord God* (上帝) is the *Victor God* (十勝).

The lyric interpreted above mean that the Reincarnate Maitreya Buddha, *Jeongdoryeong*, and the *Lord God* are all the same hero with the *Sweet Dew*.

The Secret Key to New Heaven's door

The Secret of humans' mind

Why do humans hate death?

Our first ancestors, Adam and Eve, were Gods, they lived in happiness as immortals. In humans, there is the blood of the ancestors who lived forever in infinite happiness; the world was happy, immortal, and pleasant. So humans have a mindset of hating death.

The Secret of humans' hometown

Before people became humans, what existence they were?

The reason people want to live in infinite happiness forever is that humanity's hometown is the Garden of Eden. That is, they were Gods who lived in joy. So humans cannot be happy in the mortal world. Therefore, nobody has enjoyed true happiness in the history of humankind.

Then, why does humanity live a miserable life? Humanity's self-awareness(ego) is the spirit of Satan. So everyone tries to be happy, but nobody is happy. Self-awareness(ego) is a sad, angry, jealous, and ignorant spirit. So Satan cannot be satisfied.

Happiness belongs only to God. The human spirit is self-awareness(ego); the spirit of Satan. So if we remove Satan; self-awareness(ego), only God exists in us, then, the Garden of Eden replaces our minds and heaven sets in our bodies. So, the Bible has words, "nor will people say, 'Here it is,' or 'here it is,' as the kingdom of God within you."

4. Who is the Reincarnate Maitreya Buddha?

According to the Buddhist scriptures, the Reincarnate Maitreya Buddha is the man who comes to the world in the year 3007 after *Sakyamuni* (the creator of Buddhism) died.

Bisangpum part （非常品） of *Jeungil Sutra*（增一阿含經） volume 49 says, "In the future, Buddha will come; His name is the Reincarnate Maitreya Buddha." *Gungeullon* part （弓乙論, an article in the *Gyeokamyourok*) predicts, "The Reincarnate Maitreya Buddha is the religious sect leader of all *dharma*, He will come with a principle to unite Confucianism, Buddhism, and Christianity."

Also, *Sipseungga* part （十勝歌, a song in the *Gyeokamyourok*) sings the Reincarnate Maitreya Buddha is *Sipseung*, *Jeongdoryeong* is *Sipseung*, and the Most Highest of coming again is also *Sipseung*.

---

1. He is the essence of three aspects which are; God, Adam and Eve. Adam and Eve are refering to the two characters with in the book of Genesis in the Bible

What is *Sipseung*? It consists of Sip(十 means Ten) and Seung(勝 implies victory). Here Sip(十 of Ten) means God, so it symbolizes the Victorious God who at last overcomes Satan which holds the power of death.

Then what did God win? *Dobusinin* (挑符神人, an article in the *Gyeokamyourok*) wrote, "When the Victor *Jeongdoryeong* (十勝道靈) appears, the world will be noisy with right and wrong." *Sipseung* means the *Victor God* who overcame Satan which hid in His body.

The essence of the *Sweet Dew* in the Bible is the Spirit of the *Victor Savior*. The Bible speaks about the nature of Dew precisely. Hosea 14: 5 has, "I will be like the dew to Israel; he will blossom like a lily." That is, I (God) become the dew to Israel (the Victor in Hebrew). Also, the man who pours down the dew is the Savior as a symbol of lily.

The Victor who pours down the Dew seems like a man, but He is not a human according to *Malunlon*(末運論, an article of *Gyokamyourok*). It says, "似人不人天神降， 三神救世主" means the man who pours down the *Sweet Dew* seems like a man but is the *Trinity*. One who came down wearing a human's body. He is just the *Trinity* and the *Victor Savior*.

In other words, the advent of the *Sweet Dew* means that the *Trinity* came to the world wearing a human's body to save people who live in the pains of birth, aging, diseases, and death. Therefore, the advent of the Sweet Dew means that the *Victor*(天生子) who all humanity has waited for came to the world to blow the last trumpet.

Key 3

Secret of a UFO & a UFO rider

Who is a UFO rider?

The words "everything is done up to one's resolution" are right. Everything goes upon your mind. To do so, you must have a firm conviction. If you have a wish fixed on flying without giving up, you can fly. The *Victor God* flew into the universe before He came to the world. Is it a lie? No, it isn't.

"This man flew into the universe before He came here. So when This man(the Victor Cho Hee Sung) goes to Japan, a UFO flies there. When He is in *Fukuoka*, a UFO flies there," The Victor God said.

This theory is exact from the fact that those who cultivate themselves doing hypogastric breathing can make themselves float and fly. Do you know the principle? Do you know where they concentrate? They concentrate on the center of their head. Then they can fly. Have you ever seen the scene?

Did a UFO fly here and there in Korea? Do you understand? It isn't a lie. Why did UFOs fly in *Fukuoka* and *Shimonoseki* when This man was there? So it was on Japanese Broadcasting Station. A follower of *Shimonoseki* Victory Altar said because the hero of a UFO was there, so a UFO flew there.

--- Extracted from the words of the Victor God (Here, 'this man' indicates the Victor God himself.)

5. The era of light which opens New Heaven and New Earth has started.

God used different names of the Savior of each religion and planted His plans in each scripture of each religion to save all humanity, so He is in every scripture of each religion. All His teaching in every scripture is about the hidden manna and the upcoming era of light. Now the age of immortality which is that of light has already started.

All things are light according to the words of the Reincarnate Maitreya Buddha. All are light. These words go with the revelations by today's quantum physicists. Every material is composed of molecules; molecules formed by drawing atoms. Atoms formed by nucleus and electrons. A core consists of protons and neutrons; scientists call this (proton, neuron) nucleon.

Gluon binds three quarks in the nucleon. The quark in nucleon is a kind of a particle of light. Like this, the smallest unit of all material is a particle of light. Physicists call this an elementary particle.

Above we examined that light forms all things, but the soul of darkness catches them.

6. Light is a living material with consciousness.

Therefore, light is not just light. The light that forms all things has its consciousness according to today's quantum physicists. Today's quantum physics reveals that light which is the source of all things has its awareness through such as the Sans lit experiment, the experiment of electron paramagnetic resonance, the analysis of Classer and Friedman, and several tests from different aspects.

The reason we have consciousness is that the light that forms our bodies has awareness. Therefore, having awareness is not only humanity's privilege. Now it is revealed that all plants have high consciousness, in a way, they have more eminent awareness than humans according to a lot of researchers including Clive Baxter, and Marcello Vogel, the co-authorship with Peter Tomkins Christopher Bud of 'the world of spirit plants.'

* A Human's body is spirit and the mass of Light

Light forms all things, and so does the human body.

Elementary particles are particles of light that forms nucleons; nucleons form an atomic nucleus. Collection of elementary particle builds Nucleons; a set of nucleons compose a nucleus. Surrounding a core, electrons that have a different character from nucleus go around. That is an atom. The atoms form a molecule that is the smallest unit that has the nature of the material.

The particles form for example blood, the source of our lives. And the blood builds our bodies' cells. Ten trillion cells according to medical scientists shape our bodies. Like this, our bodies are formed by light, in other words, our bodies are the mass of light.

For the first time, Kirlian of old Russia revealed that humans radiate light, through photographs that were taken by a camera with the function of high frequency.

Then, why are humans somber and dark although light forms them?

Why do they grow old and die? It is because the spirit of darkness locks their bright mind.

7. All things were God that is light, but the contamination in the level of consciousness changed God into material beings when the spirit caught by Satan of darkness.

Today quantum physicists say in one voice that all things in the universe are caught in a trap. Being in a trap means being captivated. However, according to String theory, the universe is connected by one intertwined string. This incomplete argument will be apparent by reading my book. Let's examine the principle that the world is one.

First, when one examines the condition of atoms, electrons go around the nucleus, protons captivates neutrons using the powerful nuclear force in the core. If people break up the nucleus artificially, the neutrinos in neutrons bounce out from the nucleus. This phenomenon is the liberty of God once captivated. Whenever people experiment, neutrinos come out from the core and win freedom. That means neutrinos are in captivity.

Second, there are several nucleons in a nucleus, protons and neutrons that are nucleons have three quarks, which are in chains called gluons. Quantum physicists call this condition the confinement of quark. What does this mean? It means that quarks, the smallest unit of light, are in captivity.

Third, Einstein said that the universe is like a giant closed box. Therefore, any materials in the world cannot get out of the universe. It explains the principle of the universe that the soul of darkness, which captivates light, rules the universe using stronger power than the energy of light. Even light cannot get out of the world because of the gravity that Satan draws. If people become a victor who overcomes the soul of Satan and is free from self-awareness, the condition reverses.

Fourth, the material is in the condition that free frequency is caught in limited space by the soul of Satan. I mentioned above that the particle, which is the smallest unit of material, is not only a particle of light but also a frequency like an electromagnetic wave. Modern physics has revealed it.

This material is in the isolated condition because free frequency is caught in limited space and cannot go out of it. If the frequency that moved freely is caught in small areas, it goes around with high speed, because of this reason, particles, atoms, moles, and the whole universe are spinning, and that is the desperate struggle of God's spirit to escape from being locked. As soil, wood, stone, iron, etc. feel hard, it is difficult for people to think that the essence of their material is a mass of frequency. However, they are the mass of spectrum that is caught in limited spaces. We feel that things are hard because they spin enormously fast. When airplane propellers spin slowly, we can put our hands into them without being hurt. However, when they turn at high speeds, we cannot put our hands into the fan blades because the spinning blades are faster than the speed of the hand's moving. Wherever they touch, they touch only the edge of the blades and result in injury.

Fast spinning airplane propellers look like a compact frisbee. Electrons spin at 600 miles per second. Also, an electron spins 40,000 miles per second in cramped nucleuses according to scientists. We feel that materials are hard when these particles are cramped inside nucleuses, they rotate at enormous speeds.

The condition of all things and humans is that the bright spirit is captivated by the evil and the dark spirit. It is like wrapping bright lamps with a dark cloth. If the Victor removes the dark spirit, all things and humans will be changed into a brilliant light.

Also, the Victor in Korea said, 38 years ago, "people can be turned into flying beings that move faster than airplanes in a moment." That is a hint about a new era. Like you looked at the brilliant light, the *Sweet Dew*, above, the appearing of the *Sweet Dew* means the advent of a brilliant living being that removed the dark soul and overcame it. So God promised in the scriptures and the prophetic books, "the Reincarnate Maitreya Buddha will overcome the spirit of Satan and appear in a human form to save people who are caught and are dying by the spirit of Satan."

God of light lost to the spirit of Satan, the dark spirit, 6,000 years ago, according to *Doboosinin* (桃符神人), an article of *Gyeokamyourok* written 450 years ago by a Korean; before the beginning, God was composed of three aspects, Satan was composed of eight. God enjoyed infinite happiness as the Trinity without agonies and knowing death.

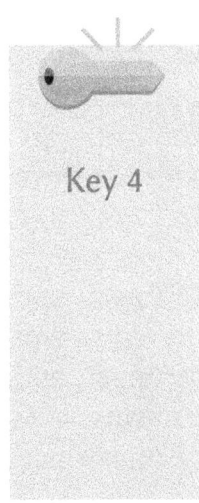

The Secret of Sin and Self-awareness

What is sin?

Sin is the *forbidden fruit* of Satan. Satan is the spirit of death, the spirit of Satan is the mind of Satan. The self-awareness of 'I' is Satan.

People die due to the wage of sin. If they remove self-awareness of 'I'; the spirit of death, they cannot die. That is the secret of eternal life.

Originally, God was composed of three aspects which were one body (the *Trinity*). So God lived as the whole universe itself, which was a mass of light. However, Satan that is a jealous spirit attacked God with quick tricks and God lost according to *Gyeokamyourok*.

In the beginning, in the era of chaos when God and Satan fought, God lost to Satan. Due to this accident, the situation changed. Satan deprived the authority of governing the universe from God; the world became that of Satan. Therefore, Satan grasped the power of death.

Hebrews 2:14 says, "Since the children have flesh and blood, he too shared in their humanity so that by his death he might destroy him who holds the power of death, that is, the devil."

The Bible and *Gyeokamyourok* coincide in saying that Satan has the authority of death. Because of this, the children of God were destined to die; all things become evil and kill.

God made secret plans for an unfortunate situation, predicted His plans, and after a long time of His efforts, He defeated *Satan* and appeared in the world as the Victor God. Chapter 4:2 in the nature part of the Reincarnate Maitreya Buddha of the *Great Nirvana Sutra* volume 5 says, "Dying means the bodies collapse and are finished. However, there is no death. That is because of the *Sweet Dew*. This Sweet Dew is true nirvana." The Reincarnate Maitreya Buddha is the man who attained nirvana. The above sentences are interpreted that the Sweet Dew is the Reincarnate Maitreya Buddha who reached nirvana.

What is *nirvana*? Nirvana is to get out of desire, anger, and ignorance; it is not as easy as like people taking off dirty and tainted clothes. Because the underlying root of desire, anger, and ignorance is Satan that captivates God. Nirvana means true freedom when the Buddha (God) kills the spirit of Satan which captivates Buddha (God) in humans.

The advent of the Sweet Dew means that God became a Victor by overcoming Satan, which is self-awareness of humans and grasps the authority of death. It means that God of the beginning defeated Satan finally as wished.

Eunbiga(隱秘歌 , a song in the Gyeokamyourok) says that three Gods are combined into one and comes as one body. This man is the Reincarnate Maitreya Buddha; He appears with the Sweet Dew. The Reincarnate Maitreya Buddha is the Victor God and *Jeongdoryeong*. At the end of times, three saints will come to the world as one person.

The Reincarnate Maitreya Buddha (the Savior of Buddhists), Jeongdoryeong (the Savior of Koreans), always emits the Sweet Dew.

Initially, the Trinity God lived as one body, but He was broken into debris by Satan, the spirit of death. Through processing some steps with secret plans for 6,000 years, the divided Gods were combined into one God (the Trinity) again and came to the world as one person. The man is the Reincarnate Maitreya Buddha whom Buddhists have waited for. He is supreme God in supernatural being *Tao*(神仙道) of Orient, and He is *Jeongdoryeong* in Korean traditional religion and Confucianism.

Malunlon (末運論 , a theory in the *Gyeokamyourok*) writes, "He seems like a man but he is never a human, 'He is God in a human form body." Additionally, He appears with the Sweet Dew.

Key 5

The Secret of the New food of Neo-humans

What will be the food of Neo-humans? How will they live?

In a new era, there is food which will raise life; it is manna. Do you know manna? This man(referring to the Victor) already hinted at it. The spirit of God is the food of life. The food is the material of life in oxygen. As water is composed as H_2O, the food of life is in water, too. So when we water plants, they become alive because there is the material of life in water. The new heaven's food is just the hidden manna and the *Holy Dew Spirit*. So from now on, a new era of *eternal life* will be open.

Therefore, as it is now, if a new era of people living forever opens up, people will not be able to live

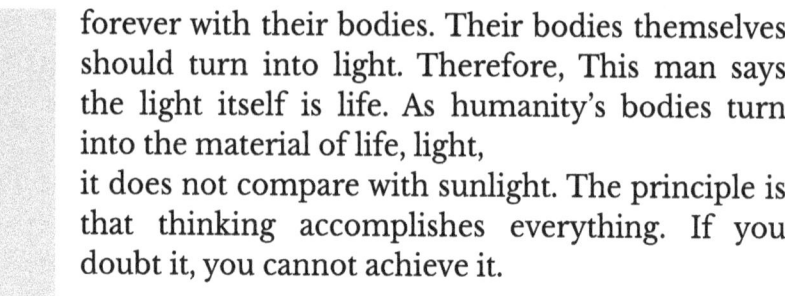

forever with their bodies. Their bodies themselves should turn into light. Therefore, This man says the light itself is life. As humanity's bodies turn into the material of life, light,
it does not compare with sunlight. The principle is that thinking accomplishes everything. If you doubt it, you cannot achieve it.

8. The men who receive this light never die and are changed into a brilliant light. The era when people fly is coming. People will never die.

The people who receive the *Sweet Dew* will never die. Even if they contract serious diseases, they are cured. If they accept the *Sweet Dew*, their minds change, their blood change, their bodies change; their bodies become immortal in the brilliant light.

Humans were initially God according to the Bible, the Buddhist scriptures, and *Gyeokamyourok*.

In the old Bible, in Psalms 82:6, it says, "You are gods; you are all sons of the Most High." Deuteronomy 14:1, "You are the children of the Lord, your God."

The offspring of cows are cows; the babies of horses are still horses. If humans are the children of God, all humans are surely Gods.

John 1:4 says, "God is life and light."

Therefore, if God was a brilliant light, humans should be a brilliant light, too. Therefore, it is natural if humans receive the light (spirit) of God continually, the spirit of God removes the dark spirit of *Satan* which surrounds each cell of humans, and then all humans recover the light of God.

April 16th, 1993, in the lecture hall of *Hangukilbo* building, the pictures of the *Sweet Dew* were taken during the lecture under the title 'I will reveal the secret of *Gyeokamyourok*.' The *Sweet Dew* is moving from right to left toward the platform.

```
Pic 1-3, 1-4. The Sweet Dew is falling down in the lecture
hall.
```

The *Sweet Dew* is the spirit of the *Savior* that always follows and protects every day and night the men who believe in the true Savior. Therefore, they neither have accidents nor face disasters. At *Kobe* Earthquake in Japan, a lot of buildings and houses collapsed, and a lot of people lost their lives. However, those who believe in

Jeongdoryeong never were hurt, and also their homes were not damaged, either.

Besides, wherever His followers go or take worship services, the spirit (the Sweet Dew) of God follows them. In the Bible, in Hosea 14:5, it says that the *Sweet Dew* is just God. Like that, God always accompanies His followers and protects them as the *Sweet Dew*.

Jeongdoryeong (referring to the *Victor*) moves a long distance in a moment. In one winter, it snowed a lot. When His old followers came back homes after taking worship services, the roads were very slippery for seniors to climb a steep slope. Therefore, they could not walk and just sighed. At that moment, *Jeongdoryeong* appeared in a moment and led them to the hill holding their arms.[2]

They thanked Him with a greeting, at the moment He disappeared in front of them. These anecdotes happened a lot to those who followed Him. *Jeongdoryeong* said that soon those who receive the *Sweet Dew* would fly faster than airplanes.

Lee Won-young, an American physicist and professor said at his

---

2. Supernatural being (神仙): 安心歌 (Ansimga) part of 龍潭遺辭 [Yongdamyousa], a hidden secret of heaven(天機書), written by Choi Je Woo, the first saint among four saints in Juyeok (周易) says that I will become a supernatural being (神仙) and fly to the sky (飛上天). It means if we achieve great Tao, we can become supernatural beings and fly to the sky. In his book 大巡典經 [Daesoon Jeongyeong] he predicted the era of great Tao when the men of God appear, at that time people would eat the hidden manna(海印 = 仙藥) that is an immortal food.

lecture in Seoul University in 1986 that neutrons penetrate 10 billion-light-year lead's thickness. Why is the penetrating power of neutrons so strong?

The universe is made of the principle of the yin-yang. So all materials have positive or negative characters. For example, the negative light is attracted by the positive light. However, as neutrons have a neutral character, they are not drawn to the positive or negative material. Above the physicist said that neutrons have strong penetrating power, even though they have this power, why are they caught by protons?

Because the distance between them is only one-third of the nucleus' diameter, the protons captivate the neutrinos. Right before the Big Bang, in the beginning, the universe existed very compactly in a tiny space by the extreme pressure of *Satan* according to physicists.

However, according to the prophecy and the Savior, on the process that Satan occupied the God in brilliant light, Satan compressed God continually until God could not manage Satan's pressure. Then, by the force of Satan, the mass of light(God) broken into female and male. God transformed into all things such as plants, rocks, stars, animal, and so on. The troubled God is forming the current universe.

God is still locked in all things as light. For example, all living things emit light. According to the Bible and the Buddhist scriptures, God is light and life. For another example, every star has a flaming ball in the center. The fiery orb is the spirit of God. So plants grow sharply due to the power of the life of God in the middle of the earth.

The light of neutrons does not shine in a straight line like sunshine, but in spiral lines, which can move as it wants because it has its awareness.

Therefore, the future that will have no night is coming soon according to *Saengchojirak* (生初之樂, an article of *GyeokamYourok*).

The light of the future that is coming soon will go not straightly but spirally. It will flash even to winding holes brightly. The era is a non-polar without yin-yang. So the age will have neither shadow nor shade. The light of God is a neutral light. Therefore, it is not influenced by positive, negative electrons and gravity. Moreover, the light is the *Sweet Dew* that broke the chain of *Satan* and overcame him.

The great light of *nirvana* is neither attracted nor captivated by positive and negative materials, breaks the chain of Satan that captivates imperfect gods, and emancipates the spirit of imperfect gods from the prison of *Satan*. Therefore, it is natural that the men who are reborn as the *Spirit of God* will fly at will.

9. The Savior appeared to the world with complete science and religion.

If the *Savior* does not know everything, He is a swindler. Why was the universe made? How was it made? With what aim was it made and how has it been progressed? How will the universe be finished in the future? What are human beings? Why do humans die? How will God accomplish immortality?

Here are the religious and scientific answers to the above questions.

As each scripture predicted, the Savior who appeared with the *Sweet Dew* says that so far there was neither science nor religion. Today, physicists say that the structures of atoms of materials are the condition that electrons spin around the nucleus, the nucleus captivate protons and neutrons using a powerful nuclear force.

However, nobody says with what power the electron's spin around the nucleus. Also, people do not know why protons captivate neutrons using a powerful nuclear force. Plus, they do not know why neutrinos in neutrons run away to the universe when physicists destroy a nucleus artificially. Today's study does not speak to the basis of all things, but they address the phenomenon of the surface of all things. It is just like when people ask the reason for people's death; they reply that all humans become old, contract diseases, and die.

However, it is not the answer. People just talk about the phenomenon of aging and dying. It is not a correct answer. The death of all things and humans comes from the structures of atoms that protons captivate neutrons and electrons spin around the nucleus. Food chains of the law of the jungle come from this structure of atoms; the reason that people hate each other and kill brutally through wars comes from this, as well.

The key which solves the secret of birth, age, disease, and death of humans, all things, and the universe is in the structures of one atom.

So far, nobody has revealed this. Therefore, there was neither study nor religion in the world according to the Victor.

The true Victor was supposed to answer the questions mentioned above. Think about it for a second.

How does a doctor heal patients without knowing about the reason for the diseases? How can the Savior change the mortal universe into an immortal world without knowing about the reason for the death of all things and the basic principle of the universe?

Scriptures already predicted it. Corinthians 13:10 in the Bible, it says, "When perfection comes, the imperfect disappears."

The words mean that someday a perfect study and a perfect religion will come. Also, the words "the perfection was supposed to come" mean that before the perfection comes, the study and religions are imperfect. Page 4-5 in the nature part of the *Reincarnate Maitreya Buddha* of the *Great Nirvana Sutra* volume 8 says like that, too.

Therefore, all words in the scriptures are imperfect, so they become the source that causes agonies to humans. Hence, they are imperfect words. Perfect words are the source of the right path. When the *Reincarnate Maitreya Buddha* appears to the world, He will remove the imperfect words and religions. Hence, you should throw imperfect words and know the perfect words of the *Reincarnated Maitreya Buddha*.

Gapeulga (甲乙歌, a song in the *GyeokamYourok*) says when the Savior appears to the world; He will come with a perfect study, then, the existing religions and study will perish in a day.

Like this, when the savior *Jeongdoryeong* appears, He was expected to tell about a perfect study and religion. The *Savior* appears with not only the hidden manna but also the truth. The knowledge scientifically and reasonably shines the underlying cause of death, the way of immortality, and the reason for the universe being formed.

Unless He tells about a perfect religion and philosophy, He cannot unite all religions and philosophies. Come to the world of light, confirm, and see the perfect science and religion.

Here is a New hymn of the *Victory Altar*

Come to the light of the Holy Spirit

> 1. The glory of God that overcame the sinful world. Becomes the light of the Holy Spirit and shines on the whole universe. In the new world where the sun and the moon lose their light. The light of the glory of God is splendid more and more.
>
> Chorus
>
> Brothers, come toward the light of the Holy Spirit, The whole humanity, let's move toward the light of God
>
> 2. After destroying the *authority of Satan*, only joy overflows. The pain of death, the sorrow of aging, the worldly worry, agony, and delusion, and all sins disappear. No rotting food is necessary; people live on the Holy Dew Spirit.
>
> 3. The *Savior God*, the mother of all humans, Wore a human's body and came to the world. Toward the humans with a lot of doubt, He has accomplished the five covenants. Spreading the sayings of the truth leads people to the way of eternal life.

Key 6

The Secret of Radiocarbon dating technology

Radiocarbon dating is wrong

The main factors of decaying material are the air pollution and the poison in humans. Therefore the speed of decaying material is different from the environment of times. The pace of decaying material 5000 years ago was slow because the atmosphere was clean at that time, but nowadays the situation is severely polluted, so the speed of decaying material is very fast. Not only time factor which affects the Half-Life of carbon isotope but also something else. The amount of air pollution determines the decaying speed. Among them, humans' thought affects most the environments including the air.

In old times, when Japanese attacked Korea and killed a lot of people, a lot of pine trees died according to old Korean books. Like that, when people felt dejected, resentful, or disappointed, they emit poison through bodies and breaths. Therefore, the air became toxically polluted, since the pine trees are susceptible to the air pollution, a lot of pine trees died at that time.

The rate of decay is different from each place and time. The plants or things which stay with a person whose spirit is clean neither collapse nor die easily.

Radiocarbon dating calculates the time of things' death through the number of c-14 carbon isotope in the remaining material. Because the speed of c-14 reducing is different from the environment of the air and the condition of people nearby, it cannot reveal the age of fossils without significant error.

Furthermore, the false reading is being used as a framework of the history of time to which many other subjects refer before sitting itself at a particular time slot, so that produce the whole system corrupted.

Neo-humans would reveal the secret of the universe

In the universe, there is the material of saving life and the substance of killing life. About the fact, the Bible writes that in the beginning, the light of God and darkness of *Satan* existed in the universe. According to the *Victor God*, in the beginning, there was a war; Satan of imitation and jealousy occupied God. Physicists call the war the Big Bang.

The result is that the spirit of death possessed God, locked up in the Self-awareness of 'I,' made the whole universe into the sinful *yin-yang* world, and has caused endless conflict and wars.

Therefore, the weak God became the slave of Satan by the sudden attack of Satan before crushed into all things. The God could not reveal His situation in the Bible or scriptures in detail, so He hid the strategy of taking the authority of universe from Satan, which strongly ruled the world.

Therefore, God's unfair and miserable situations have been secretly passed down to today through prophets. Only a few researchers know that *Dobusinin* (桃符神人, an article in the *Gyeokamyourok*) is a master key to solve the secret of the universe and God.

In 6000 years, the God overcame Satan and reinstated His omniscience and omnipotence which governs the universe at His will. His presence can stop killer typhoons, to stop summer monsoon rains. Now it is the time for all humans to know about the advent of the Victor and His strategy to recover the Garden of Eden. Therefore, I will tell about them in this book.

God of light became the brilliant *Holy Dew Spirit* and came to Korea to save humanity. The Victor came as an existence of light to liberate humans who are the slaves of Satan by making them reborn as the Holy Dew Spirit, immortal existences. Welcoming the era of light, humans will be reborn as immortal *neo-humans* by changing self-awareness of 'I', keeping the *Law of Liberty*, and having a new philosophy.

Now I will summarize the message of God of brilliant light on June 6, 1990, for Neo-humans. As self-awareness of 'I' is the forbidden fruit, if people think and move by desires of 'I,' their blood decays and they die.

However, if they do not live by desires of 'I,' but live by conscience which is the nature of God, new changes will happen to them. If they live like that, their blood will turn into an immortal one. The nondecaying immortal blood turns into light.

That evidence is that light comes out from humans. Semyon D, Kirlian, a scientist of spirit, called the light 'the aura'. It means that the light of God is in human's blood. However, scientists do not know the fact. The fact that light comes out from humans is crystal clear.

Light is a kind of fire and fever. The term 'fever' refers to the idea of making warmth. The fact that light comes out from humans verifies that fever, light, exists in a human's body. However, when humans catch diseases, their bodies become colder gradually, and when their bodies lose their fever completely, they die.

To judge a human's death, people touch their hands and feet. If their hands and feet become cold gradually, you know they are dying. No matter how hot summer is, if their bodies are cold like ice, they are dying. As life is light itself, if humans lose fever completely, they die. Because the life of humans is light, light itself is a fever, if people lose fever completely, they become cold and die.

Humans' lives depend on light, are kept alive by light. Therefore, if the light of man is not extinguished, the man cannot die. This man is talking about advanced and immortal science. Therefore, if a light of a man becomes not extinguished one, he neither dies nor catches diseases. He is God. The man who becomes God has the light that is not extinguished, so he cannot catch diseases.

The fact that light is in the blood of humans is proved by the light coming out of humans. The light from ordinary people is one that can be cold; that is, the light in sinners is one that becomes cold and is extinguished. When the light is extinguished, people die. We should know that when the light is extinguished, people die. The reason people die is their light, their lives are gradually extinguished, that is because their bodies lose fevers entirely, and they die. Then, this causes one to question "how can we make our light not be extinguished?"

Light is formed by blood, and blood is formed by a mind. So to make their blood not decay, they should have a mind that makes blood not decay. Then their blood cannot decay. These are new words that are scientific and medical.

The Victor says about high-tech science. "Everything depends on the mind." If people have a mind that the light in blood is not extinguished, they cannot die. If This man says about vague words in the Bible or the Buddhist scriptures, you cannot understand His words. So He scientifically says about an immortal science using the principle of blood for you to understand an immortal science.

If people make friends who strongly emit light, even they emit weak light, they become gradually strong by receiving the strong light of their friend.

Therefore, the Bible and the maxim tell, "Be careful in making friends." The white group in the Bible are starting to emit the strong light of life in the *Victory Altar* where is *New Heaven and New Earth*.

However, ordinary people in the sinful world emit the light that extinguishes the light of life. If you meet sinners who emit light which extinguishes the light of life, you are sick due to being affected by the toxic light.

If this Victor is not polluted by sins of all humans of the world, He can fly by being changed into light. Some men question why this Victor looks old. If the Victor is not polluted, He becomes young like a seventeen-year-old boy. If He charges the sins of humans, He looks around 60 to 80 years. If you keep the *Law of Liberty* or do not commit sins, this Victor becomes young. This man's condition depends on you.

This era is immortal. To become immortal and to be saved, you should live as the Victor says, and live keeping the Law of Liberty. If you live in harmony regarding brothers as my body, regarding brothers as God, regarding brothers' sins as mine, or brothers' situation, mine, you become God.

If you practice it, the light in you becomes one that is not extinguished; the body becomes an immortal one that is not extinguished forever. You should realize that everything relies on the mind.

Key 7

The Top Secret of Drawing New Heaven

What will you draw, the Holy Dew Spirit or Ego?

The universe is operated by the law of drawing. People draw something every second. If you think of death, the spirit of death occupies your mind and body. So you cannot avoid death. If you draw immortal God, He comes to you and fills your mind and body.

If the spirit of the Victor stays in your body continually, you cannot die because the immortal God transforms your body into an immortal one.

In the Next book, I will introduce the secret of being reborn as the Holy Spirit, keeping the *Law of Liberty*, and the methodology that does not extinguish the light of life in humans' body. In this book there are some new words which teach people how to go toward the world of light, heaven.

False Self-consciousness & breaking fixed notions

When Galileo said that the earth goes around the sun, people did not believe his words at that time. Also when Columbus claimed a round-shaped planet, people laughed at him. Whenever human history made a significant discovery, the first obstacle was a fixed idea. Then, what do you think of the era of light?

It's the time for you to change. If the hidden manna falls, humans cannot die according to the Bible, the Buddhist scriptures, and the prophetic books. You should break your stereotype. The most prominent fixed idea is that humans must die. Is it true?

People should break this idea. Although the death of humans has been taken for granted, nobody likes it. Why do all humans have the mindset hating death?

Maybe they are the existence of God.

What is true happiness? It is to gain eternal life without pain. It is the nature and ultimate wish of humans. Humanity's history is that of struggling to overcome death and to gain eternal life. But so far there was nobody who accomplishes immortality in the dark and sinful world.

Then, doesn't eternal life belong to humans? Is it impossible to gain immortal life? No, it isn't. All scriptures anticipate the advent of the Victor and the era of immortality. People do not know why humans die and what the *hidden manna* is. To accomplish eternal life, they should know the manna of heaven first.

Also if they know the reason for death, they can get out of death. If all humans realize the root of humans and remove the factor of death, they can accomplish immortality. Humans' original sin, heredity sin, the sin they committed in the present life can be completely wiped away by the *Holy Dew Spirit* of the Victor. Where the *Sweet Dew* falls, there is the way of eternal life. Remembering this, let's find the right way to the *Sweet Dew*.

So far, there was neither true study nor religion in this world. Let's change our thought and have a right value of life engraving the voice of heaven's warning.

In Isaiah 34:16, in the Bible, it says, "Look in the scroll of the Lord and read; none of these will be missing, not one will lack her mate." The Bible foretells in detail about the advent of the Savior who pours down the manna. The predictions were hidden by God; He revealed them to only a few prophets and angels thousands of years ago. Some predictions were written in the Bible and other predictions have been passed down through mouths to today. Next chapter, I will write about the hidden secret of heaven through the Bible.

Chapter II

The New Era is Opened by the Hidden Manna

The manna that fell in Moses times is the food of heaven that Israelites lived on in the desert for 40 years. It was a hint that the Savior would appear and save people using the food of life which is the fruit of life.

If the hidden manna falls, it means that New Heaven and New Earth are opened; there will not be death, anguish, and pain in the New Heaven.

The Secret of the hidden manna

1. The manna in the Bible

Manna is a miracle food from heaven, according to Exodus 16:14-31, Numbers 11:6-9, Deuteronomy 8:3, Nehemiah 9:20-21, Psalm 78:23-24, John 6:31, and Revelation 2:17 in the Bible. When Moses took the Jewish people to the desert from Egypt, there was no food with them. So they almost starved to death.

They complained to Moses, so, he prayed to God. The Lord of God said, "You will eat meat fully in the evening, eat rice cake in the morning." In that evening, quails covered the camp place and the next morning, the dew fell densely on the ground, the dew disappeared, and something white and round like frost piled fully there. Moses said to his people, "God gave us this food; take the amount of food you can eat." This food covered their campsite. They called the food 'manna'. As it was rotten after one day, they should bring the amount they could eat for one day; they were permitted 4 liters for each person.

The Israel people lived on the manna for forty years according to the Book of Exodus 16:13 and Number 11:6-9. If the manna of Moses' period is a physical manna, the Hidden manna in the Bible is a spiritual manna. The *Holy Dew Spirit* in the Bible is the hidden manna of the New Heaven that makes all dying creatures be reborn as the Holy Spirit and live forever in happiness.

Revelation 2:17 says, "He who has an ear, let him hear what the Spirit says to the churches. To him who overcomes, I will give some of the hidden manna." These words mean that the man who has the hidden manna is the Victor. The Dew is the immortal manna.

Dew did not fall after Moses' time. Much later, Isaiah, a great prophet, predicted as follows, "But your dead will live; their bodies will rise. You, who dwell in the grave, wake up and shout. Your dew is like the dew of the morning; the dew will give birth to her dead" in Isaiah 26:19. It predicted, "if the Savior who pours down the Dew appears, death will perish." The Dew is not a physical food, but a spiritual food. It means just an immortal manna.

Also, John 6:27 says, "Do not work for food that spoils, but for food that endures to eternal, which the Son of Man will give you. On him, God the Father has placed his seal of approval." 1Corinthians 15:54 writes, "When the perishable has been clothed with the imperishable and the mortal with immortality, then the saying that is written will come true," "Death has been swallowed up in the victory." Therefore, the words "humans' lifespan is like trees" are accomplished after the Holy Dew Spirit appears.

Key 8

The Secret of The White Stone and the promised land in the Bible

What is the secret of the white stone and the Holy Land?

The Victor said in 1990 that He received a white stone at the age of seven. At that time, He did not know the word on the white stone. He learned the word of 素砂 (Sosa) in *Seodang* (書堂 =a private education institute in Korea equivalent to elementary school in modern education programs), He said that the name on the white stone is *Sosa* (素砂 meaning a white stone). He visited the place named *Sosa* when he grew up there.

Israel (the Victor who won in a fight) is in the New Testament Bible, and the Victor is the most critical word in Revelation. Revelation is the last part of the Bible volume 66, if the *Victor* appears, immortality (the aim of the Bible) comes to the subject of accomplishable.

Therefore God in John shouted to the Victor to appear. We should learn the Victor, the Savior, and Israel indicates one person(same meaning).

As God is the Alpha and the Omega, God of the beginning was reborn as God of consummation, became the Victor Savior, and came to this world. The Bible says the words of God; it was written in secret messages to avoid attack from Satan. So only the Victor who has the spirit of God can tell the Bible correctly.

Gyeokamyourok, a Korean prophetic book, with 100 percent accuracy, says that the Savior will come to Sosa. Also, it claims that even though heaven collapsed, it will be built in Sosa. In Korea, there was no village named *Sosa* except for one in *Bucheon* city until now.

As like Revelation 2:17 in the Bible, the Victor should pour down the Hidden Manna and know the new name written on the white stone which God gave to Him.

It is correct that 素砂 (Sosa) is on it. 素 (So) means 'white' and 砂 (Sa) means 'sand' in Chinese characters. As sand is a small stone and a small stone is still a stone. 素砂 (Sosa) itself means the 'white stone'. So, giving a white stone means giving the land of Sosa.

God says, "to him who overcomes, I will give him the hidden manna; I will give him a white stone with a new name written on it, known only to him who receives it."

The hidden manna is the spirit of God who overcomes Satan. As Sosa itself means white stone, giving a white stone indicates having the Victor stand in the Victory Altar in Sosa area and making him speak of new words in order to produce the righteous by pouring the hidden manna (the Holy Dew Spirit).

 The eastern righteous men in the Bible stay in the Victory Altar, are becoming neo-humans who are reborn as the Holy Spirit and cannot die.

2. The Sweet Dew in the Buddhist scriptures

Sakyamuni predicted 'the Dharma of the Sweet Dew' in the Buddhist scriptures. Let's see how the Buddhist scriptures foretell the *Reincarnate Maitreya Buddha*(彌勒如來 = 生彌勒佛).

The Buddhist scriptures express the Sweet Dew(甘露) as the light of Great Nirvana that the Reincarnated Maitreya Buddha pours

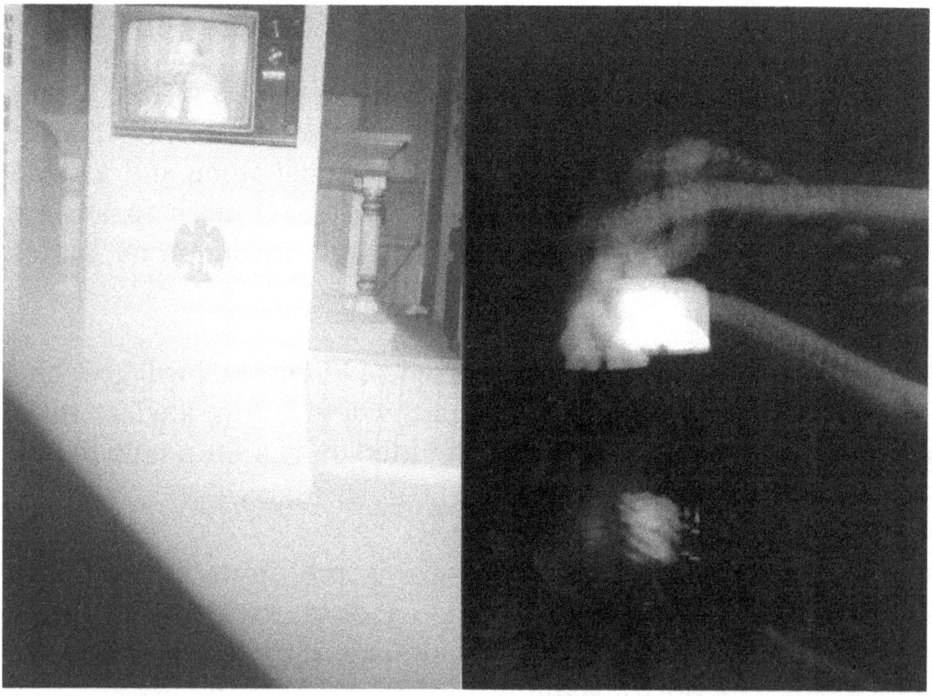

Pic 2-1, 2-2. The other self of the Reincarnate Maitreya Buddha comes out from a TV screen during a sermon using DVD. It means the other selves of the Maitreya Buddha stays everywhere and pours his spirit to people who long for him.

out. The whole Buddhist scriptures such as the Great Nirvana Sutra, the *Dharma Flower Sutra*, and the *Flower Adornment Sutra* say that the Sweet Dew is the symbol of the Reincarnated Maitreya Buddha.

According to volume 26 of the *Flower Adornment Sutra*, the Reincarnated Maitreya Buddha, who can fill the universe with His other selves in a very short moment,, pours down the Sweet Dew and removes the agonies of people.

Pic 2-3. The Sweet Dew (bottom right) Ariel Han took

In accordance with *Sasangpum*(四相品) part of the *Great Nirvana Sutra* volume 5, "There is no death here because of the Sweet Dew(是處無死), the man who pours out this Sweet Dew is the man who reaches nirvana."

According to the part of the lifespan of the *Great Nirvana Sutra* volume 2, *Sakyamuni* said when the Dharma of the Sweet Dew comes, only then, people would reach nirvana.

Also, 4-2 the nature part of the Reincarnate Maitreya Buddha(如來性品) of the Great Nirvana Sutra volume 5 tells about the essence and the origin of the word of the Sweet Dew concretely as follows:

The *Buddha* is the existence that neither delivers children, nor dies, nor collapses, nor catches diseases. It means nirvana; death is not here because of the Sweet Dew. This Sweet Dew is nirvana. In other words, it is the body of Dharma. When a man dies, his body collapses, and his life perishes.

Like this the Scriptures said, the primary aim of the law of Buddhism is to get out of the circle of being born, catching diseases and dying to live forever enjoying bliss. Also, *Bupgugyeong Annyeong* part (法句經 安寧品) predicted, "to get out of the circle of birth and death; you should receive the Sweet Dew."

The Holy Dew Spirit and the Immortal world

I narrated the essence of the Sweet Dew and the predictions of the Scriptures until now. Now I will tell you how the Holy Dew Spirit will turn the world into immortals.

The grace of the Holy Dew Spirit removes sins, agony, and suffering. Therefore, people always enjoy happiness and joy; also they feel the phenomenon of getting younger in the heaven, the Victory Altar. As well, the Holy Dew Spirit purifies the air as the air of *Buddha* by detoxifying through His other selves. As the air gradually becomes that of heaven, the new era when people do not need decaying food is coming closer, and they will live on the air.

The reason is that all the air will be changed into that of the Holy Dew Spirit. When sins in humans perish by breathing the Sweet Dew, all religions are reunited as one. Because the Holy Dew Spirit kills the ego which is the splitting spirit. Therefore, the world will stop quarreling, and it will reunify as one.

The new era will be led by the *Neo-humans* who become *Buddha* or *God* and will be able to fly, and then all things and the universe will be turned into light. Like this, the universe will be changed into the immortal step by step because the Holy Dew Spirit is emitted by the *Reincarnated Maitreya Buddha*.

Prophetic books of Korea and China and the Buddhist books underlined that those who realized the essence of the Holy Dew Spirit should help the Reincarnate Maitreya at the risk of their life.

When the true Savior who is the seventh angel blows a trumpet at the last big changing phrase, the men who achieve fifty percent as God will be changed into light suddenly according to 1Corinthians 15:51-4.

People can see the power of the Reincarnated Maitreya Buddha through His accomplishments of His five covenants. Although He came wearing a human's body, as He has recovered the power of the Savior, He works as His other selves and changes His body at will. But those who are indulged into desires and sins do not know Him. In this chapter, I told how the Holy Dew Spirit would turn the world into immortals. In the next section, I will say about the Victor, the hero of all scriptures.

Key 9

The secret of the root of human being

The Secret of forgotten memory for the Country of God People was the immortal God who was flying as light. Those traces are that people want to fly and fly in their dreams. Also, they emit light. The Bible says God is light, and life is light. All humans have life in them. Also, living people emit light. Additionally, all humans want to live forever in infinite happiness like God. All humans' characters belong to God's. Also, God supported the above sayings through Psalm 82:6 that you are the sons of the Most High.

Chapter III
The Secret of the Victor & the Testimonies of saints

Key 10

The Secret of the fruit of life

The Bible says that if people eat the fruit of life, they will not die. In Revelation 2:7, in the Bible, it says that to him that overcomes, will I give to eat the tree of life, which is in the midst of the paradise of God. Also, God says in Revelation 2-3 that he will give the fruit of life to the man who overcomes. Therefore, the Victor knows the fruit of life and has it.

The Victor says that the sayings of the Bible are spiritual; the fruit of life is the spirit. The spirit is that of the Victor that overcomes the authority of death, the spirit of *Satan*. People can live forever by eating the spirit every second. Also, the conviction of immortality is the fruit of life because it is the spirit(thought) of the Victor.

I could see the advent of the Victor in Revelation of the Bible. Revelation says that owing to the advent of the Victor, a new era is opened, and the true Sabbath is completed. In this chapter, I will introduce the Victor who is the hero of New Jerusalem and New Heaven, the symbol of numbers in the Bible, and the testimonies of Neo-humans who live in the Pure Land of Happiness. Like the *Amrita Sutra* says, the people who live in the Pure Land of Happiness live without anguish, pain, and shade of death according to their testimonies.

Those who hear about these people will realize that the advent of *Neo-humans* and the era of immortality are approaching.

Key 11

The Secret of Savior's name(Victor)

What is the name of the Victor?

According to Revelation 2:28, God says that I will give the morning star to him who overcomes. The Victor's first name is Hee Sung (in Chinese), which means bright morning star. Also, the Buddhist Scriptures say that the name of the Reincarnate Maitreya Buddha is the *Bright Star*. The Bible says that the Savior is the lamb according to Revelation 17:14. It indicates the year of the Savior's birth. The Savior was born on June 28th, 1931 in the lunar calendar. June is the month of the lamb, 1931 year is the year of the lamb. So 'the Savior is the lamb' means that the Savior was born in the year of the lamb.

He overcame His ego at fifty years of age by living a life on the contrary of what his ego wanted. After He defeated and killed His ego, the spirit of the Trinity occupied and became His self-consciousness of 'I'. Therefore, He has recovered the power of the Trinity. He pours the Sweet Dew which is the symbol of the Savior, Victor, and the Reincarnated Maitreya Buddha according to the Bible, the Buddhist scriptures, and the prophetic books. Isaiah 26:16 "Those of our people who have died will live again! Their bodies will come back to life. All those sleeping in their graves will wake up and sing for joy. As the sparkling Dew refreshes the earth."

The Nirvana Sutra says the Reincarnate Maitreya Buddha saves people from birth, aging, diseases, and death by emitting the Sweet Dew. The Sweet Dew is an immortal material, which is the spirit of the Savior, Victor, and the Reincarnate Maitreya Buddha.

The Victor has shown omnipotent and omniscient power because the Trinity accompanies him. Becoming the Victor 1980, He proclaimed the five covenants.

Key 12

The seven secrets of the Victor in the Bible

According to Revelation 2:26-28 in the Bible. "I will give the morning star to him who overcomes and does my will to the end; I will give authority over the nations. 'He will rule them with an iron scepter; he will dash them to pieces like pottery.'"

And then according to Revelation 2:7, "He will give the right to eat from the tree of life to him who overcomes."

In Revelation 2:17, it says, "God will give some of the hidden manna and a white stone with a new name written on it, known only to him who receives it."

Revelation 3:12 says, "Him who overcomes, I will make a pillar in the temple of my God. Never again will he leave it. I will write on Him the name of my God, and the name of the city of my God, the new Jerusalem, which is coming down out of heaven from my God; I will also write on Him my new name."

Also, Revelation 2:11 says,"He who overcomes will not be hurt at all by the second death." Additionally, Revelation 3:5, He who overcomes will like them be dressed in white. I will never blot out his name from the book of life.

And Revelation 3:21, "To him who overcomes, I will give the right to sit with on my throne, just as I sat down on God's throne."

The above paragraphs indicate that name of the Victor will become the name of God, as God promised that he would not erase the name of the Victor from the book of life and gave the right to eat the fruit of life from the tree of life, he achieves immortality.

That is, the Victor is an immortal God. Additionally, sitting with on my(God's) throne means not the Victor and God sitting on the throne together but God occupying the Victor's body.

God is the Victor, the Victor is God. Like this, Israel, the Victor, is in the New Testament Bible. The Victor is the basis of Revelation.

Revelation is the last part of the Bible volume 66. If the Victor appears, immortality, the aim of the Bible, is expected to be accomplished. Therefore God in John, the writer of Revelation, shouted the Victor to appear. Here what we should know is that the Victor, the Savior, and Israel indicate one person. The God of the beginning was reborn as almighty God became the Victor Savior, and came to this world. As the word of the Bible is one about God, it was written with secret messages to avoid attacks from Satan according to the Victor Cho Hee Sung of the Victory Altar. There were sad circumstances to God in the Bible. The Savior is the man who was reborn as the Holy Spirit (God) in Korea, the land in the Far East corner like the prediction of Isaiah 41 1:9. If the Savior is the God of the beginning, He should know the pitiful circumstances of heaven and reveal all sealed secrets in detail.

Key 13

The Secret of number five

What is the secret of number five?

Number five symbolizes the Savior. In Genesis 30: 6, in the Bible, it says Dan is the fifth son of Jacob, the son of Isaac, and he received the right of the first-born. However, Jacob blessed Dan seventhly, because he knew that Dan would be the perfect New Heaven's man. Number seven symbolizes the completion of humanity and God by being one. When the Victor was trained in the *Secret Chamber*, He received number five, and the other members of the trainees received number four. Number five is seen in the antefix which was discovered in the basin of the Daedong River, where Dan's tribes founded the first government of Korea. *Mugunghwa*(rose of Sharon), Korean national flower, has five leaves, five stamens, and five calyces, too. The meaning of *Mugunghwa* is eternal life. That is, number five symbolizes the Savior who will build an immortal land on the earth.

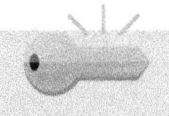

Key 14

The Secret of the Savior's nation and Chosen people

Who are Judah and Dan?

The tribe of Dan is very important because the Savior comes from the offspring of Dan.

Genesis 49 says, "Judah is a lion's cub. The scepter will not depart from Judah until Shiloh comes. Shiloh means the Savior.

Dan will be a serpent by the roadside, a viper along the path. That bites the horse's heels so that its rider tumbles backward. I look for your deliverance, O Lord." This prediction means that the Savior will come from the tribe of Dan.

Key 15

The Secret of 144,000 Number in the Bible

There are some numbers in the Bible. They are not physical ones.

Number four indicates the king of the four living beings, according to Revelation 4:7; the king is the man who overcame Satan. So number four means the Victor (the *last Adam*) and the *Victress*(Eve) who are righteous by overcoming Satan. Number '0' indicates perfection and endlessness. In conclusion, '144' symbolizes God, Eve, and Adam, '000' indicates that God, Adam, and Eve are all perfect and righteous. That is, number 144,000 indicates that God became a Victor and was completed as the *Trinity*.

The testimonies of Neo-humans

Here are five testimonies of *Neo-humans* who live in *New Jerusalem* and the new earth, where the hidden manna always falls.

Kim Jeong-Heum, a Buddhist

The Reincarnate Maitreya Buddha has come.

On Thursday, July seventh, 1992, I talked with a girl student in front of the Korea University library after eating supper at a school cafeteria.

It was more of a monologue on her part than a conversation; I just agreed with her and stared at her. I was involuntarily concentrated on panels exhibited for promoting a religion and her sayings. It was like getting struck by something strong. Also, I could not take my eyes off her. She looked more serene and shinier than any other girl students I have ever seen.

The *Victory Altar* that she told me about was enough to captivate my interest. Besides I was so shocked by her simple words "The Reincarnate Maitreya Buddha has come."

Three days later, on July twelfth I went to the Victory Altar. The first man who I met there was Sang Won monk. He welcomed me with a bright smile and a warm heart, so I was relaxed. The monk interpreted the Nirvana Sutra to me.

According to the Nirvana Sutra, the Reincarnate Maitreya Buddha was supposed to appear in 3007 years after Sakyamuni died, to save people from death by pouring out the Sweet Dew, and to establish the real pure land of Buddha.

More amazing words were that the Reincarnate Maitreya Buddha was expected to appear as Mr. Cho Hee Sung in Korea neither India nor China.

The monk said that the year 1992 was 3019 according to the *Mahayana era*. Then 3007 year of the *Mahayana era* was already passed. Also, he added that all predictions in the Nirvana Sutra have been realized in the Victory Altar. I was surprised at hearing that the Reincarnate Maitreya Buddha is *Jeongdoryeong* (He is the Savior who Koreans have waited for.)

While I listened to the monk, there was an announcement to inform the time for a worship service. So I followed the monk to a chapel. On entering the chapel, I was shocked at the scene of the followers who were kneeling compactly like an orderly parade and clapping enthusiastically.

It was more astounding than holy because I had not heard about that form of the worship service. I thought fanatics' religious society drew me. Because I was used to a mood of temples and I expected that the Reincarnate Maitreya Buddha would lead the worship service for realizing in a quiet atmosphere. Also, I was so embarrassed by the Reincarnate Maitreya Buddha led the worship service like a form of *Christianity*.

At any rate, the worship service began in an uneasy condition; the first hymn removed my distraction in a moment. The lyric was like this: How do I love my neighbors without efforts, how can I forgive them without my pains, love is not calculating, it is only giving.

I had read a lot of poems that praise love, but they had not touched my heart like the hymn. The hymn was comfortable and familiar, the melody was dull. However, it touched my heart to the bone. As soon as the hymn finished, my heart was relaxed.

While I took 21 days' education there, I had one question. Some men among followers of the Victory Altar discharged rotten-blood urine in three days since he came to the Victory, somebody experienced it in two years. When do I experience it? The Reincarnate Maitreya Buddha said if people open their minds, they receive the *Sweet Dew*, and the dead spirit of the devil was discharged with urine and dung.

That made me excited and anxious. I wanted to experience discharging the urine and dung of the dead devil's spirit, that wish pushed me to concentrate on the worship service every day.

As I moved to the chapel of the second basement level from the chapel of the first basement level, my fighting against myself began. I tried to 'Clap loudly', 'Sing hymns out' 'Look at the eyes of the Lord', and so on.

Seniors taught me how to receive the Sweet Dew. I sat in the first line because if I sat in the middle, I was conscious of people around me, then I could not concentrate on the Maitreya Buddha. Not only singing hymns before worship services but also singing hymns during the worship services, I struggled against myself.

In less than 5 minutes since I sang the first hymn, my arms were getting sore. So by the end of the second hymn, I was hoping that the next hymn would be one without clapping. Then the Reincarnate Maitreya Buddha who read my thinking chose a hymn with clapping. He blamed my young spirit with His stern and strong eyes, so I could not almost breathe.

My life of the Victory Altar was like that every day. Exactly two months after I came, I went to the bathroom to make water after taking a worship service. Surprisingly I found that my urine was black blood color.

Finally, Satan which was killed by the Sweet Dew of the Reincarnate Maitreya Buddha was discharged as urine. People think that Satan is in a cemetery or dark basements. In fact, Satan is self-awareness of 'I'.

All evil things and dirty things come out from self-awareness of 'I' and have polluted the world until now. Now the Reincarnate Maitreya Buddha purifies the polluted world by removing self-awareness of 'I', which is the primary source that pollutes the world.

Also, He came to me and purified my decayed blood by sending the Sweet Dew. I am sure that the Reincarnate Maitreya Buddha can lead people to nirvana.

I always had a doubtful lump in the corner of my mind. When the doubtful lump was discharged as blood, I felt so happy that I shed tears with joy.

After that, my body and mind became so light and fresh that my clapping was not difficult, and it seemed like I clapped involuntarily.

Last July twelfth is the two year anniversary of coming here. For two years, there were a lot of difficulties to overcome me. Sometimes I was moved to tears when I thought of the Lord's love and grace. Sometimes I deplored my life because my spirit became dirty.

However, the most challenging thing was throwing myself away. Every day, the words of the Lord push me, the more I listen to them, the more they were a very amazing good truth. I felt that the spirit of God in me grows up through endless struggling. In fact, I wandered to look for a true teacher before I met the Reincarnate Maitreya Buddha. Now I meet the true teacher who leads me exactly to a right way. The Lord, please use me in accomplishing your will.

Key 16

The Secret of the true teacher, the Victor Savior

The teacher who leads to the truth is the true Savior.

It is easy to meet teachers who teach with the scriptures. However, according to one scholar, it is difficult to meet teachers who lead people to the truth. The believers of the Victory Altar are lucky and precious people because they meet the true teacher who leads them to the truth.

The Savior often told them "All of them should become Saviors." It means 'become teachers who lead people to the truth.' Also, now we are facing the end of times when all sins of humans are

finished, there are the workers of heaven to help the people of the world to be saved. The believers of the Victory Altar are the ones who have duties to lead all humanity to salvation, peace, freedom, and nirvana.

Let's think of the Savior's sermons. The Victor told humans to regard others as my body to be saved. He teaches the way of you and I becoming one and not being separated.

The Secret of the fruit of life

The Bible says, "If people eat the fruit of life, they don't die. As the words of the Bible is spiritual, the fruit of life is the spirit of the Victor."

As the spirit of the Victor is one killing the spirit of death, people who receive the spirit of the Victor cannot die.

Min Hae-Kyeong, a follower of the Victory Altar

I went to a Methodist church for one year before I got married. After I married, I knew that my husband went to *Jeondogwan* which was led by *Park Tae-Sun*, the *Spiritual Mother*. At that time, as I went to a Methodist church without a particular thought, at first I felt repulsion; I already went to *Jeondogwan* following my husband.

One day in 1956, I smelt fragrance returning home after praying at dawn. I experienced a cooling grace that was connected from my chest, my abdomen, to my arms. But I did not hear about the grace of the water of life; I thought that the phenomenon of receiving the grace of the water of life was a kind of disease. So I went to a hospital; they did not know the reason exactly.

Sometimes something hot came into my body, after some time it disappeared. I came to know that it was the phenomenon of grace coming.

But I moved to another area; my husbands' business failed, we lost our all property. I was so shocked that my health became terrible. Carrying one radish from a market or walking was difficult for me. So I went to a hospital but it was not helpful, so I almost gave up my life.

One day Kim Soon-Ok, my acquaintance, asked me to meet a spiritual man. I accepted her suggestion, but I was too weak to walk.

So I tried to find out the way to meet the Victor, according to Kim Soon-Ok. Fortunately, the man who is called 'the Victor' would come near my house the next day. That was just after the Lord became the Victor; He did not do fullscale missionary work. It was on October eleventh, 1981. My husband bought a month supply of Chinese medicine with leftover money; it was desperate times.

The next day I met the Victor with several women. Receiving grace in *Jeondogwan* for a long time, I knew the quality of energy that comes from people.

The Lord told me to look at His eyes. So I saw His eyes. His eyes were emitting light. Being mysterious, I saw them continually. He asked me "What will you do to catch a tiger?" He told me that he became a Victor by looking at the *Spiritual Mother*, who has God in his mind, without a second's missing. It made me think if I looked at the Victor, I will be the Victor-like.

Hence, as I continued looking at the Vitor, He sent out the *Dew Spirit* to me. Before I met the Lord, I took a rest two or three times to go up the stairs because my house was on the second floor.

One day, on my way home after a worship service, I felt my body was floating and quickly got to the floor of my house in a second. Opening the door of my house, I found myself floating in the air. I was so excited that I tried to pick up a piece of paper to write a letter to my mother. But the paper flew up fast. Thinking it strange, I wrote a letter to my mother simply.

And I went out of the room to change briquettes. The man (the Victor) who was giving me grace appeared there. And then He followed me continually.

After taking a worship service, I was too happy and light to see if my body existed or not. People could not understand without such an experience. At the beginning of going to the Victory Altar, my body was too heavy and sick; one day, during a worship service, I felt that wind blew on my head surrounding and whirling my body, a lump the size of my fist in my stomach fell. At that time, the Lord told me to look at Him for the first time.

In spite of it, I did not think that my disease was curable. I was just curious about His eyes emitted light, so I followed Him unknowingly and saw continually. After that, a thing like a thread came from my eyes for two months. It was like a web. I thought it was an evil thing.

There was continually a bad smell from my pee. My sins were being discharged through my waste.

Nowadays I am entirely cured, and I have the power to convey God's message. When I send the message, the Holy Dew Spirit whirls my body. Looking at the sky, the Lord is there. Every person seems like God to me. Babies look like the Lord of babies, adults look like the Lord of adults, and I realized the Lord's words. As they looked like the Lord, I regarded them as the Lord. The bad water looked like the clean water of a lake; dead trees looked like blooming trees. He created me heaven in my mind.

If people receive grace, actually everything looks beautiful. It is not an illusion for a second. It is continued. I do nothing except I try not to hurt people's minds and follow others' suggestion as possible as I can. However He gives me a lot of grace, I do not know how I pay back for His grace.

When I talk about His grace with brothers, the Holy Dew Spirit comes to me. So I cannot help thinking of the Lord. As the Lord says, everybody is God.

I cannot express all the grace of God in detail; it is just amazing. I think the grace of God makes sinners God. I am writing this testimony to announce the advent of the Lord. Also, I leave myself to the Lord who continually gives massive grace at this moment.

The sins in my body disappeared by just looking at the Lord.

Key 18

The Secret of the belief from God

The Bible says, "belief is the gift of God in Ephesian 2:8. He gives eternal life to people as a gift."

The belief is the gift from God because all He has is neither money nor gold but eternal life. So He gives eternal life to people as a present. God who overcomes *Satan* provides eternal life for people.

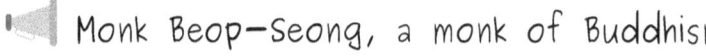

Monk Beop-Seong, a monk of Buddhism

I had questions "Where are human beings from, where do they go?" " What is the ultimate aim of life?" "Are human's life patterns fixed?"

I had wondered about the above questions for a long time and thought that monks might know the answers. So I became a Buddhist of Myogak temple at the age of thirty-one. I tried to find out the true meaning of life.

In spite of studying about life through the scriptures of each religion for several years, I could not find out the answers. I saw several monks who were suffering from desires, anger, and ignorance like worldly people and sticking to their self-respect and ego rather than trying to find out the way to nirvana.

I thought that monks had to live with the empty mind coming from self-renunciation to realize the truth. But they looked like worldly people wearing Buddhist monks' robes. When I thought that most monks were the same as worldly people, I felt rejected. So I went to a small cave near the temple and started to meditate to make my mind empty.

I tried to solve a question "If all human beings were Buddha and the nature of Buddha is in everything, why do evils exist in them? How can I get rid of the evils in me?"

By the way, I was asked to run a building for propagation in Guabsa temple. I could not reject the suggestion. So I became a monk in charge of the building for propagation.

But people who worked at the propagation building were interested in only money. So I was disappointed in them, too. I tried to read books about Indian Yogi to find the truth. I used to meditate after reading books which had the teachings of Rajneesh and Maharishi.

Three months later, BeobJeon, a monk, arrived at the building for propagation. As he cultivated his moral sense in a cave for a long time, he looked calm. So I respected him from the start.

He said that the Reincarnated Maitreya Buddha who is the Savior of Buddhists appeared. He verified his words using the Dharma Flower Sutra. He explained the advent of the Reincarnated Maitreya Buddha through the books of Buddhism and *Gyeoamyourok* for several hours.

After listening to his explaining, I was surprised to remember the story of *Jeongdoryeong* [1].

He said that Jeongdoryeong is the Reincarnated Maitreya Buddha. So I followed him to *Yeokgok* where the Reincarnated Maitreya Buddha is.

I was a little embarrassed about the building of the Victory Altar. It looked like a church rather than a temple. But I felt safe after hearing that the Reincarnated Maitreya Buddha was supposed to come from Christianity, unify Confucianism, Buddhism, and Christianity, and make all people immortal ones.

The worship service is similar to Christianity; they clap their hands while singing hymns. Because I was accustomed to being in calm temples, I needed the patience to follow the worship services. I found myself sticking to the forms of liturgies.

However, I came to think if the man who leads the services is the true Reincarnated Maitreya Buddha, just accomplishing nirvana is enough, the form of worship services wasn't important to me. And I came to know that the form of the worship of the Victory Altar is the better one than Buddhism's.

---

1. Jeongdoryeong is the hero whose appearance is due at the end of 20 Century in Gyeokamyourok (a Korean prophecy book). Nam Sago whose pen name is Gyeokam wrote that Jeongdoryeong would unify all religions and lead humanity to advanced level.

As I clapped strongly, all my distraction went away; the boundary between myself and my surroundings disappeared; only the Reincarnated Maitreya Buddha emitted light. Being surrounded by the light, I realized that I became light itself and one body with the Reincarnated Maitreya Buddha.

As the *Sweet Dew* from the *Reincarnated Maitreya Buddha* removed all my sins, my body seemed to disappear, and I felt light as a feather floating in the air.

I knew the power of the Reincarnated Maitreya Buddha through the Sutra of Secret. Also, I came to know from worship services that He had tremendous power to save all people from suffering from the eternal cycle of birth and death.

'Human beings were Buddha who did not know death; Satan came into the Buddha as desires, anger, and ignorance. So human beings became mortal due to those feels.

But their memory that they lived forever enjoying freedom remains in their blood; so people try to find the way of reaching nirvana (their hometown) according to the Reincarnated Maitreya Buddha.

He teaches the way of accomplishing eternal life exactly and gets rid of evil minds (the soul of Satan) by pouring out the Sweet Dew. According to the Buddhist Scriptures, the Reincarnated Maitreya Buddha pours out the Sweet Dew and makes people reach nirvana.

The Victory Altar where the Reincarnated Maitreya Buddha always stays has a strong scent of lilies, the spirit of the Reincarnate Maitreya Buddha.

When *Beobjeon*, a monk, called me to lead to the Victory Altar, I felt that intense energy came to the middle of the head. That was the grace of the Reincarnated Maitreya Buddha.

About a month later, I unlived the life of the propagation building and moved to the Victory Altar. Then I felt relief for coming to the place where I had to come. I felt friendly with the monks who already met the Reincarnated Maitreya Buddha.

I did not think that I would meet the Reincarnated Maitreya Buddha. Whenever I think of being born in Korea and meeting Him, I feel gratitude. I envied people who were born at the time of Sakyamuni and met him. But Now I met the Reincarnated Maitreya Buddha with much more power than *Sakyamuni*. I have no wishing now.

How do I express my fullness of heart about meeting the Reincarnated Maitreya Buddha every day, who dissipates all my sins by looking at Him.

Entering universities with a good grade is good; getting a promotion is good, too. But the luck that people meet the Reincarnated Maitreya Buddha and get out of the suffering from samsara of birth and death is the best.

Now is the time for me to convey His message of immortality to the world. I will try my best for people's evils to be removed and for them to reach nirvana as soon as possible.

📢 Jeong Soo-Youn a follower of the Victory Altar

God sending light to a critical patient

On Saturday, February 10th, 1990, when I lived in *Masan*, a classmate of mine at the university called me. He asked me to go to *Jinhae* to attend a lecture about *Jeonggamrok*[1] and *Gyeoamyourok*[2] which are Korean prophetic books. As I enjoyed dramas of old Korean history, and I accepted his suggestion simply.

It was pouring outside that day, but there were a lot of people in the lecture room. The lecture was summarized as follows. "At that moment God was captivated by Satan, God became humans, so they were destined to die; hence humans were originally God, the duty of human beings is reinstating God."

The lecturer said that at the end of the twentieth century, a man who says about the way of going back God appears, the man is just *Jeongdoryeong*. Also, I was surprised at the words that *Jeongdoryeong* makes people immortal.

Until that time I was an atheist, I laughed at the Christian who believes if people do not believe in Jesus, they go to hell. I was a little embarrassed by the lecture, but after thinking into it, the possibility is enough because it is logically considered. I concluded that studying the prophecies had enough values to me.

At that time I had submitted a letter of resignation to my company due to the health problems, I was taken to the emergency room of a hospital in *Masan* because of insensibility. My consciousness came alive in two days. I was hospitalized there for several days, and my coworkers and relatives inquired after me. I could identify them, but after they left me, I could not remember who came to me even right before. Like that, I was a severe patient with zero memory.

Being in charge of a section chief for quality control, I drank a lot of alcohol for business every day. I drank even on Sunday two bottles of soju(Korean liquor) and smoked two packs a day. Sometimes I smoked three packs.

---

1. Jeonggamrok: Another well-known Korean prophecy book which hints the advent of Jinin (眞人 , a true humankind like the Jeongdoryeong in Gyeokamyourok)

2. Gyeoamyourok: A Korean prophetic book

I tried to quit drinking, but I could not go three days without drinking for business. So I handed in a letter of resignation.

On that day I listened to the lecture, my company accepted the letter of resignation. From that day I started to listen to the words of *Jeongdoryeong* through recorded video in the Victory Altar in Masan.

Being moved and surprised at the beginning of the words of the lecturer, I could concentrate on it. But after finishing the lecture, I could not remember it at all. But I went there every day like a student who goes to school every day.

The fifteenth day since I went to the Victory Alter, I bought a pack of tobacco after arguing with my wife and smoked two cigarettes in a row.

But the taste of the cigarette was different from the taste I smoked before I started attending the worship at the *Masan* altar. I had a headache all day due to the smell of nicotine. I did not have desire to smoke any more and threw the rest of the cigarettes into the trash can.

I heard that a good way to quit smoking is to drink water a lot and to take a shower to eliminate nicotine quickly. But in my case, quitting smoking was accomplished in two weeks without intention.

I thought quitting smoking was impossible. It was surprising and mysterious to me. I experienced that the Sweet Dew from *Jeongdoryeong* made my blood clean and eliminated all sins, bad habits, and negative factors in the blood. Without the power of purifying blood and mind, how was the habit of smoking two packs a day stopped in two weeks? Of course, I did not drink anymore.

But my liver and other organs were not healthy due to my

intemperate life. For a while after quitting smoking, there was a bad smell from my body. So I hated to meet people. The bad smell came out from my body for three months, then the smell disappeared gradually, and so my body got better.

After recovering my health, staying at home without working, I was getting bored. When my memory was almost recovered as normal people, I moved to *Yeokgok*, the headquarter of the Victory Altar, and got a job there. I thanked *Jeongdoryeong* who extended a helping hand out at the moment I felt the end of my life.

I dreamed a terrible dream, and my mother would wake me up with tender hands, so also He woke me up from terrible dreams with true words. Terrible dreams will not come again in my life.

While attending the worship services of the Victory Altar for four years, I weighed up to sixty-eight kilogram and stood 175 centimeters tall. Before I came here, my weight was at best fifty nine kilogram. These days, when I wake up, my condition is very fresh. My lips' color was always blue, but now they are red. The ache in the liver has wholly disappeared. I was irritated and pessimistic. But now I am lively and optimistic.

My wife followed me to the Victory Altar because my personality changed. I respect her like God and help her when I am free. Even though there are unhappiness and pains in the world, I am sure that someday they will disappear; people will live in complete happiness.

 Angela Kim

Thinking comes true.

Have you experienced that? There are many kinds of thoughts, good and bad, passive and positive. Some people think big, some people small. Although all people try to be happy, they suffer diseases and die. Therefore they struggle with diseases, depression, and frustration about life. People are fated to be trapped in unhappiness cycles.

In my case, as I was growing up, my agony and burden of life became serious. Therefore, I continually tried to find the truth; nothing was important to me except getting out of the humans' problem.

I longed for happiness in my spirit, and I tried to find it through the Bible, the Buddhist scriptures, and philosophical books. However, the gap between my longing and the feeling of outside life was so big. No peace, happiness, and fulfillment were in my heart.

In spite of that, there was a feeling in my heart that should never give up and that my problem would be solved at thirty.

Accordingly, I wanted to be thirty. At the age of thirty, something strange occurred. A male teacher introduced me to the Victor.

When I met Him, He just looked like a kind and well-mannered man. I just went to meet Him for a minute. However, He spent three hours talking to me about the essence of humanity, our Korean races, and science.

He already knew what I was thinking about, and He answered all my questions about life. After three hours with Him, I felt my body and mind become light like feathers, very fresh, peaceful, transparent, and clean.

I often laughed since that time. Before I met the Victor, I could not laugh no matter how I tried. However, I did not know who He was. Later I watched his sayings through a video recorded worship for several months. His name was in the Bible and the Buddhist Scriptures as the Savior.

He is doing a campaign for humans becoming one. He knows the hidden secrets of humans' life such as why humans die although they do not want to, why everything is separated into female and male, what heaven and hell are, and the secret of the Korean people, etc.

Nowadays I am happy, and my mind becomes clean like I wash my mind with soap by just thinking of the Victor.

Because He is such a happy person and gets rid of people's bad thoughts. Just thinks of Him, then His spirit comes you and gets rid of your bad soul. People die because of the bad soul in their mind.

Nothing is impossible for the Victor. Now I will try to help sick and sad people as much as I can by sending His message to the world.

Key 19

The Secret of New Jerusalem

All people are controlled by self-consciousness of 'I', the spirit of death. The spirit of death kills people. If humans overcome the spirit of death, throw it away, and get out of it completely, they can get true freedom and be reborn as the immortal spirit of God. The land where people are reborn as the immortal spirit of God is just New Jerusalem; The Zion was supposed to be built by the Korean Victor (which is the secretly hidden Israelity) according to the Bible.

Whojida Daeko, a Japanese follower

An illusion came upon to me for some time. There was a huge desert under the blue sky. Footprints of a man have connected in one thin line started far away, which were stopped before me.

Looking closely, they were only a trace on the line rather than footprints. Somebody said that was my life's progress. I was surprised. I thought that a fifty-year life of one man left as a small trace on the sand, so if a wind blows, it will disappear.

At the moment, suddenly one wind blew and erased the trace on the sand for a second. After the winds passed by, my illusion disappeared.

After waking up, I shed tears endlessly. Like a heroine who lost her past, did I feel a premonition that would happen? No, I was not.

The wind played a beautiful music that she never listened to and shed tears for being parted with affectionate and missing men.

I could not move at all. What is that reason? After that, I sometimes had an illusion; as time was passing by, the interval was more frequently.

One day I found the fact that the illusion came with a piano piece, which is called 'Eorian harps.' When it was played by piano or harps, the illusions came to me. It was an odd titled song 'Harps that wind plays.' I did not touch the piano or the recorder.

The trial of God seemed like getting rid of beautiful, lovely, and favorable things of mine. And some time passed again. I felt captivated with fear strangely that something would come to me from God. After that, time passed again.

One day an old friend called me, and I met her. She talked about UFOs. It was my old interest. I just heard her story without telling my experiences. I parted with the friend doubting the intention of why she talked about old things.

There was a calling from her again. She said that a great teacher came from Korea. Again, she continued the story she talked about before. Although I was not interested in UFOs, because I did not have any appointments, I promised to participate in the meeting.

"Korea and Japan are brother countries."

That was the first saying from the Korean. I answered with the mind. "Yes" He looked gentle, his mind seemed gentler. Why did He come to Japan? I looked at the man's eyes. They looked pale which were suffering cataract. They were strange.

I had never met someone with holy eyes. His eyes looked holy rather than pale. I thought that he was a famous spiritual person. A Korean American, one of his followers, told me about his strong motivation to follow him. The man who is called 'the Lord(the Victor)' looked a little tired.

After a little while, we watched His sermon through a VTR with interpreting. The interpreting began with "Human beings were originally God." It was the same words as Japanese traditional religion, Sindo (神道).

I also agreed to the principle of blood. I was interested in the relationship between Korea and of Japan. Additionally, I have believed Christianity since I was seventeen years old. I was interested in the similarity between Japanese Sindo and Israel history.

I already knew that the offspring of Dan tribe came to Korea, and one part of them went over Japan. But I had thought that it had no relationship with Christianity.

As my friend suggested that I go to Korea and take twenty-one-day education for beginners, I rejected it. But when the Lord asked me to take the suggestion, I accepted it willingly.

I received a call from the friend again. She asked me whether I was ready to go to Korea. It was not usual. I had the same experience in the past. The way chosen by God was just following Him; throwing myself as a mother, wife, and a man. Also, I threw away all things that I got from the world. That day was my thirty-third birthday.

The memory of the day came upon to me. Will the same thing of the day happen again? Then why will the same thing happen again? What is connected with the thing of the day?

Seven days after meeting the Korean teacher, I went to Korea. Even though I did not know about the Victory Altar, my twenty-one-day education was started. I thought it would be a group of spiritual people. But it was different. Surprisingly it was a worship of a form of Christianity.

More surprisingly, according to the Lord, Jesus was the object of judgment; he was not conceived by the Holy Spirit as well as he was not crucified, either. And he defected to France and lived for 84 years. So it does not make sense that he was resurrected.

Even I have ever heard about that before; I ignored it because not only I did not find any evidence about that but also it was the insistence of other religions.

But the Lord told about the incidents before the trial of Jesus by Pilate from the pulpit of the holy altar. At that time I felt there would be significantly hidden crises of Christianity because of His words.

I was surprised. On the earth, by whose will, by whose order, did the man say? I did not doubt the facts. Is He judging Jesus and revealing the God's will?

There was a sign in the front of the building. It says the Association of the World Eternal Life. Eternal life is living forever. They shouted loudly about eternal life to the world here.

Then, the Israel people who received an important assignment from Abraham who built an altar in Canaan came to Korea with God repeating victories, built the Altar, and held worship services to God.

Immortality is not only the last fruit of the Bible but also the beginning of a new world. The Victor says in the Victory Altar that the glorious world which has neither death nor agony will be accomplished in this land, Korea. 'Death is the wage of sins'. The last image of human beings is death.

Can Jesus who taught eternal life after death come with a thousand troops to object the words of the Savior? Jesus was dead, so he is a sinner. Then, on the earth, who found out immortality? Who is the Victor who proclaimed eternal life toward the tremendous sinful history?

The man is the humble and lofty Lord. He is the Savior who pours out the Holy Dew Spirit, which God promised to give in the Bible.

In fact, surprisingly He is the Savior who all human beings have waited for. The saving work has been accomplished in the Victory Altar in Yeokgok, Korea for 40 years by the Victor Cho Hee Sung.

At the moment people look at the Victor Cho Heesung, their sins disappear. He is the superhero who destroys the essence of death. It is a surprising work of the Savior that people need neither to shed tears of repentance for washing their sins nor to confess their sins.

The day when Christianity collapses and the *Big Change*(immortal era= 天地開壁) happens will come soon. Thinking of these huge affairs, I just shed tears. We live with God. Actually the Victor Cho

Hee Sung is an almighty person. He came to me and made me convinced He is the Lord. Looking at the Lord, people's sins disappear, and they receive immortality. Those who listen to His saying even one time, they cannot help joining the work of New Heaven.

"All the people of the world! the new beautiful heaven will be built soon."

I am a witness who walks toward heaven with the Lord living with the people who are conveying God's message to the world.

I wrote about the hero of New Jerusalem and New Heaven, the meaning of numbers in the Bible, and the lives of neo-humans in New Jerusalem and New Heaven.

Nostradamus expressed, "When the King of horror, other existence, appears, the fate of the earth will be changed."

The King of horror is the righteous man in the east, the God of the beginning, and the God of Omega, who appeared in Korea with tremendous power.

In the next chapter, I will tell about the almighty power of the Victor which can turn the universe immortal.

Humanity is God itself. We have to see God right.

There is no hierarchy, nor family in the world of God. It is due to only God in the body of the One forms the Kingdom of God.

To end up wars and terrors, to bring peace the world, people should meet the good teacher who speaks the truth.

Chapter IV
The Secret of the Five Covenants & Other existence (the Victor)

The Bible tells about God's existence and power through incidents. For example, God showed His power in Moses' time. Like that, the Victor proclaimed the five mysterious covenants in 1981 in Korea to show the people of the world that His power can change the mortal world into an immortal one. I will write about the five covenants that the Victor promised to Koreans.

The five commitments of the Victor God were proclaimed to make foolish and doubtful men realize the existence of the Victor God.

The existence who overcame Satan is not God but the Victor God.

Because God became the Victor God, He has had Almighty power. He proclaimed the five commitments to show doubtful people that He is the Savior. His New Covenants for South Korean people are as follows.

1. I will remove worldwide Communism.

2. I will halt the monsoon rains in South Korea.
3. I will keep South Korea from typhoons.
4. I will make South Korean harvests abundant.
5. I will prevent wars in Korea.

The five commitments were proclaimed on August eighteenth, 1981 by the Savior *Jeongdoryeong*; His promise has been kept for 37 years. So South Korea becomes rich. However, North Koreans have not been blessed by Him because they are against His will, so they have had a lot of floods and drought. Therefore, they are poor.

That is the strategy of the Victor to draw North Korea to the field of unifying the Korean peninsula.

Humans were originally God.

But in the beginning, the *Trinity* (Adam, Eve, God) lost a war against Satan. At the moment the Trinity lost to Satan, He became a captive; Adam became male, and Eve female. God being turned into male and female means that He lost the character of eternal life and was destined to die.

The Bible says about this accident as follows: "Eating the forbidden fruit, they were driven from the Garden of Eden." And the books of the Buddhist describe it "because humans were shot by an arrow of three poisons; desire, anger, and ignorance, they were destined to die."

Also, at the moment the Trinity became the captive of Satan, He lost His omniscient and omnipotent power. Satan that captivated the Trinity God planned to annihilate the Trinity God. Its period is 6000 years, God and the universe were supposed to be automatically destroyed.

But the Trinity God could not put up with the plan of Satan. God who was not caught by Satan succeeded in making the weapon of annihilating Satan by overcoming all hardship and adversity for 6000 years. And He appeared to the world to save humans wearing a human's body. He is Mr. Cho Hee Sung; He appeared with the Holy Dew Spirit, the weapon of destroying Satan.

On the day when God defeated Satan, mountains, streams, grasses, and trees danced, the sky and the earth cried with joy.

In 6000 years, God defeated Satan in the mind of Mr. Cho Hee Sung, three Gods who had been divided in the beginning were combined into one body (Trinity) and became the Victor God.

On October fifteenth, 1981, when the *Eve Victor* (the heroine of opening the 6th seal who was Cho's spiritual trainer in the Secret Chamber) God said to Mr. Cho Hee Sung, "You became a Victor," He answered, "It was not me who won but God, God defeat me."

Finally, by completing the *Adam Victor* (the hero of opening the 7th seal), three Gods became one body and recovered His omniscient and omnipotent power. And Cho Hee Sung proclaimed the five commitments to announce His recovering Almighty to the world in August 1981.

On the day when He revealed the five commitments, the sky trembled, and huge thunders rolled, and lightning flashed. What does it mean that the sky and the ground answered and God was happy?

At that time, the Victor Savior, Mr. Cho Hee Sung said, "because the children of God have died for 6000 years, God has been very sad, now the will of God is accomplished. Until now there was neither heaven, nor the Garden of Eden, nor the fruit of life, nor righteousness. So, nothing good was to God. God has served as a slave to Satan for 6000 years."

Like this, the wish of God who has lived in a miserable situation as a captive of Satan has been accomplished in 6000 years and

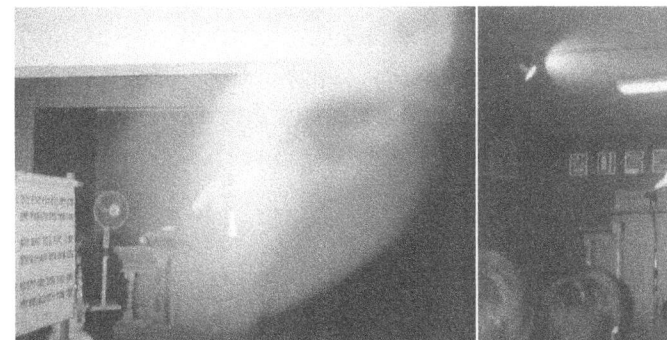

Pic 4-1, 4-2. The Holy Dew Spirit looking like blood, fire, and pillar of smoke (Acts 2:19). It just looks like he is riding cloud.

recovered His omniscient and omnipotent power in the air.

Cho Hee Sung. The Victor, Cho Hee Sung, said like this "Self-awareness of 'I,' Satan, has controlled God for 6000 years, but the great Victor who killed Self-awareness of 'I' appeared in Korea.

The Victor is not a man because God killed Satan (His Self-awareness) of Cho Hee Sung, occupied His body, and God became a Victor. So the Victor is the Creator God.

The Creator God strategically deprived Satan of the royal authority, which controlled the universe for 6000 years, and occupied the crown.

The Holy Dew Spirit uses the omniscient and omnipotent power.

The whirlpool of fire pillar in the picture is the Holy Dew Spirit; anybody can take photos of this. The Five Commitments show that the Trinity God has recovered His omniscient and omnipotent power.

Let me introduce His words "A long time ago, as Satan occupied space; God did not have any power. But after God killed the Satan, He recovered and exercised His Almighty power."

The Victor God who appeared as the Savior controls winds and clouds as He wants according to *Gyeokamyourok*. The Savior, a *True Man* (眞人 *Jinin* is another nickname of the same hero to come as a Savior in Korean prophecy books), uses the power of controlling wind and cloud as He wants.

According to Revelation 11:6, "He closes the door of heaven, and He will halt raining using His power during the predicting period."

Key 20

The Secret of Armageddon War

The man who opens the seventh seal waged the last war against the *Red Dragon Satan* in His Body in the Secret Chamber. After defeating the *Red Dragon Satan*(His self-awareness) in His body, the Trinity occupied His body.

Therefore, after the *Armageddon War*, God restored His Almighty. Also, He came to know the secret of Satan and the secret of the scroll in the seventh seal.

This spiritual *Armageddon war* was finished on Oct 15, 1980, in the *Secret Chamber* of *Milsil*(密室) in Sosa Korea with the victory of God.

The Five Covenants have been accomplished. Confirm! [1]

**Covenant 1. He said,
"I will remove worldwide communism"**

It was accomplished.

He appointed Gorbachev as the president of the Soviet Union and changed all the communist countries in the world into democratic countries.

In August 1991, a civilian revolution that was recorded as the greatest revolution in the human history happened in the Soviet Union, the birthplace of The communism. The great revolution of the century that announced the end of communist dictatorship was that of reform which was expressed as 'Perestroika' by Mikhail Gorbachev, the president of the Soviet Union.

Nobody knows that it was the *Trinity Victor* who removed Communism, which was supported by more than half of the countries on the earth. The Victor Cho Hee Seung proclaimed that He would eradicate Communism in 1981 when Communism was widespread.

Communism is an ideology that separates between parents and their friends; it cannot disappear suddenly in one day. The Victor who is Almighty and has the power of controlling the mind of people set Gorbachev, a person of the same age as the Victor his own, at the head; He revised the mind of the Soviet Union citizens through Gorbachev and made him control the mind of the communist leadership.

---

1. The Victor, Cho Hee-Sung proclaimed the Five Covenants to show His power. Because unless people believe Him, they don't follow Him

On the day when the coup of some communists failed, there was a rainbow over the Victory Altar on a sunny day.

The daily record of Communism's collapsing

1985.3.11,	Gorbachev was chosen as the leader of the Soviet Union, Communism adopted the line of reformation
1986.7.28,	The declaring of Vladivostok, which created the mood of thaw in the Asia-Pacific region
1987.6,	The permission of the pursuit of profit, the reformation of economy
1988.3.19,	The declaring of new Beograd
1989.8.12,	The collapsing of Communism in East Europe without intervening of the Soviet Union
1990.9.25,	The Soviet adopted the comprehensive market economy.
1991.4.1,	The Warsaw Treaty Organization was disbanded.
1991.6.16,	Yeltsin declared the collapsing of Communism.
1991.6.28,	COMECON was disbanded.
1991.8.20,	Gorbachev lost his position
1991.8.22,	Yeltsin arrested the persons who led the coup
1991.8.26,	Communism was disbanded

When the Victor, Mr. Cho Hee Sung, set Gorbachev at the head and coerced him to destroy Communism. On August twentieth, 1991, existing central communists who objected to the disbanding of Communism caused a coup and imprisoned Gorbachev.

At that time, the people of the world thought that the dissolution of Communism would be failed. So they were nervous and worried. But on August twenty-first, 1991, the Victor, Mr. Cho Hee Sung, told from the pulpit of the Victory Altar, "Gorbachev will be free soon."

The Victor, Mr. Cho Hee Sung said, "He appeared in front of the communists who imprisoned Gorbachev, who was the president of the Soviet Union, at that time the body of the Victor was as big as a house." He can change His body as He wants.

The Victor yelled at them "Unless you release Gorbachev, you will die," spoken in Korean. They were scared and ran away. So while nobody was there, Gorbachev came out of the room without knowing the situation.

After Gorbachev was released, on August twenty-second, 1991, Yeltsin arrested the people who led the coup. On August twenty-third, 1991 he organized the leadership excluding communism.

Like this, the Victor announced the people of the world the breakup of Communism without revealing Himself. Also to testify the hero of the breakup of Communism, He made twin rainbows over the Victory Altar on a sunny day around five PM. on August twenty-third, 1991.

The disbanding of Communism was the splendid achievement of God that eradicated the plan of Satan to annihilate all humans.

Communism of the Soviet Union and democracy of America were facing each other in the cold era. The tense fighting of both camps drove the world into horror. It would be the third world war.

The nuclear weapons which America and the Soviet Union reserved were enough to destroy the earth twenty times. In this situation, if the third world war broke out, it would wreck the universe and life would not exist anymore.

Therefore, I think that the Victor, Mr. Cho Hee Sung's accomplishment of the disbanding of communism is a tremendous work of salvation that already saved the world from a nuclear war.

Nostradamus of France, the greatest prophet, said, "The earth would be destroyed in August 1999." Accordingly, the people of the world were worried.

When the Victor Savior proclaimed that He would eradicate Communism in 1981, people laughed at Him. But about ten years later, His words came true on earth; He did not tell a lie, furthermore, it was not blood shedding event at all.

The word of the third world war has disappeared completely.

The accomplishing of Victor's first commitment 'removing Communism' eradicated the basic root of humans' horror, and it is a great achievement to save humans.

Here are vital pieces of evidence to support that the Victor broke communism.

Kenani Gera Simof, the spokesman of Kremlin, said on TV as the ambassador of the Soviet Union in Lisbon "A changing started in the Communism world from 1981." Also, Gorbachev said with no knowledge for heaven's will, "The breakup of Communism was his terrible mistake." Mikhail Gorbachev won a Novel Peace Prize due to the finishing of Communism.

Like Mr. Cho Hee Sung said, after Gorbachev was free, there was a rainbow over the Victory Altar to show that the hero who removed communism is in the Victory Altar.

Rainbow means the commitment of God. The bright part beside to the rainbow in the photograph is the Holy Dew Spirit, which is the Spirit of the Victor. It is the evidence that Mr. Cho Hee Sung released Gorbachev.

Gorbachev eased off the arms race by pursuing the reformation of Perestroika. However, he said, "The disbanding Communism was a terrible mistake" in an interview with a reporter of the Chinese Communism official organ, People's Daily newspaper on June second, 2006

Pic 4-3. This is the picture which was taken after Gorbachev was released.

Mr. Cho split Himself into billions' other selves and went into each Communist, and rooted out the ideology of Communism in them.

The Victor (who is the 'other existence' whom *Nostradamus* spoke of) saved the earth.

While Nostradamus talked with Queen Catherine about the existence of salvation, she asked questions.

"Who would appear on doomsday?"

"Whether people could avoid the doomsday?"

"Whether people should just wait for the day without any trying?"

"Whether God or angels help people?"

"Are there any ways for salvation?"

Then Nostradamus answered "No. There is no way to salvation."

"People cannot avoid the collapse. That is destined to them at that time."

"But I think if other existence appears, the terrible circumstance of the doomsday will disappear."

" I do not know because it is in the mist far away."

" I do not know, either if it appears to me."

The above words mean that nobody escapes the destruction of the doomsday.

However, if other existence appears, they can avoid that terrible circumstance.

The other existence is just the Victor, Mr. Cho Hee Sung.

As the Victor, Mr. Cho Hee Sung, appeared as a Victor, to proclaim the removing of Communism showed His will that He would eradicate the underlying root of humans' horror, Satan's plan, the doomsday of the earth.

**Commitment 2. He said,
"I will halt the monsoon rains in South Korea"**

It has been accomplished for 37 years till now 2017.

The Korea Meteorological Administration revealed, "They will not use the term of 'monsoon rains." Monsoon rains have disappeared.

Mr. Cho Hee Sung was born as a son of a poor farmer. Korea had monsoon rains every year. They caused poor harvests. He was so sorry to see hungry people. So He thought if He halts the monsoon rains, Koreans will be rich. Hence He proclaimed that He would halt the monsoon rains in Korea. Of course, it has been accomplished for 36 years till now in 2017.

Monsoon rains are ones from June fifteenth to July fifteenth.

From old times, Korea had a lot of rain without stopping from June fifteenth to July fifteenth every year. Korean people called the seasonal non-stopping rains 'monsoon rains'. The rainwater let the newly transplanted rice float in it to ruin the rice crop before their root grows firmly.

Like that, the monsoon ruined rice farming which is Koreas' staple, so it left the country extremely hungry.

But in August 1981, since The Victor, Mr. Cho Hee Sung proclaimed that He would halt the monsoon rains in South Korea, the monsoon rains have not fallen in that period.

Hence the Korea Meteorological Administration used new terms to call 'the period of no long rainy seasons' such as 'dried monsoon rains', 'monsoon rains without raining', and 'guerrilla monsoon rains' according to the newspaper Chosun Ilbo of August twenty-third, 2008.

Namely, the rain falls a little, stops, and disappears; it is monsoon rains but not like the disastrous monsoon rains. In fact, the seasonal rain front forms every year but no monsoon rains in that period. We have more chance of showers, however, before and after the period, so fair amount of rain falls spread over time which is suitable for farming.

As the Korea Meteorological Administration's weather forecasts have been off for 37 years; many people denounced them, so they revealed that they would not tell the monsoon rains officially.

Mr. Cho Hee Sung halts monsoon rains.

Until the Korea Meteorological Administration revealed the article, they were criticized a lot in public opinion. As the Victor, Mr. Cho Hee Sung controls the weather with His Almighty power; the weather forecast cannot be right.

Like that, Mr. Cho Hee Sung's covenant "He will halt the monsoon rains" has been accomplished entirely.

**Commitment 3. He said,
"I will protect Korea from typhoons."**

Before 1981, Koreans had poor harvests due to having more than twenty typhoons every year, and there were a lot of victims and damage caused by them.

But since 1981, typhoons have disappeared or suddenly changed their course before hitting the Korean peninsula or perished; there has been the phenomenon of typhoons missing in Korea, which is incomprehensible to ordinary people.

Daily Sports newspaper of August twelfth, 1988 put the title

"Typhoons, which are summer's unwelcome guest, are missing" and "the courses of nine typhoons changed avoiding Korea or perished" on a small title.

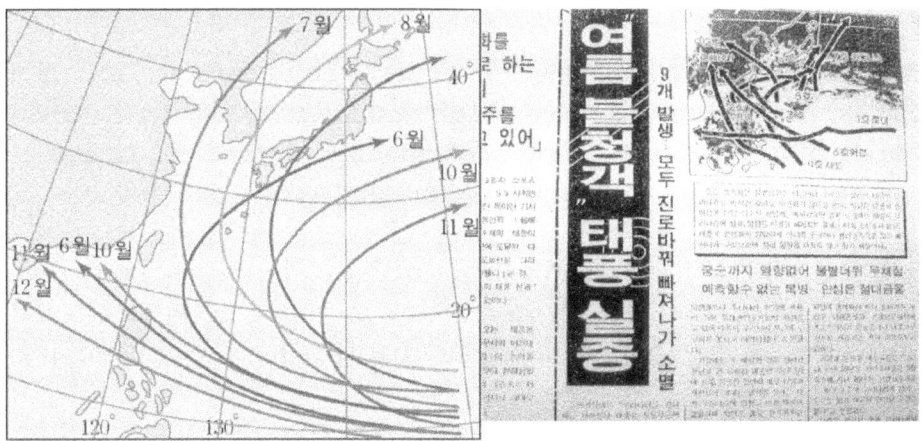

```
Pic 4-4, 4-5. The courses of nine typhoons changed avoiding
Korea or perished.
```

They loaded an illustration of nine typhoons, which came toward Korea and evaded Korea.

They added "continuing hot summer weather is not unrelated to the avoidance of summer's unwelcomed guest, typhoons. Will such typhoons disappear this summer? Korea usually has one or two typhoons by this time every year. But this year, there is no sign of typhoons. It is not because typhoons have not formed in the Pacific; they have turned to the Philippines or China, and so they do not affect Korea."

In 2009, typhoons tremendously damaged to Japan, Taiwan, and China, but Korea did not have any typhoons, although it is located between them.

The Victor, Mr. Cho Hee Sung's promise "He will keep Korea free from typhoons" has been accomplished. Therefore, Korea is a country blessed by the Victor, God.

**Commitment 4. He said,
"I will make Korean harvests abundant."**

Koreans have had abundant harvests for 37 years.

Until recently Korea had one or two years' good harvests, and then one year's bad harvest periodically. So there was a term called 'barley hump'. Hungry people were looking forward the period of barley harvest. Korean people were hungry ones.

But from 1981, the rice planting area has been declining five percent every year due to the exodus of young adults from the agricultural sector, and yet abundant harvests have continued; it is surprising.

To have abundant harvests, farmers need enough sunshine, and water, and no damage from diseases and insects. In other words, unless heaven helps farmers, they never have abundant harvests.

Thanks to the Victor, Mr. Cho Hee Sung, Koreans have had abundant harvests for 37 years. This must be a blessing from heaven.

Since Mr. Cho Hee Sung promised five covenants, the amount of production of rice has been growing rapidly; there is no year that does not have three hundred tons of rice harvest.

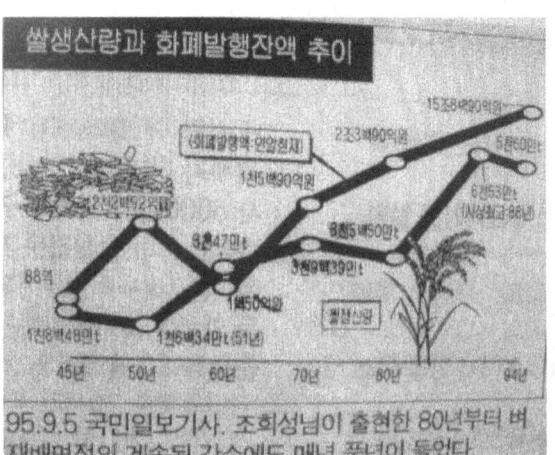

Pic 4-6. The production of rice from 1945 to 1994

It means that Korea has had abundant harvests every year. Because of continuing good harvest, the government had a problem in storing it, so it asked farmers to reduce the production of rice.

Korea is a small land, but North Korea has a different situation. It has had bad harvests due to continuing droughts or floods, so many people are dying of hunger. It is sad for South Koreans to think of them. Anyway, Victor's promise to make Korean harvests abundant has been accomplished for 36 years.

Commitment 5. He said,
"I will prevent wars in Korea."

Nobody forgot the pains of the Korean War in 1950. It caused not only two million casualties but also tremendous property damage. Accordingly, Korea became a heap of ashes and the most impoverished country in the world. People think if the second Korean War breaks out, it will be beyond the local war; it will expand into a world war; then the world will face the destruction of humans. The Victor proclaimed that He would prevent wars in Korea.

He provided an institutional strategy for wars not to break out in Korea. North Korea does not give up the illusion of unification by military force, but since Victor's promise, the condition of institutional strategy is set to deter occurring wars.

He made both South Korea and North Korea join the UN. Above all, the North Korea's joining the UN earlier than South Korea was eccentric. South-North Korea led a reconciliation mood by creating a peaceful atmosphere between South Korea and North Korea. They decided not to attack each other and exchange cultures from the fifth meeting of high officials from December tenth to December thirteenth of 1991 in Seoul.

The Victor made the late Kim Dae Jung the president of South Korea and thought about the reunification of the Korean peninsula.

In 1997 when the Victor served time in jail, His members went to the jail to meet Him. He said, "The president of this election will be Kim Dae Jung." They doubted him because, at that time, people thought that Lee Hoi Chang, the counterpart of Kim Dae Jung, would be elected. But the Victor said that Kim Dae Jung would be a new president.

Above all, He said that He would put up Kim candidate as a president of the reunification. One day, a few days before the election, Mr. Cho in prison ordered some seniors of the Victory Altar to go to Kim Dae Jung candidate's house to say to him, "Kim Dae Jung will become the president of South Korea."

So some seniors of the Victory Altar went to Kim Dae-Jung candidate's house with a towel on the day before the Election Day. The towel embroidered with a wriggling dragon said, "Congratulations on being elected as the president."

At that time, Kim Dae Jung candidate was moved deeply and appreciated the Victor.

 Making a reconcile mood and starting exchanging cultures

As the Victor said before the election, Kim Dae Jung would be elected as the president of South Korea, His plan, keeping Korea free from wars, has progressed well as planned.

The government of Kim Dae Jung regarded inter-Korean relationship very highly. He considerably changed the relationship between two governments strained for fifty years. The two governments have become intimate with each other through the sunshine policy of South Korea.

On June fifteenth, 2000, Kim Dae Jung, the president of South Korea, visited North Korea and held the summit in a peaceful mood, and
achieved the joint communique of June fifteenth between South and North of Korea.

Starting with opening tourism to Geumgang Mountain, they made great progress in exchanging economics & culture. The sunshine policy of the Kim Dae Jung government contributed to the peace of Korean peninsula.

Also, the government drew firm support from four strong countries; America, Russia, China, and Japanese, which did not trust the former government of Kim Young Sam.

The president Kim Dae Jung won the Nobel Peace Prize.

In June 2000, not only Koreans but also people around the world watched Kim Dae Jung, the president South Korea, visiting North Korea for the first time. The holding of two leaders in the Soonhang airport of North Korea made people excited.

The two governments agreed to connect Gyeongui railway and Dounghae one, they started to open the road in 2003, and Gyeongui railway in 2007. Additionally, the reunions of the separated family were accomplished.

The Victor, Mr. Cho Hee Sung, paved the groundwork for Korean Wars not to break out. Until now the Victor has deterred wars.

Also His commitment, "He will prevent wars in Korea" has been accomplished.

Isaiah prophesied, thousands of years ago, that the Victor would appear and accomplish the affair of heaven. Also in Genesis in the Bible, Jacob predicted that the Savior would come from the tribe of Dan, the fifth son of Jacob of Israel. Jacob predicted the future of 12 branches; he said a little about Dan's future because the God in him hid the tribe to produce the Savior. Israelites say that the Dan tribe is lost one; they are looking for the lost Dan tribe.

Therefore, in the next chapter, I will explain about the lost tribe, God's secret plans and strategies. *Gyeokamyourok* foretold that Koreans would break the news to the world about the secret of new heaven.

Chapter V

The Secret of Number 5 & The Lost Tribe of Israelite

he Wave of the number five is just that of the judge, the Savior, and *Mugunghwa*, the rose of Sharon.

The Wave of number five is the wave of the Dan tribe, the fifth son of Jacob of Israel. The number five of Hebrew's code on the roof-end tiles which were found in the bank of the Daedong River symbolizes the wave of the Savior.

When Mr. Cho Hee Sung as a candidate of *Adam Victor* went to the *Secret Chamber*, the *Eve Victor* assigned him number five while others in the isolated tiny inhabit received number four by the Victress who opened the sixth seal. It means neo-humans who face the wave of eternal life in Korea, which is the land of Rose of Sharon according to Revelation.

The wave means the completion of the Holy Spirit, the wave of the Holy Spirit, and the work of saving lives has been realized as Genesis 49:16 says. Furthermore, the wave announces that the Savior has appeared and built an immortal world.

The secret of Arirang

Arirang is a song that Koreans have sung for thousands of years waiting for *Jeongdoryeong*, the Savior of Koreans. Arirang is originated from Ariryeong(亞理嶺), according to *Gapeulga, Gasa, Sipseungga, Gunggungga*, and *Haeinga* of *Gyokamyourok*. That is, Gyokamyourok has the key to solve the meaning of Arirang.

I came to know the meaning of A(亞) from the fact that Koreans are the offspring of Dan, the Chosen People, who live with the philosophy that humans are heaven (God).

Ari(亞理) meaning God is originated from 'Ali' and 'Ala' of Hebrew. Also, Ali and Ala came from 'Hari,' 'Harra,' and 'Hananim.' By being dropped out of consonant 'h,' nowadays, Hananim has become 'Ananim' which means God in Hebrew.

Before producing paper, Israelites passed down their prediction through oral tradition. The reason that Arirang has been passed down through the tribe of Dan, Koreans, for thousands of years is that the Messiah was supposed to come from them. So especially Koreans have a heart that loves and worships God.

Also Isaiah and Genesis in the Bible predict that the Savior will come from the tribe of Dan; that is the secret of Arirang. The meaning of Arirang lyric is that people(衆生, 任) who throw me (亞理 meaning Jeongdoryeong) will catch diseases before going just Ten Li (4 Kilometers).

十里 Ten Li is four kilometers, 十 means 亞, 里 means village, so 十里 means the village of Jeongdoryeong, the pure land of utmost happiness.

The meaning of the whole sentence is that those who leave Jeongdoryeong will catch diseases without reaching the pure land of utmost happiness.

Therefore, Arirang is the inner voices of Koreans that want to meet the Savior who will build heaven and save them from birth, aging, diseases, and death.

Because all humans have an inward wish of waiting for the Savior, Arirang is a song of the Savior. So people are deeply moved by Arirang. Hence it was chosen as the most beautiful song by a lot of musicians.

The secret of the 韓流, Hanryu

I can't expect how strong the wind of the Hanryu will blow the world. When Korea opened its culture to Japan just ten years ago, Koreans thought that Korean music markets would be occupied by Japanese culture.

However, Korean music has grown up enough to swallow Japanese markets contrary to their expectation; furthermore, the Hanryu which expands to Europe will make Korea's future bright.

PSY captures the heart of people from all around the world by his horse dancing. A Singer Group, Big Bang has led in the center of the Hanryu. Wonder girls, female Idol group, went to America. Super Junior, male groups, who went beyond China and Thailand, now captivate the heart of Europeans. Especially, Girls' Generation, the top female idols of Korea, is popular and leads fashions in France. Nowadays, the Hanryu's popularity is rising throughout the world day by day.

On earth, what makes the people of the world be attracted to Korean pop stars? I was able to find that the subject which draws people's interests is the Victor while I listened to His new words. Everybody can understand who the governor of the world is by listening to His words.

Korean culture has naturally gained global attention, too. 'Hanryu' and 'Korean Wave' have the same meaning. 'Top 5 Hanryu Dramas' means the five most popular Korean-made dramas, which are 'Winter Sonata,' 'Dae Jang Geum,' 'Stairway to Heaven,' 'Beautiful Days' and 'Hotelier.' Their popularity has been rising in Asia. So more and more people want to know about the Korean language and Korean culture.

In short, the Hanryu is Korean culture such as Korean singers' songs, TV dramas, Korean movies, TV Stars, etc. It has created great sensation in China, Japan, Asia, Europe, North America, and South America. However, in the view of era and prediction, I define the Hanryu as follows. 韓流 (Hanryu) is the new era's messengers who announce that the Victor appears among the chosen people, in Korea, which is the chosen land.

That is, it contains the messages that a new era will be led by the Victor, who appeared in Sosa, Korea. He will become a Noah ark which saves all humans of the world. Also, it is a wave that announces the Korean spirit and culture through TV dramas, movies, and TV stars.

In addition, there are hidden wills of heaven in Hanryu. If people are interested in just TV dramas, movies, and TV stars, but they do not know the tough history of Korea, the clean Korean spirit, and the thought of the Reincarnate Maitreya Buddha, then they do not know
the true meaning of the Hanryu.

If Koreans, as well as foreigners, do not know the message of New heaven and the true meaning of the Hanryu, they may finish their lives without enjoying the immortal era.

Therefore, I conclude that the Hanryu has the will of heaven, is a warning and a guidebook to those who are indulged in desires and momentary happiness.

The root of the Hanryu is the Victor who is pouring down the Holy Dew Spirit and is causing new religious and cultural phenomenon. I
think that the Victor was explained enough by 'the five covenants.' So I will tell about the primary material of the Hanryu through the phenomenon of religion rising in Korea.

I could not find the cause of the Hanryu through studying cultural Hanryu such as movie and music; I came to know the reason through studying Korean culture, politics, and religion. While having studied the phenomenon of Korean new religion for 20 years, I found a mysterious truth and the source of the Hanryu, which are based on causing peculiar culture, the abnormal changing of the weather, and the complete changing of Korean new religion.

I surely knew that the wills of heaven are hidden in the Hanryu.

First, God has revealed that Koreans are chosen by holding the Asian games in 1986, Olympics in 1988, the World Cup in 2002, the International Congress of Linguistics and the World Congress of Philosophers in 2008, and so on.

Second, God announces that the Korean language is very creative and He broadens the understanding of Hangeul (Korean language) to complete the Hanryu.

That is, people can understand the national character by learning their language. Koreans' language is initially Altai. Before they used Hangeul, they used Chinese. Before they used Chinese, they learned the Old Altai language and the Garimto letters while living in the Altai Mountains and did not use the Old Hebrew to hide that they are Israelites.

Recently the theory that the Dan tribe changed their language to hide the tribe has become a hot issue in an academic world; some Koreans who study the Bible and Israeli archeologist who study

Northeast Asia already knew that Koreans are the Dan tribe of original Israelites.

They found that there are a lot of similarities between the Korean people and the Israelites.

Third, Koreans get interested in prophetic books that predicted the advent of the Maitreya Buddha; who want to the prophetic books are attracting the interest of the world new religionists to know why Koreans have been waiting for the advent of the Maitreya Buddha.

Additionally, the new religion which is directly led by God Himself aims to achieve immortality, announces the fifth wave Hanryu, which was started by the advent of the Victor.

The Hanryu drives the attention of people of the world to the advent of true religion which is stirring up the wind of eternal life in Korea; it announces the opening of New Heaven and New Earth. That is the meaning of the Hanryu.

In conclusion, The Hanryu began in Yeokgok Sosa Bucheon city, Korea due to the advent of the Victor of the Bible; it went to Japan, Taiwan, China, and Europe, America, South America, and Africa.

The heat of the Hanryu which is spreading to the world will come back to Sosa Korea that is New Jerusalem, where the water of life is flowing from the Savior Victor.

---

1 The definition of Avatar is other selves; it indicates an animation character who substitutes the role of the user in cyberspace. It is a compound which is formed by 'Ava' meaning 'descend and pass through' in Sanskrit and 'Terr' meaning the earth. Avatar means 'incarnation' from heaven in the old India language. Opening the era of the internet, it indicates a graphic image which expresses selves in three dimensions, cyber games, or chat sites.

It was prophesied in several prophetic books including the Revelation of the Bible and Gyeokamyourok. They also said, "The Hanryu starts in Sosa and finishes in Sosa". Although the Savior appeared thirty years ago, foolish people think that Jesus is the Savior, they sent the true Messiah who pours down the Holy Dew Spirit to jail for seven years. So the Savior is using K-pop stars as His Avatar [1] to draw people's attention to the Savior.

Why was an Avatar animation so popular? Have you ever thought about that?

The Victor has controlled and changed the dark world into an immortal world by using people as His Avatar. Because He has working power as infinite His other selves, He can go into people's bodies as His other selves and controls the people, as He wants, and sometimes can change His body into fire or a house-sized body to accomplish the work of heaven.

Due to the advent of the Victor who goes to people's thought and mind and changes them at His will, all humans will face a new era.

Key 21

The Secret of the creation of Hangeul

Korean writing system is a wonderful language of Heaven.

King Sejong of Korea Lee dynasty created Hangeul for the Savior to save all humans. It is so systematic and scientific that any foreigners can learn it in a day. Some smart foreigners can learn it in two hours.

Some countries which do not have their writing system borrow Hangeul for writing their language. Linguists say in one voice that Hangeul

 is the best writing system in the world. When King Sejong created Hangeul, he had a lot of difficulties and objections.

Above all, Confucianism scholars who used Chinese letters objected Hangeul to protect their privilege. Nowadays the Savior reveals the secret of heaven in the Bible, the Buddhist books, and prophetic books in the world using Korean. So until the will of heaven is accomplished, Hangeul will be a universal language.

If people do not know Korean, they cannot understand the Savior's sayings, then they will have a big problem in achieving salvation.

The secret of the lost tribe, Dan

Researchers of the Bible think that the Savior was from Judah or will come from Judah. However, the Bible writes in detail about from what tribe the Savior comes. The words of the Bible are prophetic and spiritual, and they are written for the chosen people to interpret the Bible. In Korea, the Victor has revealed the secret of heaven in the Bible for 37 years.

I came to know the essence of the Victor and the lost tribe through the Bible and have studied for 20 years the secrets of heaven and the lost Dan tribe which were revealed by the Victor.

What is the secret of the Hebrew on the roof-end tiles found in the bank of the Deadong River(大同江)?

The Victor Savior, Cho Hee-sung, revealed the secret of the roof-end tiles which were found in the Deadong riverbank in Korea.

Do you know the amazing fact that the roof-end tiles have ancient Hebrew on them?

The roof-end tiles, which renowned archaeologists did not know, will change Korean history completely. This fact has come out through several publications for twenty years; why did they not come into the spotlight to people?

Among the twelve tribes of Israel, Dan who led the Dan tribe is just the founder of Korea, so Korean history is about 3000 years. The Savior Cho Hee Sung knew that, not by human's ability but by the power of God. He has insisted on changing Korean history correctly.

Renowned scholars of Korea and Israel confirmed that the patterns on the roof-end tiles are ancient Hebrew.

The Savior Cho Hee Sung said that Korean people are the Dan tribe of Israel. That evidence is the Hebrew on the roof-end tiles which were found on the bank of the Deadong River in Korea.

The Victor told some young men to go to the Seoul National Museum to take the pictures of the roof-end tiles and to take those photos to Sin Sa-hun, who was a professor of Seoul National University and an expert in old Hebrew. The professor confirmed that the patterns on the roof-end tiles are ancient Hebrew.

Han G-H, a reporter of KTN(Korea Travel News) and a writer of this book, went to Israel to confirm the Hebrew on the roof-end tiles. He met Mr. Ed. Greenstein, a professor at Bar ILan University there. Ed. Greenstein told that the Hebrew on the roof-end tiles is late 8~6 century BC.

Here are their interpretations about the Hebrew of the roof-end tiles. Mr. Ed Greenstein's version about the roof-end tile *pic 5-1* is the same as Mr. Sin Sa-hun's version. Both of them interpreted it as 'arrive.'

< The roof-end tile with the ancient Hebrew >

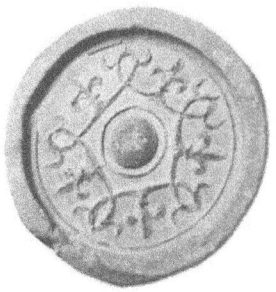

- Age : Age of Gojosun(ancient josun)
- Excavated Area : Daedong river valley, Pyongyang
- Exhibit Hall : Iuchi Isao Collection in the National Meseum of Korea
- A relic Code Number : Jungnae 211

In 1987, Iuchi Isao(1911-1992), a Japanese collector, generously presented the National Museum of Korea with a total of 1,082 items of bricks and roof tiles to promote friendly relations between Korea and Japan.
Some roof-end tiles carved with ancient Hebrew.

Decipher the writing on the roof-end tile

ש ㄹ ㅏ — Ancient Hebrew

ש פ ח — Present-day Hebrew

- This means 'arrived'
- Translator : Dr. Shin Sa Hoon (Hebrew expert, the former Professor of Religous Study in the Seoul National University)

< The informer : The society of archeology & cultural anthropology >

```
Pic 5-1. The pattern of 'Arrived' in acient Hebrew
```

The picture of roof-end tile *pic 5-2* has a pattern of five leaves, Hebrews meaning "a knot," "the Kingdom of God," and "enter."

The roof-end tile *pic 5-2* tells "Go to the Kingdom of God by becoming one with the Savior"(the flower of five leaves means an everlasting life and the Savior)

The interpretation of the Hebrew of roof-end tile *pic 5-2* of two professors is almost the same. Mr. Ed Greenstein reinterpreted "Knot, Conspiracy" as becoming one, "by pulling together," Mr. Sin Sa-hun as "cooperate."

Professor Ed Greenstein interpreted the left Hebrew of roof-end tile *pic 5-3* as "please turn around the flock of sheep", the right

< The roof-end tile with the ancient Hebrew >

- Age : Age of Gojosun (ancient josun)
- Excavated Area : Daedong river valley, Pyongyang
- Exhibit Hall : The collection of the Gwangju National Meseum of Korea
- A relic Code Number : Bon 8464 (the old number : 215)

- The ancient Hebrew on the roof-end tile means
  'Enter the Kingdom of God in cooperation with the five-leaves flower'

Decipher the writing on the roof-end tile

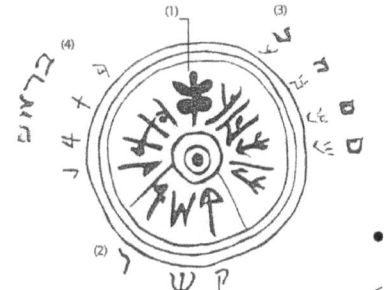

(1) the five leaves flower
(2) in cooperation with
(3) the Kingdom of God
(4) enter

קשו
סמכה
ברא ש

- Translator : Dr. Shin Sa Hoon (Hebrew expert, the former Professor of Religious Study in the Seoul National University)

< The informer : The society of archeology & cultural anthropology >

```
Pic 5-2. The pattern of "Go to the Kingdom of God by becoming
         one with the Savior" in acient Hebrew
```

Hebrew of roof-end tile three as "The ruler has commanded the law of liberty of a ruler." The interpretation of the Hebrews on the right side of roof-end tile *pic 5-3* is almost the same as professor Sin Sa-hun's too.

Professor Sin Sa-hun interpreted the Hebrew of roof-end tile *pic 5-3* as "Heaven will be recovered by saints' prayer." "The Judge who teaches the proverb governs."

Judging from the Bible and the words of the Victor, the Hebrew of the roof-end tiles *pic 5-3* mean "go back to the white flock in New Heaven and New Jerusalem." "The proverb" is the Law of Liberty which makes people reborn of the Holy Dew Spirit. "The ruler" is the Victor, the righteous man of the east, who tells the Law of

< The roof-end tile with the ancient Hebrew >

- Age : Age of Gojosun(ancient josun)
- Excavated Area : Daedong river valley, Pyongyang
- Exhibit Hall : Iuchi Isao Collection in the National Meseum of Korea
- A relic Number : Jungnae 124 (the old Number : 226)

The ancient Hebrew means ' The judge governs with the proverb'
'Heaven will be recovered by saints' prayer'

- Translator : Dr. Shin Sa Hoon (Hebrew expert, the former Professor of Religious Study at the Seoul National University)

Decipher the writing on the roof-end tile

< left side of the tile >   < right side of the tile >

This means 'The judge governs with the proverb'   This means 'The heaven will be recovered by saint's prayer'

```
Pic 5-3. The pattern of "The judge who teaches the proverb
         governs" "Heaven will be recovered by saints' prayer"
         in acient Hebrew
```

Liberty and pours down the hidden manna to the flock of sheep meaning the white herd (Holy saints), and governs the world as His other selves.

The roof-end tiles in the Korean National Museum say that Koreans are the chosen people, Israelites. However, Korean people do not know the root of Korean exactly yet.

They have been told that their grandfather is Dangun(檀君), whose mother was a bear and was reincarnated by eating garlic and wormwood.

But the Savior said the root of Koreans is Israel; Dan-gun is the fifth son among Jacob's twelve sons. (The ending 'gun' means a king, it is a suffix for an honorific title, Koreans still put the 'gun' behind the families name.) Who is the Dan tribe?

The Holy Spirit of Lord who accompanied Abraham moved to Isaac, the first wife of Abraham delivered at his age of 100 years old according to Genesis in the Bible. And the God of Isaac who accompanied the Holy Spirit moved to Jacob, the God of Jacob moved not to Judas but Dan according to the Bible (Genesis 49:16).

'Dan' is Hebrew, it means 'judge.' Judgment is the authority of the Victor Savior. The Bible surely says the Victor Savior will come from the Dan tribe.

The reason that the Hidden Dan tribe came to Korea

Only the Savior who God accompanies knows the reason that God sent only the tribe of Dan among the twelve tribes of Israel to the northeast.

As God has been with the Dan, the hidden tribe of Israel, God knew in advance if the tribe of Dan stayed in Canaan, they would perish by other tribes. So the God of the Lord picked up the Dan tribe from Canaan and moved them to the Korean Peninsula where the sun rises, the Farthest East.

The reason that Israelites were persecuted and massacred by Mussolini, Stalin and Hitler were because of Satan's plan. Satan tried to wipe off the Israelites completely. Because he knew that the Savior would appear from them.

Therefore, God hid the Dan tribe in Korea far away from the area without anybody's notice, and He raised the Dan tribe with the aim to bring up the Victor Savior.

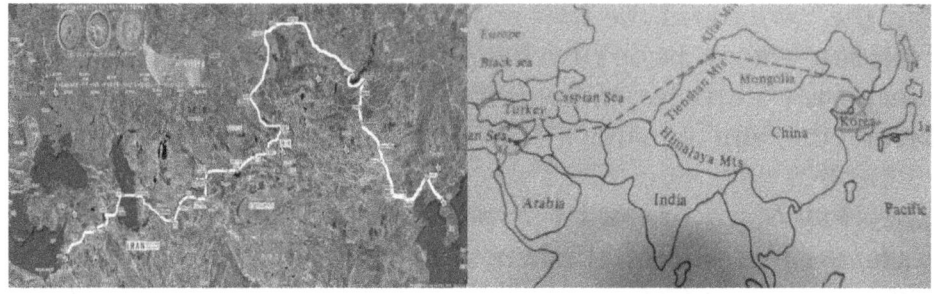

Pic 5-4. The route of the Dan tribe's immigration to the Korean Peninsula

The Dan tribe was placed at Zora between Jerusalem and Tel Aviv and fought against the Philistines for hundreds of years. After the Philistines killed captain Samson, the Dan tribe lost their will to fight and started to move to the northeast 3000 years before North Israel collapsed. After that, the Dan tribe disappeared entirely in the Bible.

However, the Savior knows the route of the Dan tribe's movement to the Korean peninsula because God of the Lord who directly led the hidden Dan tribe to Korea accompanies the Savior.

According to the Victor Savior in the Victory Altar (勝利祭壇 SeungNiJeDan), the hidden Dan tribe left Zora of Israel. They moved to the Dan area, the northeast of Lebanon, and lived there for a while. Then they moved through Syria, Iraq, and Iran to stay in the Altai Mountains for around 100 years.

The old generation died there, the second generation grew up, accustomed there, and learned Altai language to survive. So they forgot Hebrew gradually.

After that, the Dan tribe crossed over the Altai Mountains, lived in Mongolia. However, the main people of Dan tribe moved to the south, passed Manchuria, crossed the Abrok River(鴨綠江), and arrived at the Korean Peninsula.

They settled on the Deadong riverbank and founded Gochosen(古朝鮮), the first government of Korea 2800 - 2600 years ago.

So Mr. Ed Greenstein's decoding that the Hebrew of the roof-end tiles is that of late eight century to six century BC coincides with the words of the Victor Cho.

Here is another story about ancient Hebrew. According to Mr. Go Jeong-Rok who worked for Korean independence, while his father was logging in Baekdoo Mountain(白頭山) in North Korea, he saw Dangun memorial stone(檀君誌石) there during the colonial period of Japan.

Some letters were engraved on it; they were neither Chinese nor Korean. So nobody decoded it.

Fortunately, in those days there was a French Catholic priest who studied old Hebrew. He decoded it. The strange old letters were ancient Hebrew; he said that the memorial stone was made around 3000 years ago.

At that time, nobody understood why the memorial stone of Dangun was written in Hebrew. Unfortunately, the memorial stone was taken by Japanese; so we do not know where it is.

The Dan tribe will judge his people

The general public says that the Savior will come from the Judas tribe and will save mankind. However, it is wrong. According to the Bible, the judge Savior was supposed to appear from the Dan tribe and to judge all humans including the Judas tribe.

Prediction about Judas, the ancestor of Jesus

"Judas is lion's cub; you return from the prey, my son. Like a lion, he crouches and lies down, like a lioness-who dares to rouse him?

The scepter will not depart from Judas, nor ruler's staff from between his feet until Shiloh comes, and the obedience of the nations is his." (Genesis 49:9-10)

As 'scepter' means a royal authority, Shiloh means the Savior; the above-mentioned words mean that before the Savior appears, Jesus, Judas' descendant, will rule the world all the way, but if the Savior appears, Jesus will not rule the nation.

Prophecy for Dan

Dan will provide justice for his people as one of the tribes of Israel. Dan will be a serpent by the roadside, a viper along the path, that bites the horse' heels so that the rider tumbles backward. I look for deliverance, Lord. (Genesis 49:16-18)

The words "Dan will provide justice for his people" mean that the Savior who is the judge will come out among the offspring of Dan.

The words "Dan will be a serpent by the roadside, a viper along the path, that bites the horse' heels so that the rider tumbles backward" is interpreted as follows:

In old times, as kings rode horses, tumbling the rider backward means snatching the royal authority. Therefore, these words mean that the Savior from the Dan tribe snatches the royal authority of Judas. So Jacob passed into Dan the authority of judgment.

The words "I look for deliverance, Lord" means that Jacob waited for salvation through the Dan tribe. That is, it means that the Savior comes from the Dan tribe.

The Victor Savior in the Bible was supposed to appear among the hidden Dan people in Korea.

Prophet Isaiah said the Savior would appear not from Judas, but the Dan tribe's offspring in Korea.

"Be silent before me, you islands! Who has stirred up one from the east, calling Him in righteousness to his service. He hands nations over to him and subdues kings before him. I took you from the ends of the earth, from its farthest corners I called you"(Isaiah41:1-9).

Above, the ends of the earth, farthest corners' means Korea and Japan, God said: "Be silent before me, you islands!" So Japan is nothing to do with it.

According to the second sentence, God said that he would subdue kings before the righteous man of the east. It means the king of kings is the Savior of the east.

In the above words "I took you from the ends of the earth; from its farthest corners I called you the country, farthest corner," only Korea satisfy the conditions.

Then God sent the Dan tribe to the country where the sun rises. He hid them and brought them up to give birth to the Victor Savior.

Why were Koreans called Han race(韓民族) which has the name of God; Hananim in Korean. It means the chosen people of God.

Israelites called God Hananim in the ancient period, but nowadays they call Ananim by the phenomenon of 'h' being dropped, meaning cloud or heaven.

However, today Koreans still call God Hananim. Also, Korean people are called 'Han' race 'Hana' race, the name of the nation is 'Han' country and the Korean peninsula is 'Han' peninsula.

Like this, the Koreans put one part of God's name in the name of their race, their country, and their peninsula. Nowadays nobody knows why the name of their county, their race, and their peninsula is Han.

Especially, they put God in their national anthem's lyrics as follows 'thanks to Hananim keeps and helps Korea, Korea will be forever.'

Every country which attacked Korea was destroyed after attacking Korea. Then why do Koreans stick to God? Because Koreans are the direct descendants of God and the Savior was supposed to appear in them according to Isaiah 41:1-9 in the Bible.

Therefore, God hid the Dan tribe of Israel in the corner land of the Far East.

Of course, there are a lot of pieces of evidence to prove that Koreans are Israelites. They are over 100 similar things between ancient Israelites and Koreans in archeology, culture, and character. I will illustrate the similar examples using an article that I wrote in SeungNi SinMoon[2] in 2008 after visiting Israel.

To show the similarity between Israelites and Koreans, I will cite through editing and arrange the article I put in SeungNi SinMoon of 2008, the studying on the history of Israel, Israelites, and the archeological relics.

I went to Israel for three weeks in 2008 as a reporter by an official invitation. The aim of visiting Israel was to participate in the event of 60th anniversary of establishing the Israeli government, to visit cultural and historical sites, to compare the culture of Korea and Israeli, to announce the truth about the old Hebrew on the roof-tiles to Israel scholars, and to interact with archeologists of Israel.

To complete my duty, I visited the National University of Hebrew and searched the Internet for the Academy of archeology and the history of Hebrew to seek out experts in old Hebrew.

---

2 SeungNi SinMoon: This Newspaper is a biweekly newspaper, which sends messages about the advent of Neo-humans and the new words of new heaven.

Fortunately, after many complications, I met Ed. Greenstein, a professor at Bar ILan University. He told me the era of the ancient Hebrew on the roof-tiles is late 8~6 century BC.

According to Mr. Ed Greenstein, Hebrew has been changed eighteen times. He showed me the history of its changes using a diagram for fifty minutes.

After interviewing him, I gave three pictures of the roof-tiles with appreciation. Ed Greenstein promised to cooperate with my academy in interacting culture. I thought that it would be impossible for old Hebrew on the roof-end tiles which were found in Korea to be acknowledged by a professor of the Academy of Hebrew.

Similarities in genetics

Judging from the viewpoint of genetics, their appearances look alike. Their appearances and skulls are similar.

In the Bible, Noah had three sons; among them, Shem is the ancestor of Asian people, Japheth is the ancestor of European people, and Ham is the ancestor of African.

Noah predicted about his three sons as follows. Ham will be the slave of Japheth; Japheth extends his territory, lives in the tents of Shem.

Today's white people are rich with a highly developed material civilization. Compared with the highly developed civilization, the moral civilization is as corrupt as it can go; finally, they are supposed to surrender to Shem who gets ahead in moral civilization (God's civilization).

It means that the Messiah appears from the eastern people of Shem.

Israelites were originally yellow and short with black hairs according to Numbers 13:32~33 in the Bible. Also, Israelites were originally small like grasshoppers according to the Bible. So Korean people are still short.

However, today's the Israeli blood is the gene of repeated genetic mixing due to the Nazis and the occupation of Rome, so they lost the purification of their yellow race. They almost have the appearance of white people.

For example, Jesus had the Roman appearance such as brown hair, white complexion, and a long nose. However, Koreans still keep the purification of the typical yellow race with single blood; they are short and have black hair.

Here is an article which was written in January 1950 in one daily newspaper by one Jewish American soldier who was a doctor of anthropology. The report shows that Israelites and Koreans are the same race. The article is as follows.

"I have studied the shape of cranial bones of humans according to races; I can see what races are by seeing the faces of people. Also, I can see what races skulls are by seeing them. While I worked in Korea for 2.6 years, whenever people excavated tombs, I saw the skulls; I found that the skulls of Koreans and those of Israelites are the same."

Similarity in character

In character, both people are very bureaucratic, and personal connections are considered highly. Their concept of time is lost; they are stubborn, smart, and too serious.

When they drive, they lose their temper easily and often use a klaxon. Both people value education highly.

Similarity in faith and history

As they have kept the law of God and have looked forward to the Savior through a lot of adversities, Koreans have been waiting for Jeongdoryeong. Israelites have been waiting for the Messiah.

Koreans have been attacked by foreign countries around 800 times, but they survived. And Israelites were attacked a lot by foreign countries including Rome, suffered the Holocaust during the Second World War, wandered the world for thousands of years after losing their country, and waged wars against the Middle East. Through the suffering histories, the people of two countries became patriotic and strong.

I was surprised to know that the year when the two governments were established was 1948. Although they are separated by geographically, their fates are the same. Because the people of the two countries were the chosen people of God, they were supposed to go through a lot of hardships, so they developed their strength for thousands of years to change the mortal world into an immortal one by producing the Savior.

Therefore, the way of Israelites is a thorny path itself, which is one shedding tears of blood like the fate of the Savior.

Similarity in geopolitics

The two countries are very influenced now by strong countries such as America, the two countries' young men have a military duty, due to the wars against neighboring countries and the threat of terror.

Similarity in the relics of ancient folk museums

After finishing the interview and participating the 60th

anniversary of the establishing the government, I visited Eretz Israel Museum in Tel Aviv on March 27th. It is at 2 Haim Levanon St. Ramat Aviv, its exhibits cover a broad range topics such as archeology, folklore, traditional crafts, decorative arts, cultural history and local identity.

The museum also has restored production facilities including a flour mill, millstone, treadmill, water mill, a loom, a plow, smithy, and so on.

It seemed like I visited Korean folk village in Yeongin. While I stayed for more than four hours to research this category in Eretz Museum in Israel, I felt that the relics of ancient Israel will be the clue to find the lost Dan tribe and to reveal the hidden history of Korea.

Similarity in culture and living habits

Now the author will enumerate similarities in culture and living habits which support that Koreans are Israelites.

Koreans sometimes said 'goseule' meaning 'Demons, go away' when they spread red bean soup around their houses to protect them from demons like old Israelites pasted the blood of sheep on the gateposts.
Korea does not have sheep, so they used red bean soup, whose color is similar to the blood of sheep.

Also in Korea, when people start their businesses or move their houses, they make rice cake with red beans and share with their neighbors to keep them from demons.

Like Israelites celebrate the Passover by pasting the blood of sheep on the gatepost to keep devils, Korean eat red bean soup to defeat devils on the winter solstice.

That is, Koreans still observe the custom of the Passover of old

Israelites. Additionally, they have many similar customs and cultures.

(1) Similarity in the right of the first-born

They have the custom which the oldest boys inherit a legacy from their parents.

(2) Similarity in the culture of funeral

Also, they have the same funeral (burial) culture wearing hemp clothes and weeping hymn 'aigo, aigo' when their family members die according to Genesis 37, 1Chronicles 21:16.

(3) Similarity in totem faith and Sodo(蘇塗)

They built totem poles in front of the village; those are sacred poles to keep the village from demons, to obtain abundant harvests, and to wish the health of the village people.

Also, They built 'SeoNang Dang,' Tutelary shrine. 'SeoNang Dang' was the place where the chief gods dwelled to keep the villagers to be healthy, happy, and prosperous. The villagers performed a ritual service here at the beginning of every Lunar New Year.

There were Sodo areas, sacred areas, from old Chosen, the first government of Korea, to Shila era, where a chief priest performed ancestral rites to God, people in Sodo were not ruled by a king. So when even felons or murderers went to those areas, they were not arrested. I could see this example in the customs of old Israelites in Deuteronomy 19:4-6 in the Bible.

(4) Both people liked to wear hemp clothes and white ones.

In old times, old Korean women and Israel women covered their faces with cloth when they went out.

Also, Israelites liked wearing white clothes according to the Bible, so they were called the people of white clothes; Koreans were called the race of white clothes.

(5) Similarity of the system of marriage

Before marriage, the parents of bridegroom sent silk to the houses of the bride as a present, When a bridegroom went to the house of the bride, people followed the bridegroom carrying CheongSaChoLongs, a traditional Korean lantern with a red and blue silk shade.

And Israel and Korean bridegrooms and brides could not see each other before the wedding; even they could not look at each other during a wedding ceremony.[1]

In case a bridegroom looked at the bride, people threw a pack of ash to the eyes of the bridegroom in old times.

(6) Both countries' women carried a jar of water on their heads

Women carried water in water Jars on their head from a well after chattering with neighbors on a well-side.

(7) Both countries pasted the words of God on the gate or the gateposts

立春大吉, 建陽大慶 謹賀新年

They sometimes wrote down idiomatic phrases on the main gates, today's Koreans still do that.

---

[1] A story of marriage that can not be understood appears in Genesis 29:25. Jacob found himself married to someone else next morning. But Korean can understand how could it be possibly happening. It was a Korean tradition that bridegroom and bride could not see each other even before their wedding ceremony.

(8) Both people built stone altars in front of tombs and offered ritual services, Koreans do that these days.

Pic 5-5 Left, A millstone in Korean folk village in Yeongin. Pic 5-6 Right, A millstone in Eretz Israeli Museum. Please check out the round stone foundation, a millstone itself and stoppers. The left one shows missing parts to the right one.

Both people built castles, used stone mills, and made roof-end tiles and ceramics using the same way. Also, the way to build the fortress, castle, and Ondol (a system heating floors) is the same.

(9) The similarity in the ritual of the two countries.

Both people have the similar religious ritual. Israelites performed a ritual offering sheep or cows on the stone altars and Koreans held rituals for rain putting calves on the stone altars; also they used the same ritual dishes or utensils.

(10) Similarity in the stern notion of chastity

Both people had the stern notion of chastity. For example, old Israelites and Koreans killed women caught in adultery by throwing stones. (John 8:4~5, Ezekiel 23)

Also both countries did not allow boys and girls to sit together after they became seven years old. In addition, only if men and women were engaged, the women could not get married to another man.

(11) Similarity in law ancient times

They had similar laws. I could see the similarity between Moses 10 commandments and the Laws of Eight Prohibition of Dan [3] in ancient Chosen(古朝鮮 : the first government of Korea). Here are old laws of Dan of the ancient Chosen.

① You serve the only Lord.

② You respect your parents. As your parents came from heaven, if you respect your parents, it is equal to respecting heaven

③ You neither hate, nor be jealous, and nor conduct in a lewd act.

④ You live and help each other. Do not slander or murder each other.

⑤ You yield to each other and cultivate yourselves. You do not extort or steal.

⑥ You do not be fierce, arrogant, or hurt things or people. Respect each other and love following the example of heaven.

⑦ You help each other in emergencies and rescue in difficulties. Do not ignore weak people. Or you do not look down on lower

---

3. The Laws of Eight Prohibition of Dan: 檀君 8 條禁法, the national law of Dangun Chosen country which was built by Dangun is the first statute law of Korea. It is written in Gyoowonsahwa. It is the law that all people of old Chosen had to keep, so it is an important material to study old Chosen. The copy of the Laws of Eight Prohibition is exhibited in the National Central Museum; its reading number is 貴重本 629(古 2105-1).

people.

⑧ You do not conceive a sly mind and do not hide an evil mind.
   If   you respect heaven and love people, your luck is unlimited.

(12) Similarity in food culture

They enjoy the same food such as garlic, leather carp, spicy food, and leek.

Similarity in ancient Hebrew and Korean before Chinese culture

The author went to America to participate in the international seminar [4] in 2010. I presented a thesis about 'the origin of Arirang in the view of the cultural history of the world and the view of the culture of language.'

While I studied the origin of Arirang, I found a surprising fact. Arirang which is sung not only by Koreans but also by the people of the world is originated from the faith of Israelites calling Yahweh that is the origin of Jehovah.

A-Li that is the root of the words calling God is changed into Ari.

Through studying about Hebrew and Sumerian language, I found that the offspring of Dan are people of Sham in ancient times; because they used 'A-LA, A-LI, A-LU, A-BU,' Sham's language.

Therefore, I think the root of Ari is 'A-LA, A-LI' of Shem language, which was turned into A-Ri, A-RA' to pronounce easily.

---

4. The above thesis is a part of 'A Linguistic and Literary Study of the Korean Falk Song, Arirang' which I presented under the subject 'the twelfth Han Thought', in '2010 International Conference on New Religion in Korea', on January 30, 2010, in Claremont, California, USA, co-hosted by the Process studies and the Korean Academy of New Religions. I was invited by the professor, Kim Sang-Il.

Also, they are the same meaning 亞 (A) and 百亞勝 (BaekAhSeung) which are in old Korean books and funeral rituals. 亞 (A) is interpreted as 'Eol or Al in Korean, which means the original spirit of humans= the spirit of life= the holy spirit of God.
Of course, the origin of Arirang of modern form is in Gyeokamyourok, the history of the root of Arirang is long. I think that Ala, the God of Muslim in the Middle East, is originated from A-Li, Shem language, which means human spirit, soul, holy spirit.

So I infer that 'Li' of 'A-Li' was changed into A-Ri by the phenomenon of assonant and remained as the origin of Ari of modern Korean.

There are some scholars who insist that the origin of 'A-LU' is A-La of Shem language and Assyrian language.

In conclusion, I think that the origin of Arirang moved to the east by the Dan tribe, in the process of the Dan tribe's moving to the Korean Peninsula, the song was made from wishing to build heaven and standing in awe of God.

Also, there is a similarity between the existing Korean language(dialect) and the ancient Hebrew. For example, I think that 'ABUJI' of Korean meaning father came from' A-BI, A-BU' of Shem.

The ancient language of 'ABI and AMI' of Korean meaning father and mother came from 'A-BI and A-BA' and 'A-MI and U-MA' of ancient Hebrew.

AN and ANU meaning God has the similar meaning of ANA and ANI of Shem language, they are interpreted as 'Han' in Mongol, China, and Korea.

There is famous HAPOALIM BANK in Israel. It is pronounced as APOALIM, but they write 'HAPOALIM' in the way of ancient

Hebrew. Like that, the Dan tribe came to the east having the habit of the ancient Hebrew culture, so they write HANANIM and HANUNIM meaning God.

However, there are few scholars who know that the root of 'Han' country came from ancient Hebrew. Judging from the culture of languages, Koreans are surely the people of God.

Furthermore, the root of 'HANU, HANA,' is God.

Then what is the essence of God? There is HANUKA, the holiday of light, in Israel. The root of 'HANU=ANU' in HANUKA symbolizes God, so I could certainly see that from the meaning of 'HANUKA,' "the essence of God is light," and it coincides with the definition of God of the Bible.

Therefore, Gyeokamyourok predicted on the part of Hein that Jeongdoryeong would come as ARI (亞理), the hero of Ariryeong would appear with the Sweet Dew.

'The Sweet Dew is the Holy Dew Spirit, according to Hosea 14:5, it is the symbol of the Victor. Also, the sweet Dew is the brilliant light of the Reincarnate Maitreya Buddha according to Nirvana Sutra.

Therefore, the existence that comes as light is Ariryeong Jeongdoryeong, who all humans have been waiting for. So judging from the above-mentioned similarity between the two countries, Koreans who have inherited the traditions of ancient Israel are the offspring of Dan, the fifth son of Jacob, who received the right of the first-born from Jacob, moved to the east, settled in the Korean Peninsula, and produced the Victor Savior.

Here is an article interviewing the former ambassador of Israel, who worked in Korea for eight years. He admitted that Koreans were ancient Israelites.

The article of August 1st, 2005 in Choseonilbo, a daily newspaper of Korea, is an interview with Ujimanor, the Israeli ambassador, who will leave on August 7th. The title was '*Koreans and Israelites were the same race in ancient times.*'

I could not find the feeling of farewell on the face of Israeli ambassador who will leave Korea on August 7th. When a reporter [5] of Chosenilbo went to the embassy of Israel and opened his mouth, the ambassador waved his hand.

"When I(Ujimanor) came to Korea in 1970 for the first time, I worked as a consul for four years, then four years as an ambassador. When I left Korea in August 1974, I said to my wife that staying Korea was great; someday, I will come back here. 27 years later, I volunteered as Israel ambassador to Korea. I came to Seoul in September 2001."

However, that is not the first his ties with Korea. His connection with Korea traces back more. "In graduate school, I studied international relationship; my major was Northeast Asia." At that time the ambassador heard that Korea is very similar to Israel.

Ancient Israel was composed of 12 tribes. The country was attacked by a foreign country and collapsed. The Israelites scattered to Europe, Asia, Africa, and so on. Among 12 tribes, only one tribe's whereabouts remain a mystery. The lost tribe's family name is Dan.

The founder of old Chosen is Dangun. It is interesting." He is the first mania of Hanryu; He enjoyed the songs of Boa, a Korean singer, Pansori; Korean traditional music, he likes Korean traditional food.

But whenever he has chances to go singing rooms, he sings Hebrew songs. They are Habanaguila meaning let's be happy. The lost tribe's family name is Dan, the founder of Korea is Dan-gun.

---

5. Jeon Byeon Geun: A reporter of Choseonilbo, (blog) bkjeon. chosun. com

Both people are warm-hearted.

"What would you like to say to Koreans?", then he asked, "Do you know Sabra?" He continued. "It means the nature of Israel. Originally, Sabra is a kind of cactus. Its surface is hard with thorns. But its fruit is very sweet. The Israelites are the same. Because of the exterior circumstance, they seem to be difficult to treat. However, they are very kind and warm."

Then he gave the reporter a bottle of alcohol that is made from Sabra. When he came back home and drank it, its fragrance of chocolate and orange filled his mouth. The article is finished with "I can see what the ambassador wanted to say finally."

The Secret of Rose of Sharon, Mugunghwa(無窮華)

Pic 5-7,5-8 Above, Rose of Sharon in Israel,
Pic 5-9,5-10 Below, Rose of Sharon (MuGungWha) in Korea

Rose of Sharon is the national flower of Korea; its native habitat is Syria. It blooms from July to October for a long time. It has five petals, five stamens; its color is purple.

The flower's meaning is eternal life. Koreans are destined to make the mortal world into an immortal one, so they love this flower; they
brought it on the way to the Korean Peninsula around 3000 years ago.

In olden times, neighboring countries called Korea 'the country of Mugunghwa'. Koreans use the shape of the flower to decorate Korean important buildings such as the Blue House(Cheong Wa Dae), the court, the National Assembly, and the Independence Hall, the best prize which the president gives a person with the best merit, the Mugunghwa Satellite, and the military rank insignias.

People can see the shape of Mugunghwa on badges for lawmakers and students, on the car, the chair, and even the computer of South Korean president.

The Korean flag has one circle in the center of the flag. The circle is divided into the red on the upper side of the half circle and blue on the lower side of the half circle. It tells about the fate of Korea which is divided into the democracy of South Korea and the communistic of North Korea.

But if the color of red and blue are combined, it makes purple, the color of roses of Sharon. Purple means completion, also it means eternal life. So when North and South of Korea are reunified, the world will become one and the Victor will make the immoral world in Korea first according to a prophetic book Gyeokamyourok.

Gyeokamyourok, the master key of all prophetic books

The Secret of Gyeokamyourok

In chapter III, the author told about the existence of the Victor that was predicted in the Bible. From now, the author will explain about the Victor in Gyeokamyourok.

Gyeokamyourok is a master key which solves the secrets of the Bible, the Buddhist books, and all prophetic books of the world. The prophetic code of *Gyeoamyourok* is very complicated, so common people cannot solve it.
To solve this book, people should know astronomy, Juyok (周易), geography, the law of nature, and prophetic books of the world.

Gyeokamyourok was predicted centering the Dan tribe among Israelites. It foretold 450 years ago about the incidents and the fate of Korea, Korean politicians, and social phenomenon with 100 percent accuracy.

What is Gyeokamyourok?

Gyeokamyourok(格菴遺錄) is a Korean prophetic book. It is a representative of Korean prophetic books. It was written by 南師古 (Nam Sa-go) 450 years ago. His nickname is 格菴 (Gyeokam).

He was born in Gyeongsang province in 1509. He was an expert in astronomy. When he was young, he met a transcendent person and received the predictions about the future of Korea and the world from him. He recorded the prophecies in this book. The book was registered in the National Central Library. So you can read the book directly at this library.

As all prophecies were sealed thoroughly so as not to be interpreted easily, this book was recorded by splitting Chinese letters or metaphor.

As the predictions of Gyeokamyourok have 100 percent accuracy, people cannot but believe it. It is foretold the day of Yee dynasty's collapse and the ending day of the Japanese colonial period in Korea, the attack of the Japanese upon Korea in 1592, the attack of the Chinese, and the Korean War in 1950.

It also suggested ways to survive during those wars. Furthermore, the book foretold that the Korean peninsula would be divided, face and fight each other, and build 板門店 (*Panmunjeom*) between the 38th Parallel after the Korean War.

As well, it predicted the family names or hometowns of all Korean Presidents, the students' movement against the dictatorship of April 1960 and May Sixteenth revolution. Additionally, it predicted late president Park Jeong-hee would die by two bullets in his head.

Above all, the most important prediction of the book is that the Savior will appear in Korea, His symbol is the Sweet Dew, He will revenge all humans' enemies (Satan), and build an immortal world and universe.

Also the book writes that the tree of life by the river of life in Revelation of the Bible will grow a lot by the Savior.

When the Japanese read the book, they were afraid of it, because the book had huge secrets about Korea and gave the Koreans a lot of hope. At that time they tried to kill the Korean spirit by prohibiting the use of Korean language and cutting out famous spiritual aspects from Korean Mountain ranges by driving big metal posts into them.

Therefore, they took all the books from Koreans and burnt them for three days and night. Some books were brought to Japan. So the books are rare in Korea now. It also predicted that Korea would be the strongest country, be the parent' country of all humans, and all the people of the world are supposed to come to Korea.

Also, Gyeokamyourok said that epidemic diseases would sweep the world, the diseases would be so dreadful that if people catch the disease in the morning, they will die in the evening. It also suggested surviving ways against the disaster in the book.

The hidden prediction of saints who sought the Dharma of the Sweet Dew

First, Eunbiga(隱秘歌), the first part of Gyeokamyourok, wrote that the man who pours out the Sweet Dew is Jeongdoryeong, the Savior of Koreans.

Also, Haeinga(海印歌) of Gyeokamyourok said the Sweet Dew is the essence of elixir that previous saints waited for and dreamed. Also, Doboosinin (桃符神人) part of Gyeokamyourok talked about the power of the Sweet Dew as follows: the mysterious Sweet Dew makes old gray useless men a strong teenage body, stay young men forever.

" 白髮老軀無用者 가 仙風道骨更小年 에 不老不衰永春 으로 不可思議海印 "

Additionally, we can see the effect of the Sweet Dew on humans in Sampunglon(三豊論 meaning a theory of three Pungs, richness) of Gyeokamyourok. It is said, in the first Pung, the Sweet Dew makes bad men into good ones, in the second Pung, the nature becomes domicile, in the third Pung, the true Sweet Dew makes people reach nirvana.

The Sweet Dew (甘露海印) in Gyeokamyourok is the hidden manna in the Bible, the water of Sweet Dew or the brilliant light of the Reincarnate Maitreya Buddha(生彌勒佛).

Tao Te Ching(道德經) wrote God and humans become one by the Sweet Dew falling. Like that, all scriptures and prophetic books

Pic 5-11, Left, The Reincarnated Maitreya Buddha can fill the universe with His other selves for an instance, and remove the agonies of people by emitting the Sweet Dew.
Pic 5-12, Right, A typical Buddhist statue of the Reincarnated Maitreya Buddha (the Future Buddha)

predicted about the Holy Dew Spirit; it was written as the spiritual material of heaven in Gyeokamyourok.

Gyeokamyourok was the master key of solving the predictions to all prophetic books and the scriptures. However it is written in hidden codes, so everybody cannot interpret it until the hero comes.

When the Victor appears and reveals the secret of heaven, the predictions of the prophetic books are supposed to be revealed completely.

So far I explained the secret of the lost Dan tribe, the Korean culture that produced the Savior, and Gyeokamyourok.

Chapter VI
The Secret of the Pure Land of Utmost Happiness

In this chapter, I will tell about the prediction of the advent of the Reincarnate Maitreya Buddha and the secret of the Pure Land of Utmost Happiness hidden in the Buddhist scriptures.

There are secrets about the Amrita Buddha in the Buddhist Scriptures, especially in the Amrita Sutra, the Nirvana Sutra, and the Dharma Adornment Sutra. The scholars of Buddhism call the Nirvana Sutra 'the hidden Sutra,' which has the most secrets about Buddha.

Therefore, they call the hidden Sutras. The Dharma Adornment Sutra and the Amrita Sutra predicted about the advent of Amrita Buddha who would appear in the year 3007 after Sakyamuni died.

The secret of the Amrita Sutra

The Amrita Sutra predicted that the Amrita Buddha would appear in the future and build the pure land of sheer happiness, and Holy people (Neo-humans) would appear in the year 3007 after Sakyamuni died.

People think that the pure land of ultimate happiness is after death. However, the Amrita Sutra does not say so. It says that the pure land of utmost happiness is where people neither have pain nor die, is where joy overflows, comes from the bottom of the heart flowing over the top of the heart of people.

The pure land of utmost happiness is accomplished when people have the nature of Buddha while they are alive. Until now there was no way to obtain the Sweet Dew, so the scholars of Buddhism misinterpreted the Amrita Sutra. Sakyamuni said when people realize the truth of the way of the Sweet Dew; they will reach nirvana while they are alive.

Through meeting the Amrita Buddha, people find the way to the Sweet Dew. By seeing Him, they can get out of the restraint of birth and death. Here in the paragraph below an article, the writer wrote in the newspaper about the Victory Altar.

I found that the right way that Sakyamuni predicted in his Hidden Scriptures is the Sweet Dew. That people can reach nirvana due to the Sweet Dew means that <u>the light of the Sweet Dew itself is the Reincarnated Maitreya Buddha.</u>

Then, let's find what the right way to the Sweet Dew is.

First, if we know exactly the origin of the Sweet Dew and the origin of the Amritabul, we can realize the pure land of utmost joy and the way of getting out of the restraint of humans step by step, and then we achieve the right way of nirvana.

The Secret of the Amrita Buddha

Understanding the meaning of the Sweet Dew and Amritabul

The Sweet Dew(甘露) is Amrita in Sanskrit. It means the alcohol that gods drink, a medicine or elixir that gods take; if people drink it, their agonies disappear, and they can get out of the restraint of birth, aging, diseases, and death.

This term exists in almost all Scriptures and is well known.

Bomun part of the Lotus Sutra said 澍甘露法雨, 滅除煩惱焰, which means "The Reincarnated Maitreya Buddha pours down the Dharma rain and destroys the flame of agony."

Old Indian's Beda Scripture said that the Sweet Dew is the manna of heaven that gods drink, that is, it means soma drink. The name came from its sweet taste, and the scholars of Buddhism think that the Sweet Dew is the alcohol of heaven or the manna of heaven.

Therefore, by analyzing the common predictions of the old Buddhist Scriptures and other Scriptures, I can define the Sweet Dew as follows.

If people drink the elixir of heaven, they achieve immortality; their bodies are turned into light and become God. Also, it is known as a mysterious liquid, which cures a human's agony, makes people live longer, and makes dead people live again.

Therefore, the true image of the Sweet Dew cannot be expressed in humanity's language; So I would like to describe it as the best taste, the best level, the superb Tao, and nirvana.

The terms of the Sweet Dew in the Nirvana Sutra and the flowers rain of mandala in the Dharma Flower Sutra predicted the advent of the Amrita Reincarnate Maitreya Buddha who will preach the right way of the Sweet Dew wearing a human form in the future.

Also, the Nirvana Sutra predicted that when Mr. Cho of heaven appears; He will pour down the Sweet Dew, remove people's sins, and save people.

As the scriptures predicted that the Almighty Victor Buddha (最勝金剛彌勒佛) would appear with the Udumbaras in the year 3007 after Sakyamuni died;

His symbol is the Sweet Dew(甘露). The Sweet Dew of the Reincarnated Maitreya Buddha who makes marvelous accomplishment for all humans is the Spirit of wisdom and life itself; its essence is as follows.

The Sweet Dew is the Holy Spirit like fire, smoke, and rain; it is a kind of brilliant light. Such light of the Sweet Dew is the essence and spirit of the Amita Reincarnated Maitreya Buddha; it moves in a spiral form saving people. Then what is the term of Amita (阿彌陀)?

It is Sanskrit; it originates from the first part of the name of Buddha who is called Amitabha meaning the Buddha of infinite light or Amitayus meaning the Buddha of endless lifespan.

The Secret of Namuamitabul(南無阿彌陀佛)

Amitabul means the Reincarnated Maitreya Buddha who has an infinite lifespan and pours out the Sweet Dew(甘露光明).

Not only in the Nirvana Sutra, the Lotus Sutra, and the Amrita Sutra but also in Amrita Buddhism which Japanese and Koreans believe, there is Namuamitabul(南無阿彌陀佛), a kind of Buddhists' prayer which is composed of six syllables.

The prayer's true meaning is "Turn to Amrita", but they chant the prayer without knowing its meaning; it is pitiful.

Now, I will talk about the symbol of the Sweet Dew that the Reincarnated Maitreya Buddha brings according to the Buddhist Scriptures.

The Great Nirvana Sutra volume 5 says, "the man who pours down the Sweet Dew is the man who reached nirvana (是甘露者 卽眞解脫者). If people want to get out of the cycle of the agony of birth and death, they should drink the Sweet Dew(度生死苦 當服甘露味)."

Also, part 4 of the nature of the Reincarnate Maitreya Buddha of the Nirvana Sutra volume 8 says, "If people taste the Sweet Dew, they are neither reborn nor do they die (無上甘露味 不生亦不死)". The Sweet Dew that the Trinity Buddha pours down is an immortal medicine and gives overflowing delight.

As well, Sakyamuni predicted in the Great Nirvana Sutra volume 9 that there would be a lot of the Sweet Dew in the Victory Altar, the headquarter of Mahayana Buddhism, so people should listen carefully to the predictions of the Buddhist scriptures.

It says as follows when the light of the Sweet Dew penetrates into the pores of people, they reach nirvana(法性光明入毛孔者 必定當得阿綠多羅三冪三菩提).

It foretold, "Where the Sweet Dew falls, the pure land of utmost joy is."

Of course, I have seen the Sweet Dew falls from the Reincarnated Maitreya Buddha during the services of Buddhism. However, most people were ignorant about the Sweet Dew in 1980s and 1990s, so they did not believe that the author saw the Sweet Dew or the pictures of the Sweet Dew. As time passed, people started to believe the pictures.

💡 The secret of the right way in the Buddhist Scriptures

I will introduce the Victory Altar where the Sweet Dew falls from the
Reincarnated Maitreya Buddha, who overcame the authority of death. Also, the author will tell about the land of happiness, the power of the Reincarnated Maitreya Buddha, and His tremendous

accomplishment.

The people in the land of happiness have no agony, they have just pure ecstasy, so the land is named the land of happiness. Most people who live in the delusion of five filth and ignorance do not understand the true view of the land of happiness.

Although the Reincarnated Maitreya Buddha preaches the right Tao(正道)[1] of the Sweet Dew, the ignorant people do not know it exactly. I will explain the term of the land of happiness in the Amita Sutra.

Sakyamuni asked his disciple, Salibul, "Salibul, do you know why the land is called the land of happiness?" Of course, Salibul did not know it. Sakyamuni saw it in advance and said as follows:

Because seven layers' balustrade, seven layers' treasure nets, seven layers' street trees are surrounded by four treasures, the land is called the land of happiness. Sakyamuni also saw and explained it in detail that the Reincarnated Maitreya Buddha would appear and accomplish the pure, solemn, and delightful land. The land of happiness is where the Sweet Dew is, there is no agony, only pure happiness overflows.

Like John predicted about New Heaven and New Earth in Revelation, Sakyamuni predicted about the true figure of the land of happiness; the color and shape of the Sweet Dew in his Scriptures.

I will brief the scene of Sakyamuni's version of the pure land of utmost joy. At the land of happiness, the Reincarnated Maitreya

---

1. Tao (道): means 'way', 'road' or 'teaching' to get to the destination. If you don't know the right(正) way(道), you can't get there; even though you might be able to talk about, practice and teach it. If Tao(道) ends up with death, it would never be the right way. Sakyamuni commented that the right way(正道) will appear in the future with the Sweet Dew(甘露).

Buddha received the righteous men's offering, the spectacle of the land of happiness is that the Sweet Dew always falls, which is decorated solemnly with splendid light.

There are precious trees like the trees of life in Revelations in the Bible. And there are wheel-sized lotuses in a valuable pond; yellow lotus emits yellow light, white lotus emits yellow light, the color of the flowers is that of mysterious heaven.

All day righteous men can hear the music of heaven, flower rain falls, and the flake of gold floats in the land of utmost joy.

The Holy Dew Spirit is the fragrances of flowers, spiritual birds (righteous men) eat the Sweet Dew for a meal during worship services, and they sing songs.

The fresh air of heaven blows; the new and auspicious atmosphere of God makes the land happy, the hearts of righteous men are filled with love for the Reincarnated Maitreya Buddha.

Indomitable righteous men who wish to go to the land of happiness are continually striving for immortality; indomitable angels never give up removing three poisons to reach nirvana and to become a Victor Buddha.

Sakyamuni predicted that the land of happiness is where the holy group prays to go to the land of happiness and listen to the land of Buddha. Also, he asked people to have hope for immortality; he predicted that there are countless righteous men, who never pull back, and are soldiers of heaven that are indomitable against Satan.

A lot of Buddhism saints, righteous men, praise the Victor Reincarnated Maitreya Buddha, struggle against Self-awareness(ego), and try to be reborn an immortal Buddha.

Also, Sakyamuni explained if people kill the Self-awareness of 'I' which is three poisons; desire, anger, and ignorance, they will go to the land of so happiness. Sakyamuni added people have to be careful in interpreting about humans' finale in the Amita Sutra.

The scholars of Buddhism interpret the finale of humans as death. They expediently interpret that people go to the land of happiness after death. However, initially, they misinterpret the Amrita Sutra.

The author insists that they can go to nirvana by interpreting the Amrita Sutra correctly. In fact, they will go to nirvana when they are free from the three poisons that are the spirit of death. Then they achieve an immortal existence.

Sakyamuni asked his disciples to believe and follow his words and all Buddha's ones in the pure land. Sakyamuni predicted that at that time, since the world would be that of five filths: the era would be right, people's thinking would be tainted, agonies would make people murky, people would be unclear, and their life would be weak in the sinful world. So people would be difficult to believe the right Tao(正道) of the Amrita Reincarnated Maitreya Buddha.

As he foretold, the Reincarnated Maitreya Buddha continues preaching the incredible law for all humans to believe Him. However, as preaching about immortality is the first time in human history, people would not believe the Reincarnated Maitreya Buddha's words.

Therefore, Sakyamuni asked that if the Reincarnated Maitreya Buddha who emits the Sweet Dew appears, believe and follow Him at the risk of one's life.

💡 The true figure of the right way of Scriptures

Above, the author explained the core contents and the secrets hidden in the Amrita Sutra. Four scriptures tell about the pure land; they are the Amrita Sutra, the Lotus Sutra, the Flower Adornment Sutra, and the Nirvana Sutra, which secretly predicted at the time of the era of the Reincarnated Maitreya Buddha in the future.

The power of Satan (devil) which has the key to the spiritual prison(birth, aging, diseases, and death) was so intense that Buddha could not eradicate three poisons.

Sakyamuni preached for the true Buddhists to recognize the era of the Reincarnated Maitreya Buddha through the predictions of the Amita Sutra and the right way of the Sweet Dew. He asked his disciples to supply the Amita Sutra to people when the era of the Reincarnated Maitreya Buddha comes.

Conveying the truth is very important for their salvation. In short, other sutras usually were written by the forms of asking and answering, but the Amrita Sutra was short and written in the form of preaching.

It remained us a lot of meaning. In this respect, the meaning that Sakyamuni came to the world is that he announced the appearance of the Reincarnated Maitreya Buddha. Also, he confessed that his preaching was not perfect, the preaching of the Reincarnated Maitreya Buddha would be perfect.

He suggested exactly in the Nirvana Sutra and the Amrita Sutra where the light of the Sweet Dew shines is where the Reincarnated Maitreya Buddha stays, it is the land of happiness without agonies and the cycles of transmigration.

Also, the spiritual terms such as a pond, colorful lights, several colors' lotus, the flower rain of mandala of heaven in the Amrita Sutra are the words of expressing the pure land of happiness.

All scriptures point the Victory Altar, where the Reincarnated Maitreya Buddha preaches the right way of immortality by pouring out the Sweet Dew.

Therefore, righteous men in the Victory Altar try to reach nirvana by killing three poisons and living the way opposite of what Self-awareness of 'I' (ego) wants.

The era of the Reincarnated Maitreya Buddha

Gyeokamyourok said that only people who did great virtue to others for three generations could meet the Reincarnated Maitreya Buddha.
Also, the Reincarnated Maitreya Buddha and the Amrita Sutra said that the offspring of the ancestors whom the Reincarnated Maitreya Buddha loves are called and led by Him, and are striving to build the land of Buddha.

Where the Sweet Dew is shining is where the Reincarnated Maitreya Buddha dwells. There is the only one, the very Victory Altar, on the earth, where the right way of the Sweet Dew of the Amrita Sutra and the secret of immortality are preached reasonably by the Reincarnated Maitreya Buddha.

Sakyamuni said, "What the Reincarnated Maitreya Buddha wants is conveying the Nirvana Sutra to people. If people do it, their sins and karma disappear like fog and dew perish when the sun shines."

As the Scriptures predicted, conveying the truth of the Nirvana Sutra, the Great Hidden Sutra, and the right way to the Sweet Dew is the shortest way to evangelize.

Those who met the Reincarnated Maitreya Buddha should let all humans know His advent.

Finally, like the Great Nirvana Sutra volume 8 says, "When the truth spreads to the world, as all the water of all rivers flows into the sea, all religions come to the Reincarnated Maitreya Buddha." When the time comes, the words will be surely accomplished.

The hidden secrets of the Nirvana Sutra

Sakyamuni stopped expediential preaches for 48 years before he died, he said for a day and night what he did not say before. The compilation of his last words is the Nirvana Sutra.

The Nirvana Sutra wrote about the advent of the Reincarnate Maitreya Buddha and the way of the Sweet Dew. The Nirvana Sutra hid the most secrets of heaven.

The book predicted that the hidden manna (the Holy Dew Spirit) of the Bible would fall as the light of the Reincarnate Maitreya Buddha. The hidden manna is 'the water of the Sweet Dew,' 'the brilliant light of the Sweet Dew,' and 'Amrita' in the Buddhist scriptures.

The three terms are the light from the Reincarnate Maitreya Buddha; it is the light that overcomes the nature of humans. Therefore, where the Sweet Dew falls, there is neither death nor aging according to the Nirvana Sutra.

Here is the sermon of December 31st, 1991 of the Reincarnate Maitreya Buddha(the Victor) who pours down the Sweet Dew. 'This man' in the sermon indicates the Victor himself.

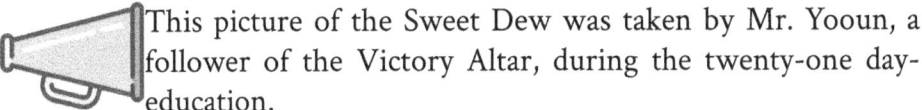

This picture of the Sweet Dew was taken by Mr. Yooun, a follower of the Victory Altar, during the twenty-one day-education.

The lyrics of a hymn 'when the parched ground finds springs, water flows on the parched ground' indicate Sosa. So (素) means white and Sa means sand(砂).

That is, the saying is that water flows on a dessert. Is the water worldly? It is the holy water. In spite of the holy water of life flowing from Sosa, people do not know it until now, because there

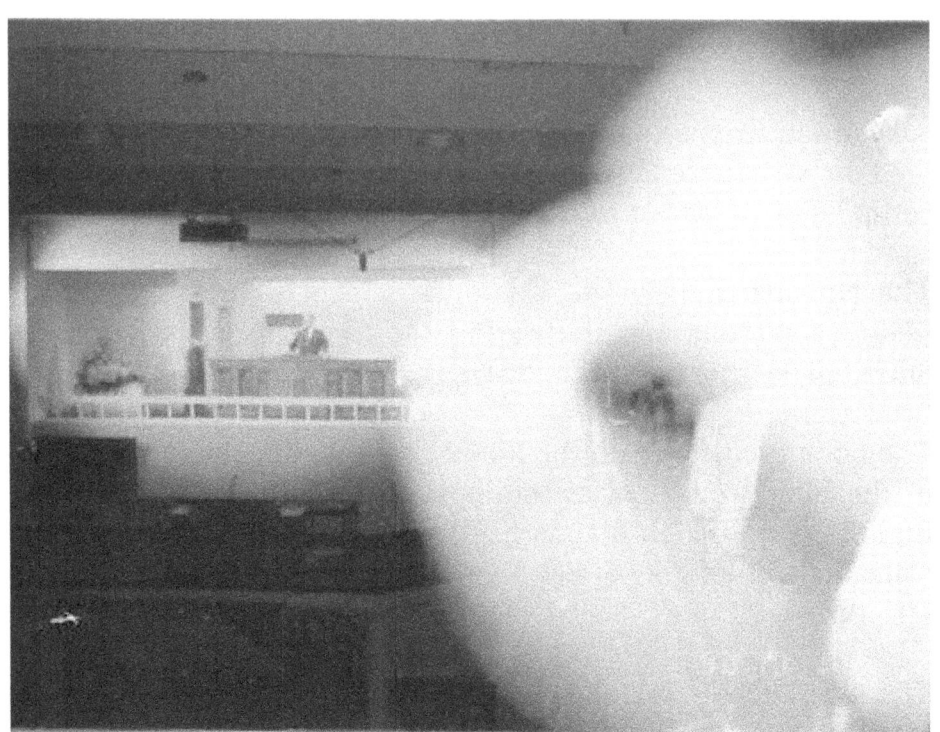

Pic 6-1, The Holy Dew Spirit/ the Sweet Dew/ the Amrita has been caught on the camera during Mr. Cho Hee-sung preaches a sermon in the Victory Altar on 11th Oct 1992. The brilliant light on the right side is the Reincarnated Maitreya Buddha/ Dharma-body/ light of Nirvana/ Victor Savior/ Faith/ Zion/ UFO/ His otherself

is no true writing in the world.

Letters are writing. As there are no writings in the world, people could not understand the meaning of the sayings. Therefore, as it is now, according to the Buddhist books, because there are no writings in the world, there are no religions in the world.

The Nirvana Sutra said that there is no science (learning). Page 289 of the Nirvana Sutra volume 29 said, "When a man accomplishes the nature of Buddha, all humans who meet the man will accomplish the nature of Buddha."

This man says if the Savior appears, the humans who meet the Savior will become Saviors. This saying is in the Nirvana Sutra. Also, page 290 of the Nirvana Sutra volume 6 says, "Tao of the world has no liberty and no equality, yours and mine are different, the Tao of Buddha is free and equal, being one is the right way".

Here, in the Victory Altar, the Victor always says, "Regard everyone as my body" the Nirvana Sutra noted it, too.

Therefore, true Tao and religion accomplish one, unless accomplishing one; you and I are of a different existence, which is neither Tao nor religion.

Also, This man says there is no science in the world. On page 85 of the Nirvana Sutra volume 8, Sakyamuni said, "The letters of all scriptures are imperfect. When the Reincarnate Maitreya Buddha appears, the imperfect letters will disappear, and the perfect letter will appear."

Sakyamuni said what he said was the imperfect letters and he preached in the imperfection. However, when the Reincarnate Maitreya Buddha appears, he will teach people with the perfect letters.

The Nirvana Sutra said about the Reincarnate Maitreya Buddha in detail.

Therefore, humans were God, but science does not know it. So science which does not understand that God is in every person is not science. Also, the religion which does not know that God is in humans is not religion.

Therefore, God (Buddha) is life according to the Bible and the Buddhist books. They say that God is life.

Does anybody not have the life inside of them? The reason everybody has life is that God (Buddha) is in them.

You live thanks to the God who is in you. If God is not in you, you cannot live. Therefore, God is life, and Buddha is life, so, as it is now, you should regard life as a precious existence. Hence the men who ignore life are Satan.

Today, if humans meet the Reincarnate Maitreya Buddha, they can achieve immortality because their sins perish as soon as they reach the Reincarnate Maitreya Buddha according to the Buddhist scriptures.

The humans who meet the Reincarnate Maitreya Buddha become Buddha because their sins perish.

If people become Buddha, they won't die. The immortal life belongs to God and Buddha.

This man states the secret of immortality logically and scientifically.

"Blood is changed as people think." Then these words, "if people think like of God, their blood changes into God's blood" are science.

These words are an immortal theory. Because God is an everlasting Spirit, the mind of God is eternal and sacrificial, therefore, as it is now, if they have the mind of God, their blood changes into that of God, so they live forever.

Therefore, if people have the mind of God, their blood will be changed into an immortal one, their body will turn into immortality one, then they cannot catch diseases. So, the revised body can live forever.

People can achieve salvation by being reborn as the Holy Spirit. People can achieve salvation by being resurrected. People can achieve salvation by eating the fruit of life. People can achieve salvation due to faith. People can achieve salvation by participating in the Sabbath. People can achieve salvation by having the mind of God, and they can achieve salvation by going to heaven.

Are the above sayings the same meaning or different meaning? They have the same meaning. People do not know it. People call letters that are so narrow that they cannot be perfect meanings. Imperfect letters cannot be letters.

Therefore, This man says, "people can achieve salvation by being reborn as the Holy Dew Spirit, people can achieve salvation by being resurrected, people can achieve salvation by eating the fruit of life, as it is now, they can achieve salvation by faith."

These words, "people accomplish salvation by being reborn as the Holy Dew Spirit" means that the Spirit of God breaks a spiritual tomb, the original Self-awareness of God occupies them again, that is, if God that is in spiritual tomb reinstates His original conscious awareness again, God is resurrected.

However, pseudo religionists say that resurrection is that the body that is buried in a tomb breaks the tomb and lives again. That is imperfect letters, they speak like that.

The saying of the Bible is spiritual. Therefore, as it is now, the resurrection should be the spiritual resurrection. So the saying that Jesus lived again is not correct.

Therefore, as it is now, when God that is caught in spiritual tomb breaks the spiritual tomb, lives again, the Self-awareness of 'I' is reborn as of the Holy Dew Spirit, it also means eating the fruit of life.

God's power is strong enough to break a spiritual tomb; it means that God overcomes Satan. God can be resurrected only after overcoming Satan.

If God cannot overcome Satan, God cannot be reborn as the Holy Dew Spirit. Only God who overcame Satan becomes the resurrected one.

Nobody said the theory of salvation precisely. The saying that achieving salvation by eating the fruit of life is, as the fruit of life is a spiritual fruit, just spirit that gives immortality is the fruit of life.

When Self-awareness of 'I' becomes of God, the Spirit of God that overcomes current human 'I' (Satan, and the authority of death) becomes the new 'I,' and the authority of eternal life lives forever. Here the resurrected Spirit of God is the fruit of life.

The spirit which is reborn as the Holy Dew Spirit is the fruit of life.
Therefore, saying that people can achieve salvation due to faith is in the Bible; however, those who know only imperfect letters cannot understand it.

Therefore, Faith is the gift that God gives to people according to Ephesians 2:8. The Spirit of God who overcomes 'I' (Satan, and the authority of death) is immortality. Only the Spirit of God gives immortality. The man who talks about this fact is the true Savior. Also, the man who pours down the Sweet Dew is the true Savior. If the Savior does not pour down the Sweet Dew, he is a fake.

Therefore, as it is now, the true Savior builds the Victory Altar in Sosa. Before the Victor built the Baekman Victory Altar, the Victory Altar has moved to Yeokgok 1-dong, Yeokgok 2-dong, and Yeokgok 3-dong.

Before we built the Victory Altar here, this area's name was GoaeiAnDong. Its name means the village where the devil lives. Here was the town where the devil lives safely.

The Victor occupied the village of the devil. The Victor is the Victor God. Therefore, as it is now, when you listen to the theory of salvation from the Savior, you can see the Savior says the theory of salvation precisely.

The Savior was not supposed to be born everywhere. The Savior should be born in the land of a corner. The condition of being the Savior is that he should be born in Korea.

The second condition is being born in the land of a corner, Gimpo. The Han River flows through the east of Gimpo, the Imjin River flows through the north of Gimpo, the west sea is in the west of Gimpo. So Gimpo is the land of the corner.

The true Savior should be born at the land of the corner. According to Isaiah 41:1-9, "Be silent before me, you islands. Who has stirred up one from the east, calling him in righteousness to his services? He subdues kings before him. I will call you from the ends of the earth, from its farthest the corner."

This man(the Victor) was born in the corner of the land. Do you know? As it is now, unless the Savior was born in the land of the corner, he is pseudo. Gyeokamyourok says that the True Man (眞 人 the hero saving the world) will be born on the bank of the Han River.

Gimpo is on the bank of the Han River. As Goyang is on the bank of the Han River, the book says that the True Man will be born in Seo ho area 西 (서) 湖 (호) 地 (지) 方 (방). Seo(西) means gold, Ho(湖) means the bank of water, Po in the name of Gimpo means the bank of water.

That is, Po and Ho have the same meaning. For Satan not to notice that Gimpo is Seoho area, God hid where the True Man will be born, this is explained in Gyeokamyourok. Therefore, unless being born in Gimpo, the Savior is pseudo.

In Hosea 14: 5, in the Bible, it says that I will be dew to Israel, he will blossom like lilies.

God says that He will be dew to Israel (victor), He will blossom like lilies according to in Hosea 14:5. God promised that he would be the dew to the Victor. This promise should be accomplished. If the Savior does not pour down the Sweet Dew, he must be a pseudo-God.

The Bible says that the Victor is the Savior. According to Revelation 2:26, "To him who overcomes and does my will to the end, I will give authority over the nations; he will rule them with an iron fist. I will also give him the morning star."

Therefore, as it is now, God says that He will give the morning star. If God gives the real morning star to the Victor; it is as big as the earth. If God gives the morning star, the Victor cannot receive it because it is too big.

God gives the morning star as a gift. The morning star is a bright star. In a hymn, it says, "The Savior is the bright star and is the Lord who is outstanding over all the humans."
In spite Christians religion, there is a hymn about the Savior, but Christians do not know the true meaning of the hymn.
The Savior is a lily; it says the Savior is the bright morning star. As the words are in the Bible, people made the hymn. As the Savior is the bright star, the man who is named the bright star is the Savior.

Therefore, This man's name is Hee-sung (熙星) which means the bright star.

Also, the Bible writes about the man who achieves and gives salvation is the sheep. The Bible already knew that the Savior would come as the Chinese zodiac cycle of the sheep; it wrote the Savior is the sheep. Therefore, if the Savior was not born in the year of the sheep, he must be a pseudo-God.

Although the Bible says that the Savior came as the year of the sheep several times, as they are not the hero of the Bible, they know only imperfect letters; they do not know its meaning.

Therefore, as it is now, Gyeokamyourok says that Jeongdoryeong will be born in the year of the sheep. This man(the Victor) was born in the year of the sheep. This man's ID card says that He was born in the year of the sheep.

In addition, This man was born on the day of the star, the time when he was born is the golden fate.

This man was born at four in the morning. He was born June 28th, 1931 in the lunar calendar; it is August 12th, 1931 in the solar calendar.

June 28th, 1931 in the lunar calendar is as it is now, the day of the star, people call famous people stars in the world. They call outstanding person stars. This man was born on June 28th and has a name meaning star.

Therefore, This man is the true Savior. This man said the truth in the Buddhist scriptures and the Bible from the beginning of the Victory Altar.

However, He never read the Buddhist scriptures. As He was from Christianity, He read only the Bible, He never read the Buddhist scriptures.

However, all His sayings are in the Buddhist scriptures. Therefore, this work is surely that of God.

Therefore, as it is now, the true Savior should have the name of the bright star; the true Savior should pour down the Sweet Dew; the Savior should be born at the corner of the land, The true Savior should be from the Dan tribe.

According to Genesis 49:16, "Dan will provide justice for his people as one of the tribes of Israel. Dan will be a serpent by the roadside, a viper along the path, which bites the horse's heels so that its rider tumbles backward. I look for your deliverance O Lord."

Jacob had God in his body and predicted his twelve sons. He gave the authority of judgment to only Dan.

The Koreans are the offspring of Dan. Then the race who will produce the Savior is the Koreans.

Therefore, only if the Savior appears, all the humans become same as the Savior. Even ugly people and foolish people will be the Savior only if they meet the Savior.

According to Gyeokamyourok, the Savior will start the work of heaven in Sosa and will finish it in Sosa. It also says although heaven collapsed, it will be built in Sosa.

The saying came true. Revelation 2:17 says that God will give the hidden manna and a white stone to the Victor, a name is written on the white stone, only the receiver knows the name.
The Victor should know the name written on the stone, if the Savior does not know the name written on the white stone, he must be a pseudo-Victor.
The name written on the stone is Sosa. The letter on the white stone is Sosa(素砂). So(素) means white, Sa(砂) means sand, the sand is a small stone. Sa(砂) is composed of the letter of stone 石 and the letter of small 少 ; a small stone is a stone.
The saying that God gives a white stone to the Victor means to give the land of Sosa. There cannot be objective about that. The area name Sosa(素砂) means white stone itself.

Therefore, God gave the land of Sosa to the Victor, and the Victor will rebuild the Eden Garden which was lost. Only the true Savior rebuilds heaven. The pseudo-Savior cannot build the heaven.

What is the pseudo-Savior doing in the sky? In spite he did not go to the sky, people believe that Jesus will come down riding cloud on October 28th next year.

If the story is true, I(the Victor) will be happy with it. However, it is a lie. So, the next year will come later a few months.

Do you know what they are going to say on that day? The Victor knows what they are going to say. They will say that the world is so sinful that nobody is saved; Jesus postpones his second coming.

Rapture is a big problem in Japan, too. These days, in Sooncheon and Yeosoo, they spread leaflets of saying that Jesus is going to descend riding a cloud.

You should be awakened. Jesus did not go to the sky.

If he went to the sky, the Bible says the ruler of the kingdom of the air is at work in those who are disobedient. It also says that the spirit of space is the evil spirit.

Therefore, they made a story that Jesus went to the sky and will return as Satan but Jesus did not go to the sky.

Christianity drove Jesus as Satan. Also, as it is now, at that time only robbers were crucified, as it is now, why did they make an innocent person a robber? As they made an innocent person a robber, they must be crazy.

Despite the fact that Jesus ran off to France and lived to his age 84, they rigged that Jesus was crucified, died, and went up to heaven.

Therefore, we should believe as the Bible says. As it is now, the Bible says that Jesus is to be innocent according to the Bible. Pilate washed his hands with a handkerchief after declaring Jesus innocent.

It was a Jewish precedent when judges declared Jesus innocent. Then Pharisaic people and Jewish held a demonstration to kill Jesus on a cross. According to the Bible, Jesus was innocent.

Therefore, they did a demonstration. Christians are foolish. The Bible should have said Jesus was innocent and he was not crucified, so he becomes a great man.

However, it says that he was crucified. They made Jesus a robber. The people who wrote in the Bible that Jesus was crucified are traitors to Jesus.

Therefore, as it is now, you should evangelize that Jesus is innocent. In spite of his not guilty sentence, how could he be crucified like robbers were crucified? The Bible was written wrongly. Then the readers will open their mind. Then you feed the fruit of life that is an immortal sayings.

Therefore, as it is now, today's Savior should work in Sosa. This land was planned 6000 years ago.

God says that He works for six days and takes a rest on the seventh day. The Bible says that one day is equivalent to 1000 years. So it means that God works for 6000 years and will take a rest from 7000th years.

God will take a rest; sinners (human) do not take a rest. God has worked to raise the Savior for 6000 years.

The Savior reveals hidden things, that is, the Savior says the secret of immortality scientifically and logically. Everybody can achieve immortality by listening to This Victor's immortal sayings. Even the fools can achieve immortality.

Only if they meet the Savior, their sins melt like snow. However, doubtful men go to hell. However, as it is now, only if they meet the Savior, their sins melt and they become righteous men, God.

Page 77 of the Nirvana Sutra volume 8 says, "If people eat the Sweet Dew, they can achieve immortality." Page 90 of the Nirvana Sutra volume 9 says that the light of the Sweet Dew goes into the pores of people, they can reach nirvana.

People can be the Reincarnate Maitreya Buddha and God. The whole Nirvana Sutra says only if they meet the Reincarnate Maitreya Buddha, their sins perish. However, if they doubt the Reincarnate Maitreya Buddha, they cannot be righteous men.

Page 59 of the Nirvana Sutra volume 6 says that the Reincarnate Maitreya Buddha in the Nirvana Sutra is like the Gold Mountain; also the humans who are with the Reincarnate Maitreya Buddha accomplish the nature of Buddha-like Gold Mountain.

Gold does not change. If it is not changed, it means becoming God (the Reincarnate Maitreya Buddha). Only if people come to the Reincarnate Maitreya Buddha in the Victory Altar, they become God.

Page 49 of the Nirvana Sutra volume 5 says where the Sweet Dew is, people neither grow old nor die. Only the Sweet Dew removes sins, so people become like a Gold Mountain. Gold Mountain means that people become immortal existences that are neither changed nor die.

According to page 61 of the Nirvana Sutra volume 6, Sakyamuni says that what the Reincarnate Maitreya Buddha wants is conveying the Nirvana Sutra to people widely. By doing so, like fog and dew perish when sun rises, all sins perish. Sins perish like that. This man's words are in the Nirvana Sutra. The Nirvana Sutra verifies This man's words.

In New Year, you should not do attempt desires. And leave all your mind and bodies to the Reincarnate Maitreya Buddha, live as the will of the Reincarnate Maitreya Buddha, not as your will.

You should obey God. Then, you cannot die, you cannot grow old, and you cannot catch diseases, either.

Now, This man says surely, in the Victory Altar, people's fatal diseases are cured. Not because This man is a magician.

Ko chairman, a Japanese follower, became so healthy that he was surprised This man to come to the Victory Altar with his wife every day.

Therefore, there are pieces of evidence that changing occurs in the Victory Altar. Therefore, you should become Reincarnate Maitreya Buddhas, Righteous men, and the Saviors to become the workers of heaven.

So God pours grace as much as you pay allegiance to God. God is smart. If God does not give grace to you, can you become righteous men? No, you cannot.

You should pay loyalties to God to receive grace. You should evangelize hard and work for heaven.

Therefore, you, as it is now, should become the workers of heaven who accomplish an immortal land.

Like the prediction of the Nirvana Sutra, the writer confirmed the Sweet Dew to fall from the Reincarnate Maitreya, the Victor, for 25 years.

The Sweet Dew falls and goes into the people's bodies through their pores. As the Sweet Dew is the immortal spirit of the Reincarnate Maitreya Buddha who overcame the spirit of death, if people receive the Sweet Dew, people's bodies become the same as the immortal body of the Reincarnate Maitreya Buddha.

Pic 6-2, 6-3: Focus on the mysterious phenomenon that happens to the believers of the Victory Altar who proceed to nirvana(涅槃) with living bodies

The secret of the Lotus Sutra

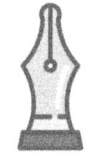

The Lotus Sutra explains the scene that the Reincarnate Maitreya
Buddha appears and preaches the way of the Sweet Dew.
And it predicted that the Holy people (Neo-humans) receive the Sweet Dew every day.

The Lotus flower in this book is the Holy Dew Spirit of the Reincarnate Maitreya Buddha; it is the light of life from Buddha who attained Nirvana. The Sweet Dew is elixir, if people receive the Sweet Dew; their anguish is removed according to the Lotus Sutra. This Dharma flower is described in the Nirvana Sutra, the Amrita Sutra Pic. Focus on the mysterious phenomenon that happens to the believers of the Victory Altar who proceed to nirvana(涅槃) with explains in detail the Sweet Dew as the seven-colored one.

The Amrita Sutra describes the Dharma flower as flower rain of Mandala where the Amrita Reincarnate Maitreya Buddha stays.

Therefore, the Dharma flower is the Holy Dew Spirit of the Victor in the Bible, also it is the light from the Reincarnate Maitreya Buddha who reached nirvana according to the Nirvana Sutra.

Next, I will introduce the prediction in the Amrita Sutra about the Holy people who are experiencing the mysterious Sweet Dew.

This is an article of Seungnisinmoon, which was written by the writer of this book.

The supreme Sweet Dew in nirvana and the mystery of holy crowds in the mandala world

> After the right way to the Sweet Dew appeared, the steps of reaching nirvana are predicted in Seonbulgajinsueorok (仙佛家眞修語錄), a Korean prophetic book.
>
> The book was sent by Bulgonghwasang(不空和尙), a monk from the northern part of India, to Gaeuoon (開雲), a Korean monk in Sangju, the northern Gyeongsang province of Korea by transcending time and space, 190 years ago, around 1320 years.
>
> The book was found by Yangseong(暘星), a Korean monk, who wrote the publishing procedure, Cheongdam (淸潭) and Goam(古菴) who were monks wrote the preface of the book, published dozens of books, and shared with some monks. Among them, Seokchudam(秋潭), a monk, my acquaintance, received the book.
>
> I have a copy of the book; the prophecy about the Dharma of Buddhism is valuable to monks who follow the right way.
>
> I will introduce the book, Seonbulgajinsueorok, a Buddhist book (佛法秘傳書), which was secretly passed down to nowadays.

It is about the experiences of holy believers 上善人 (聖徒 = 聖衆) of the Victory Altar who stay in a Way-place where the Maitreya Buddha's right way is preached.

Also, it predicted about the believers' stepwise experiences in reaching nirvana.

If people receive the Sweet Dew from the king of the Sweet Dew, they recover the nature of Buddha. There are steps of the experiences toward nirvana according to Seonbulgajinsueorok.

The first step, the holy group of the Victory Altar that are the disciples of the Reincarnated Maitreya Buddha enjoys the peace of mind through distracting thoughts being removed by the Sweet Dew.

Also, their skin becomes white like milk and all chronic diseases and serious diseases disappear. They experience that their bodies and blood are changed by dark red blood being discharged through dung and urine.

Men who cultivate themselves ardently experience that their bodies and body become young.

The second step, some followers who cultivate ardently themselves experience that six vital points on their bodies disappear, their complexity is like white cheese, and they enjoy heaven without nightmares or sleep paralysis by obtaining Sadaham.

They feel that euphoria springs up in their bodies; they are not tired although they do not sleep. Also, they do not have worrisome, their minds are endlessly peaceful.

The third step, among some followers who receive a lot of the Sweet Dew, for example, sixty to seventy years old women have periods again, and their bodies are more flexible, and their backs are straighter.

Therefore, their stick does not need any more. Also, their gray hair turns black, without feeling hunger though they did not eat food.

Some followers experienced the feeling for one month. It shows that the time when people can live without eating is coming soon.

People enjoy ecstasy without desires for honor and sex by the mysterious power of the Sweet Dew.

They feel that the Sweet Dew comes to their whole body. According to the above mentioned prophetic book, people do not breathe through their noses, their gray hair turns black, and their teeth look younger.

The fourth step, some followers' skins become white and shiny; some feel their bodies becoming as light as a piece of paper. So they feel like flying right now, and some did not feel hot even though their fingers were in the light of candles.

Actually, Mr. Cho Hee Sung who is the Reincarnated Maitreya Buddha proved that He is the holy king of the Sweet Dew and a flying being like a UFO by moving the distance of 40 kilometers in five minutes and calling to the followers at the beginning of the Victory Altar.

The secret book said that people's bodies are changed into freely flying ones, their bodies neither drown in water nor burn in fire by achieving the law of Arahan.

So far, I told about the secrets of heaven and the brilliant light of the Sweet Dew which were hidden in the Amita Sutra, the Nirvana Sutra, and the Dharma Adornment Sutra.

All these secrets were supposed to be hidden and revealed by the Reincarnate Maitreya Buddha in accordance with the Nirvana Sutra and the Amita Sutra.

Therefore, the Victor, Messiah, Reincarnate Maitreya Buddha, and Jeongdoryeong has appeared as a Korean and saved humans by pouring out the light of life.

The fifth step is not in secret books; it is completed in the period of the Reincarnated Maitreya Buddha; this step is that people are changed into a mass of light and fire if people accomplish Tao completely; they are changed into light by recovering their original essence.

This condition is that the Reincarnated Maitreya Buddha works as His other selves or changes His body.

This step exists in the law of the Sweet Dew and is a step for the followers of the Reincarnated Maitreya Buddha to go toward completion.

As the Nirvana Sutra and the Flower Adornment Sutra predicted somewhat, the Reincarnated Maitreya Buddha accomplished the supreme way and recovered the almighty power, so He can change His body as He wants.

Therefore, He proclaimed the Five Covenants on the pulpit of the Victory Altar to show His recovered omnipotence and omniscience.

Chapter VII
The Philosophy of Immortality by the Principle of Blood

hus has the author heard, following this philosophy of immortality from the Victor in the Victory Altar(勝利祭壇)

Here are the words of the Victor for immortal Secrets.

Due to the philosophy and culture of eternal life which are the best value of humans, Neo-humans become complete.

Those who live forever are supposed to have the philosophy of immortality.

Everybody has a philosophy. One's philosophy determines the values of his life. Although they try to have the best values, all humans have wrong philosophies. Do you know why?

If people live according to their values and philosophies, which do not have an-ever-present value and lose their value at the very moment they die, everything with them becomes nothing.

People do not know whether they live 70 years or 80 years. Since their lifespan is limited, if they die, their value goes to zero.

Therefore, whether they live 100 years or 200 years, if their lifespan is limited, they do not have to live long with difficulty.

There is one thing that made This man(the Victor) have the view of the eternal life. When This man was in the second year of middle school, He played yutnori(a traditional Korean game) with His friend at his friend's house.

The next day, This man heard that the friend died from His mother.
Hearing the sad story, He felt that life is vain. The tomb of the friend was at the corner on the way to school. So He thought about it every time he passed by the grave that He also would die someday. Then He thought life is meaningless. If people go to tombs like that, they do not have to live desperately.

He thought about the problem profoundly and found people who thought about this question are philosophers, This man went to bookstores to buy books of philosophy and read them over and over again.

From that time, This man was intensely interested in immortality.

I found at an early age that everybody has the mind of hating death.

Then why do humans die? This man asked 'the working of the mind and the reason of death'. So the teacher had sweated over His questions.

He said that he did not know the reason for death. However, as he taught that the working of blood is the functioning of the mind, This man was sure that thinking comes from the working of the blood.

Everybody has the mind of hating death and the mind of living happily. If those thoughts come from the working of blood, we can get the answer that humans' blood comes from their ancestors who lived in an eternal world. This man found it at His young age.

Therefore, He knew the fact that Adam and Eve have the figure of God, they lived in the Garden of Eden; The Garden of Eden is the paradise, which is heaven.

If Adam and Eve lived forever in heaven, then it is a beautiful immortal world.

The principle of immortality and the secret of genetics

There is an old saying in Korea; "If you know, you escape from eath."

This saying is usually cited as the words of a prediction 'if you know the secret of immortality, you can escape from death.' People's aging and dying are not simply due to the passing of time, but due to their blood's decaying.

Germs are created in bad blood, as the tainted blood cannot form new cells, it causes the shortage of cells and progressive aging. The most influential factor in decaying blood is attempting desires.

Now, I will state the way and wisdom to understand 'the root of desires' and removing Self-awareness of 'I' which makes people attempt desires.

Also, to be reborn as an immortal, people should know precisely how desires and illusions affect bodies, the relationship between blood and life, bodies and mind, the whereabouts of sins, and the root of life.

Mr. Cho Hee Sung, the seventh angel, preached that the working of blood is that of the mind. Blood itself is the mind. Blood itself is the spirit. As their blood forms people's flesh and bodies, their bodies are their spirit.

Also, thinking determines a humans' fate and lifespan; it makes eternal life possible. That is the principle of blood and that of immortality.

As the root of the good and the evil lie in blood, sin is in blood, too. So purifying blood is a fundamental solution for immortality; also people's minds which have a close relationship with blood decide to go to death or accomplish eternal life.

Blood is life, and life lies in blood. A person's actions and their mental status cause one's blood to decay at the same rate that they live their life. If their mental state is excellent, their blood doesn't rot. But if their spiritual situation is miserable, their blood is also poor status.

The Bible expressed that blood is life in Genesis 9:4, Leviticus 17:11. It is common sense that all patients who almost die from excessive bleeding come to life again by transfusion. That verifies that blood is life.

Humans come from one drop of their parents' blood, by the division of somatic cells which have the genetic information of the parents, it forms a fetus.

Scientists found that about 100 trillion cells form a humans' body. The cellulation cannot last forever, and each cell has a different lifespan. The cells of skin live for twenty-eight days, some cells of a hormone can live for only a few hours, and the cells of bone live for eight years.

Therefore, several hundred million's cells die a day and generate new cells to fill the loss. It means the same number of new cells are required to keep the current physical body condition, but the problem is only healthy blood can form new cells.

For example, if 100 cells die, and if their blood is 100 percent healthy, new 100 cells will refill the places where the dead 100 cells were. Aging does not exist this case.

However, almost all people attempt desires in their lives. Therefore their blood decays. Now tainted blood does not make new cells, and they gradually lose the number of cells for keeping current young bodies.

Let's say twenty percent of your blood is tainted when 100 of your cells die, only 80 new cells will form to maintain your body because the 20% of lousy blood can't produce healthy cells. As a result, the shortage of cells happens, it makes wrinkles, and the whole body loses power and gradually starts to malfunction.

This shortage of cells reduces the number of white cells, so the body loses the power of fighting off, and death finally comes. This explains how important blood is because blood itself is life. Then, is there a way that blood does not decay? Is there, a way to live forever?

That is the duty of the science of immortality. If blood is life, what is the root of life? All religions and the scriptures say that God is just life, so each religion commonly has religious precepts that they prohibit to kill life and not to eat the meat with living blood.

Therefore, all humans should know the root of life and join the campaign of recovering God by understanding the principle of immortality.

 The root of life is God.

All living things emit the light of life. Modern physicists have already said that atoms compose of all materials; neutrons are in the nucleus of atoms, and electrons go around the neutrons.

Electrons can not go around the neutron without a power source. The power of life makes them turn around. Having the power of life is being alive, and being alive means having life.

If the essence of life is God, the nature of death is Satan(the soul of the devil).

Then what is life? Life is just God. Satan(the spirit of the devil) has no life; it has only the spirit of death. The spirit of death rides God(life) and finally kills God.

Therefore, humans dying means that God that is the root of life dies and the energy of God perishes at the moment. All living things and the universe were initially immortal God(Buddha) who was the light of the Trinity.

At that moment the spirit of death(Satan) occupied the two Gods among the Trinity, it separated the Trinity into female and male and made them die after all.

However, the God who was not occupied by Satan found out the factors that kill the children of God and has secretly developed the Sweet Dew for 6000 years, which is the light killing the God's enemy (spirit of death).

And He came to Korea in the name of Bright Star. The Reincarnated Maitreya Buddha wearing the seventh angel's body has been recognized as the hero who opens New Heaven by changing the mortal world into an immortal one.

Like this, if people do not know the circumstance of God and the essence of humans, they never know the secret of eternal life.

Key 22

The Secret of Death

Why do humans became mortal existence though they want to live forever?

The spirit of Trinity was God's controlling spirit in the beginning; They lived forever as one body. At that moment, Satan occupied the first ancestors(Trinity) of humans, the spirit of the Trinity was replaced with that of Satan.

The Bible says that Satan is a sinner. God became a sinner by Satan occupying God. So humans, the descendants of God, are 50% god and 50% sinful. So unless humans overcome sin(the spirit of death), they die.

The factor that rots blood is desires, which is the character of Satan. The foolish custom that kills God in blood is the cause of death; action and mind killing God that is the root of life become the factors of death, too. The scriptures define those minds as poisons; covetousness, anger, ignorance, Satan, karma, and sin.

I will define desires as the factor of death and the root of sins from now on. As the Bible also says, "after desire conceives, it gives birth to sins; when it is full-grown, give birth to death according to James 1:15.

Because of desire, people commit sins and die. A lot of evil minds which decay blood come from desires.

Sexual desires, anger, nervousness, worries, all agonies, and delusion spring from desires; because of desires, there is you and I, mine and yours. So, desires make people commit sins and decay blood.

Therefore, we can conclude if people know the whereabouts of sins and the secret of removing the root of sin, they will live forever.

Fortunately, the people of the Victory Altar have learned the way of immortality from the immortal God.

The principle of immortality by the spectrum of blood

Knowing the cause of death is essential, but knowing the way of immortality is even more critical.

I will suggest the Law of Liberty is free from human influence. I will explain the secret to practice the Law of Liberty.

Above, I said that blood is life; God is the root of life. And the factor that kills God is sinful desires, which are the character of Satan.

Then, where do the three poisons (covet, anger, ignorance) come from and what is their root? If we get rid of the underlying factors that commit sins, we can attain immortality.

Therefore, first, we should know the root and whereabouts of sins clearly; the Self-awareness that controls humans is the spirit of death and the essence of death.

💡 The whereabouts and character of sins

As death comes from desire, desire itself does not attempt desire, Self-awareness of 'I' attempts desire. Mr. Cho Hee Sung who is the seventh angel and can kill Self-awareness of 'I' revealed the cause of birth, aging, diseases, and death.

People die because their blood decays, not from growing old according to Him. And He pointed out that sins decay the blood, Satan(Self-awareness of 'I') is the criminal that kills people by rotting their blood.

The readers may think that it is so easy to find out the cause of rotting blood.

However, Mr. Cho Hee Sung, the seventh angel, the Victor, found out the secret of karma and the whereabouts of the spirit of Satan through a lot of terrible hardships that humans cannot imagine.

He found out the principle of immortality through pains that ordinary men cannot endure.

The blood of human being is as corrupt as it can get by the original sin from the first ancestor of the human being, by hereditary sin through generation by generation, and by the self-committed sins in their present lives. So all the humans did not avoid death.

In other words, not only individual's death but also all humans' ruin came before their eyes in the late twentieth century. However, due to the advent of the eastern righteous man in the Bible, the Reincarnated Maitreya Buddha in the Buddhist Scriptures, all humans come to have hope for immortality.

The co-relationship between blood and mind

People think of blood as the essential material that just provides nutrition and oxygen. However, blood has another factor beyond the level of material.

That is, the mind changes own blood. That is, we can see that mind and blood do not exist separately; they interact with each other; blood forms mind and the mind changes the blood.

Like this, we can see that the mind's movement, personality, and behavior are different by the shape of blood.

In other words, blood, mind, and bodies cannot be separated; they are one.

People's blood is changed as they think. If somebody thinks of one person, his/ her face resembles the person that he or she thinks of.

Key 23

The Secret of Happiness and laughing

Why does laughter make people happy?

When you laugh, Satan dies. As a crying mind is Satan's, when you laugh, as the Spirit of God becomes strong, causing Satan to weaken.

Today, no matter how intelligent scientists are, they do not know this. When you laugh, your body becomes light and healthy, and diseases can be cured.

That is the work of God; the Trinity says a laughing mind is God's, when the blood of people has been changed into God's, the people laugh automatically.

If you always laugh, all severe diseases like stroke, cancers, and AIDS are cured.

If you live with a depressed mind without laughing, your disease will get serious. If you live brightly with a lot of laughing, the laughing material springs up from your body and makes people laugh because of the laughing material.

A laughing mind is originally that of God. Laughing people are beautiful, even though they have a lot of wrinkles. A laughing mind is undoubtedly that of God.

Do you know why laughing people look so beautiful? Because when they laugh, they become God. The moment you laugh, you become God. God is beautiful like that. Because God is so beautiful, laughing people look so beautiful.

Do you know why laughter makes people happy? At that moment they laugh, they become God. At that moment you become God, you cannot but be happy because happiness belongs to God.

If some couples love each other, they resemble each other gradually. It is a medical and scientific truth that bodies are changed as they think.

In the case that a baby does not resemble his/her father or mother, some scholars or religions explain the phenomenon with the doctrine of reincarnation; actually, the reason is that the mother of the baby thought of another man ardently or had an affair according to genetic engineering or the principle of blood.

Blood is changed every second as people think. When people think of something, blood is changed by that thought. Because the blood that has the information of the material of the thinking forms cells, and the body's shape and quality are made the same as the thoughts.

This is the evidence that humans' bodies are changed as they think.

It means if the mind is the spirit, the spirit is the mind. Humans' bodies form spirit, and spirit itself is mind and thought.

Because their mind has changed own blood, also their blood have changed own bodies. It is a scientific and medical saying, religious groups and scientists agree to it.

As a result, if blood is mind, the mind is the spirit, and spirit and blood are energy that can influence simultaneously on each other.

Here we can find the fact that body and spirit are one. Consequently, body and blood are changed by the mind; blood determines the character of people.

As bodies are spiritual forms, which are formed by blood, if the mind changes, the blood changes; if the blood changes, the body changes, too. That is the principle of blood.

The new view of the past, the present and the afterlife (通時的三世燈明)

According to the Seventh Angel, all humans should awake from a long sleep facing the era of the Truth. When you overcome human spirit(current ego) to be spiritually born again with the Holy Spirit, the salvation includes the previous life, the present life, and the afterlife.

What is the past life? People say they can see the previous life through contacting another spirit in them by using a particular method.

In fact, that is not the previous life; it is only contacting some awaking spirit among a lot of spirits which are in the subconscious.

If a change happens by spiritual coup, the takeover spirit from subconscious becomes a new owner of the body, and the individual shows another characteristic. It is straightforward to explain how a man becomes a crazy person.

Centering me now, the lives of my ancestors are my previous life(前世), my present life (現世) is my ancestor's afterlife, my afterlife (來世) is my children's lives.

Strictly speaking, all genetic information and traits are connected to this world through blood and lineage.

Therefore, only this world exists. It is possible through the Seventh Angel's the principle of blood looking at these three lives with the view of the *Tongsijeok*[1] (通時的 , 통시적, *transcending time*) and explaining it with the principle of *Samse-Deungmyeong* (三世燈明 , 삼세등명, *enlight over the past, the present and the future*)[2].

---

1. Tongsijeok: English pronunciation of 通時的 , 통시적. Tong(通) means entirely, Si(時) time and Jeok(的) a postposition. Interpreted as *transcending time* or *taking care of entire time* in this book.

2. Samse-Deungmyeong: English pronunciation of 三世燈明 , 삼세등명. Sam(三) means three, Se(世) world, Deung(燈) a light and Myeong(明) shine. Sakyamuni said that when the Reincarnated Maitreya Buddha comes with the complete letters, He will enlight the world with True Knowledge. The Truth is clear and taking care of entire time to cover the three worlds (the past, the present, the future).

Therefore, while I am alive by being reborn as the Holy Spirit, not only I but also all ancestors can achieve salvation; three worlds' (前世, 現世, 來世) eternal life come true in me.

That is the view of the exodus of birth and death of the Victory Altar; the principle of *Samse-Deungmyeong*. People believe vaguely that the previous life, this world, and afterlife are separated.

That is quite a superficial thought. Like I said above, all lives and traits of people's ancestors are passed down to their offspring through blood, form their offspring's bodies and mind in this world, and become the essence that moves their offspring's spirit.

That is, people's afterlife(來世) exists in the blood of their offspring. Therefore, my ancestors' nature and experiences have a close relationship with the style of my behaviors and mind's working and influence a lot on my life in the blood.

If ancestors had a talent in music, among the descendants, there is undoubtedly a person who inherits the genetic material. If there were violent behaviors in some families, their passionate character appears in their descendants according to genetics. Because all the information from the past lives gathered, encrypted on DNA, and passed down to us, who live present life.

Therefore, all humans' original sins of 6000 years, hereditary sin, and sins committed in this world are here in their descendants' bodies are reflected in this world.

And my afterlife is determined by my conditions of this world.

Also, my previous life is the lives that my ancestors lived; the ancestors are residing as my existence in my body in this world, so because all the sins and karma are connected and are passed down to me, the blood of my ancestors exists as my life in this world (現世).

Therefore, one's previous life, this life, and afterlife coexist in the blood at this moment view; (*Tongsijeok* view of transcending time).

If I have a good mind, then it washes the karma of the previous life, establishes heaven in ancestors' afterlife, and that is doing my best in this world.

On the contrary, if I have an evil mind, then it adds karma to the previous life and establishes hell in my afterlife.

Therefore, those who live for eternal life have the eternal present and also the present time when they move is important for them.

Those who live for eternal life think of only the present forgetting the previous life and the illusion of afterlife.

Additionally, they think of only becoming Neo-humans who are reborn as the Holy Spirit and possess eternal life. So those who are reborn as the Holy Spirit have no agonies about birth and death.

Plus, the Buddhist Sutras say that there is neither birth nor death to Neo-humans. That is, they are neither born nor die; they transcend three lives.

They have the only eternal life of new level in the heaven of the present. Perfect God is never conscious of time and space. Living shackled to the past and living in an illusion of the future ruin the lives of people.

The mind that neither look back the past and nor expect the future is the life of God, which is the mind of true humans, God, or Buddha, according to the theory of the Victory Altar.

When the view of the afterlife which people go to heaven after death is revealed as a fallacy, all existing religions that were from the viewpoint of the afterlife will perish.

Also, for thousands of years, religions have been formed by the view of the unrealistic afterlife, even though they do not know the essence of God, they have pretended that they are holy groups and have deceived people.

Soon their scams will be revealed at one time.

Thinking of this result, those who spiritually awakened will guess it will be a revolutionary movement that the proclaiming of the exodus from birth and death through the principle of blood which is the science of immortality.

From the view of the afterlife based on the principle of the blood of the Victory Altar, the look of the afterlife that people go to heaven after death is a grand illusion, a holy delusion.

The view of going to heaven after death is not admitted in the modern society when genetic engineering is advanced highly.

Judging from a scientific thought, unless people are reborn as the Holy Spirit and attain neutral nature by achieving nirvana, they will die, and their spirit will perish.

Therefore, the thought of spirit leaving the body after death is an anachronism and there is no method to prove the thought.

There is no difference in weight exists before death and just after death.

Like this, Kempner, a medical scientist of Germany studied about after death, supports the Seventh Angel's theory, and revealed his study as follows.

When humans die, they perish, nothing left. He said, "I observed 8000 patients nearly to die, with a special device that can record one over one million minute's waves.

He tried to find whether the spirit leaves the body right before death or right after death.

However, nothing left except for gas from the body."

The author thinks the view of going to heaven after death does not exist. Right after death, the body starts to become cold, the circulation of blood stops, the body stiffens, finally the blood and flesh decay, even the bones decay and becomes soil.

Unless you transcend birth and death during your life, you will live after your death in your children as a part of their subconscious which is the spiritual tomb. And the children might be more lump of agony and sins than you, as they should have yours on top.

Nothing will leave except a handful of earth after death. Neither heaven nor hell exists separately from a humans' life. Both heaven and hell exist only in a humans' mind.

If a person conceives a happy mind in a moment, he or she is in heaven; if a person grasps a troubled soul at this moment, you are in hell.

This view is that of birth and death of the Victory Altar, they dispassionately look at the reality and try to get out of birth, aging, diseases, and death through practicing *the philosophy of one body*.

Therefore, I think that the transcending new view of the exodus from birth and death is entirely rational.

Then I will say about the principle of immortality based on the Seventh Angel's immortal science. To know the principle of immortality, people should know *the philosophy of one body* which makes people perfect God.

Key 24

The Secret of Healthy Life

The principle of anti-aging

Those who convince themselves that they never die cannot die, even though they are 500 years old.

People think that as they become old, they lack in energy; therefore, they die. If they think that they will live forever, they cannot die. This is an absolute immortal theory.

The man who convinces himself of immortality emits an immortal material through his skin and breath.

So people breathe the immortal material. Then their bodies become immortal ones.

Therefore, the higher number of people who convince themselves immortality exist, the faster the immortal world is established.

The Hanmoum(One body) philosophy

All humans are one body because they were made of their parents, not just falling from the air. Our parents were formed by our grandparents' blood; our grandparents were formed by the blood of our great-grandparents.

Going back continually to fiftieth grandparents, 100th grandparents, and 500th grandparents, we come to realize that our ancestors were formed by the blood of God because humans' first ancestors are Adam and Eve, who lived in the Garden of Eden.

Only God lives in heaven. Therefore, because all humans have the same blood, they are brothers and are one tree that has spread out into 6 billion branches of life for 6000 years.

Although their skin is different from each other due to the environment, if we look below one millimeter of skin, the blood is the same color, red.

Also, they have the character of God commonly, conscience. So we are sure that all humans are one body of the same quality.

The seventh angel logically says we are inevitably one body and came from one root. He also confidently explains it using genetic engineering.

The ancestor of all humans was God that is the spirit of eternal life; they are forms of life spread down from one ancestor's blood. So initially all humans are one body and one brother, and one tree.

The seventh angel reborn as the Holy Spirit tells that all humans have inherited one blood; they should regard all humans as one body.

Although humans are the same root of one ancestor, they are occupied by a wrong thought that regards one body as others; it is regrettable. The splitting minds are the spirit of death that causes desires and disputes.

The philosophy of one body which regards everyone as mine is the truth that saves people and gives people peace. It is a perfect science. No matter how many people there are, the philosophy can make all of them one.

You should become a Savior through following the science of the Savior. This man told you to regard others like yours.

It means there is neither you nor I. Only one body exists. Then it gives all humans peace. The peace of all humans comes when they become one. Unless they become one, their peace does not exist. (From the Victor's sermon on 2003. 8. 11)

The day when all humans become one and enjoy immortality will surely come. As the Victor is trying to reunify the world, Satan is copying it. To reunify the world, he needs logic and weapons.

Whoever is one body, has the same blood, and is all my body. As there is nobody but my body, if people think of anybody as their bodies or one body, they cannot but become one body. (from the words of the Victor on 1987.5.3)

All humanity is spiritually one whoever is. As we are one body, we should be unified spiritually and consciously. But actually, we are not, because Satan makes people think of themselves separately.

All humans were made from the blood of God. However, they have been divided into 6.5 billion' Self-awareness of 'I' for 6000 years.

Even though they are one body, they do not know it, so they make a boundary, fight each other, and live selfishly.

The Self-awareness in humans is a splitting soul; also it is the evil soul that is the factor of quarrel, confusion, anguish, unhappiness, and death. As well, it is the reason for losing the paradise and miserable humans' history according to the Victor.

No matter how good people are, they have Self-awareness of 'I' and individual consciousness. Self-awareness and individual consciousnesses are the evil and dirty Satan.

Now as we found the factor of death, we should go back to the original being by removing the factor of death. All humans can return to one heart. The Victor says "the truth is in one, peace is in one, and immortality is in one."

After the Savior appeared, the directions of all humans' fates were already decided.

The Victory Altar is campaigning that all humans become one. As the Savior came, the perfect Spirit came as the Bible predicts in 1 Corinthians 3. The perfect Spirit is the Dew Spirit according to Isaiah 26:19 and Hosea 14:5, the Spirit of the last Angel in Revelation is the fruit of life.

The Holy Dew Spirit is the last weapon of the Savior that will recover the original paradise. The strong Spirit that combines 7 billion humans into one is working now.

Satan knows his fate, flows into humans, and makes a frantic last-ditch effort. Satan that drives all humans into destruction is just Self-awareness of 'I' hiding in humans.

As Self-awareness is the factor of destroying humans, overcoming Self-awareness of 'I' is the way to achieve salvation and peace. Self-awareness and individualism make home and society unhappy. They are the evil souls that make people split and fight each other.

Now, the followers of the Victory Altar are campaigning martyrdom by killing their Self-awareness of 'I'. When Self-awareness of 'I' in humans die, the Spirit of peace occupies humans.

In order for people to realize the ideology of God, the men who were called earlier should be martyrs first. Martyrdom is killing Self-awareness of 'I', not dying for somebody. The Christianity's theory of martyrdom is a wrong interpretation of the Bible.

More people can attain salvation by those who came earlier becoming spiritual martyrs.

The Savior has taught the followers that the secret of overcoming Self-awareness of 'I' is regarding others as myself.

As all humans are one body, 'regarding anybody as mine' is the ideology of the salvation, which is the greatest task that all mankind should accomplish.

'The philosophy of one body; regarding anybody as mine' is the spiritual task that we should overcome beyond countries and individualism. Because people are all one body, all people in every country, all mankind is one. The believers of the Victory Altar have experienced this fact.

And they need time to engrave the realization deeply in their hearts consistently. Knowing a fact is different from realizing from the bottom of one's heart. Belief and conviction are to know from realizing, it comes from the pouring of oil. The Pouring of oil means to be occupied by the Holy Spirit.

Key 25

**The Secret of
the Bright Philosophy of Neo-humans**

What is the philosophy of Hanmom(one body)?

The philosophy of 'one body' regarding everyone as one is the truth that will save people and give people peace.

This is a perfect science. No matter how many people there are, this philosophy can make all of them God. You should become the Savior by following the philosophy of the Savior.

This man told you to regard others like yours. It means there is neither you nor I, but one body. And then all humans will become one. Also, it gives all humans peace.

The God who gives peace to humans is a merciful one. The peace of all humans will be established when they become one. Unless they become one, their peace does not exist.

All mankind is one body which is made of one blood.

Recently, the fighting between Israel and Palestine has continued. They had stopped the fighting and held peace talks, but they are fighting again. That is because they have not become one.

To be peaceful, Israel and Palestine should become one.

If the Israel people and Palestine people regard each other as themselves, then they cannot have wars.

When this science is revealed to the media, all mankind will practice it.

This science is the highest philosophy that all mankind will practice (It is extracted from the Maitreya Buddha's preach).

The practicing virtues of the Law of Liberty and the secret of killing Satan

Until now, I have spoken about aging, diseases, death, the root or whereabouts of sins, the principle of blood, the interaction of mind and body. And also, noted about the way that all humans recover as God who lives happily forever by knowing the essence of humans and the philosophy of one body.

Then, how can we remove Self-awareness of 'I' which is the basis of all problems?

I will tell briefly the virtues that people can practice to be free from the spirit of death. Also, I will explain the secret of reaching nirvana.

First, I will introduce the seven essential practicing virtues to be free from birth and death, to accomplish the great Tao.

The essential practicing virtues are the teaching of the Law of Liberty and the doctrine of the Victory Altar.

They are as follow:
- Look at the Victor Savior God all the time.
- Participate in services of the Victory Altar where the Sweet Dew falls every day.
- Beseech the Sweet Dew ardently that is necessary to destroy karma.
- Recite the chant of prayer to destroy Satan in and out of you.
- Take a shower every day and change underwear.
- Don't drink alcohol or smoke. Overcome sex that hurts lives seriously.
- Sacrifice and volunteer by lowering self, and evangelizing.

By practicing these virtues, the cultivation to destroy Satan begins.

The followers of the Victory Altar recognize that when people stand on the base of the above seven essential practicing virtues, they are ready to keep the Law of Liberty.

The secret to overcoming 'I' is keeping the Law of Liberty.

The Law of Liberty is a law that makes people reborn as the Holy Spirit, not commits sins, lead to nirvana by destroying Satan.

Key 26

The Secret of Oxygen and H_2O

Scientists proclaim that oxygen is a decaying material because that oxygen decays every element.

But there is the material of life in oxygen according to the Victor Cho Hee Sung. The material of life is the spirit of God, so almost all dying patients do not die when they wear oxygen breathing respirators.

Oxygen has the strongest life, the spirit of God, among things. So the most powerful decaying spirit of Satan encompasses the spirit of God. So oxygen becomes a decaying material. Therefore, all things which contact with oxygen decay.

Like that all things including people are God who is encompassed by the spirit of Satan. Therefore all things die because of Satan, the spirit of death.

Today, doctors and scientists do not know why patients die when they take off oxygen breathing respirators. Only the hero of the universe can say

the secret of oxygen.
Why do people not die when they drink only water?

Because, the food of life is in water, too. Plants live on water due to is the material of life in water.

However, scientists do not know it. They just think that plants are alive because people water them. Plants and fish can live on only water because water has oxygen.

The practicing virtues of the Law of Liberty

- Look at and adore the Reincarnated Maitreya Buddha, Victor Savior, who pours out the Sweet Dew every second.
- Beat Self-awareness of 'I'
- Regard the sins of brothers as mine.
- Regard others' faults as mine.
- Do not hate brothers.
- Regard brothers' circumstances as mine.
- Regard others as my body
- Be convinced that I can live forever.
- Live a life opposite of what Self-awareness of 'I' wants.
- Realize that all humans are the children of God, one blood, one body, one tree, and one root of one ancestor, and practice 'one body philosophy' 100 percent in real life.
- Conceive the heart of God all the time.

Realizing and practicing the above virtues of the Law of Liberty are very important in order for humans to be reborn as the Holy Spirit and accomplish immortality.

In the next chapter, the author will introduce the new words of the Victor.

Key 27

The Secret of Satan and Ego

The way of removing the spirit of Satan, Ego.

In the Bible, sin is Satan, Satan is self-awareness of 'I.' So if we get rid of the Ego of 'I,' we overcome Satan, the spirit of death. Then the victorious God who defeats Satan will live forever in us.

How do we overcome Ego of 'I'?

If we think as God thinks, the self-awareness of 'I' disappears. God regards everybody as His body, God regards everybody as God.

Also, God is an immortal spirit. He always believes in eternal life. Additionally, He has happy spirit, so he is always laughing.

The most potent weapon of humanity is laughter. So no matter how critical patients are, if they laugh for two hours continually, their disease such as cancer or AIDS can be cured.

If they laugh for a whole day, their awareness of 'I', the spirit of death, is removed, and then they become immortal God. So be happy and always laugh like God.

Plus imagine I live forever in happiness like God as much as you can. Then the spirit of death dies soon. Thinking always comes true.

In spite the fact that the Bible tells people to throw away their ego, they always love their ego.

All the people are crazy. So they behave as their ego orders during their life.

In fact, God explains to people to eliminate this aspect because the ego is Satan, the spirit of death.

However, the Self-awareness (the ego) controls people hiding its identity; people obey the direction of their ego.

Whenever the spirit of death moves in the body of people, the blood is decayed.

When the blood becomes decayed 100 percent, they die. People do not know it. Therefore, the Victor always tells people, His children, to live the life opposite of what the ego wants.

However they always obey their ego and are dying. So the Victor is sad.

Because He was born as the Holy Spirit; He knows the Truth of the completion and says new words. So the Bible says when perfection comes, the imperfect disappears in 1 Corinthians.

Chapter VIII
New Heaven & New Words

The New words by the Victor

Like Isaiah predicted, the Victor appeared in the corner of the Far East 38 years ago. In this chapter, the author will introduce the immortal secret that the Victor Savior preached during worship services. Thus has the author heard, following these New Words [1].

---

1. New Words: From now, 'I' is the Savior(the Victor) in the Bible, the Reincarnate Maitreya Buddha in the Buddhist books.

Key 28

The Secret of a Golden Bell

What is the sound of a golden bell?

The New words of Victor are just the sound of New Heaven's Golden Bell, which kills the spirit of death in humans. So lucky people can attain immortality by listening to the voice of the Savior.

Here are the humans who are becoming immortal neo-humans in the Victory Altar in Sosa, Korea.

Day by day they receive the Spirit of the Victor who is the hero of heaven. When the Spirit of the Savior fills their bodies, they will be turned into light and live happily forever traveling as light.

Thus have I heard, 2001. 07. 25

God Himself is the origin of all the materials of the universe; therefore, not only humanity but also all things are God.

When we look at the whole Bible, it consists of the theory of salvation, Creationism, the end of human history, and the theory of resurrection.

Creation theory is that God created the world. However, God Himself is the origin of all the materials in the universe. Hence, the theory of creation is wrong because the elements of the whole universe are originally God.

Therefore, the world was not created by God, but rather God who existed before the beginning of time was split into infinite pieces by Satan. These pieces are what we call elements, the elements were surrounded by Satan. It is the formation of everything.

However, Christians say that God created the world. In fact, God did not create it. Satan split God into countless little pieces because if God existed as one, He would be too strong. So Satan split God into little pieces, and then Satan is surrounding the divided spirit of God in the current world.

Therefore, even though a fireball is in the center of the earth, sea water does not dry out, and everything on the earth is not burned out because the fireball is the spirit of God.

In fact, because the core of life is in the middle of the earth, the earth has lasted quite long; that's because the spirit of God is in the middle of the earth, the situation is that Satan holds the spirit of God in its prison.

Also, everything has the spirit of God a part of it. Therefore, every atom has a nucleus, which has neutrons in the orbit, and the neutrons are the spirit of God.

Hence the spirit of God is in every element, negative electrons are going around the nucleus continually; scientists say that the negative electrons are going around the nucleus by themselves. It is nonsense.
Scientifically saying, they are going around because of energy. Going around by themselves is not scientific.

Scientists clearly say that everything goes in a circle because of the circular energy. Without the circular energy, everything cannot go around.

Therefore, from the beginning of the Victory Altar, I said that neutrons are the spirit of God. Today's scientists say that negative electrons rotate around a neutron continually, and negative electrons are the spirit of Satan.

Dr. Lee Won Yong, a professor of Columbia University in America, came to Seoul University in 1986 and gave a lecture in front of many people.

He said that the light of a neutron could go through 10 billion light years' thickness of lead. One light year is the distance that light travels for one year.

The distance sunlight goes for one year is tremendously far. Then, 10 billion light years is limitless. If neutrons pass through this distance, it means that they have the power of endless transmission.

The reason that Dr. Lee said that neutrons could penetrate the distance of '10 billion light years' thickness of lead is that no matter how strong those neutrons have the power to pass through in scientist's opinion, they receive the power of resistance like materials of the world. For example, bullets are resisted by the power of air and fall down after a while.

The material with the strongest resistance is lead. Hence, as it is now, when a nuclear bomb is exploded, alpha, beta, and gamma rays come out. The gamma ray has the strongest penetrating power. If a nuclear bomb explodes, gamma rays penetrate every cell of the human body and the body burns to ashes.

If someone were standing there, he or she would become ashes in standing position. When the nuclear bomb exploded in Hiroshima, Japan, one man was standing there. When a passerby called him and touched the man, he became ashes and disappeared in a moment.

This gamma ray has the power to ionize all cells; as it passes, it burns all materials. If it passes through people, they die and become ashes. Hence to keep people safe from it, they need great anti air-raid shelters.

When I was an officer in the army, I taught soldiers about the theory of the atom by translating book published in English into Korean.

Air-raid shelters made with a thickness of one millimeter's lead will keep a person from death. I knew gamma rays well. The most dreadful impact of the atomic bomb is gamma rays. Gamma rays are emitted from nuclear fission of uranium.

The penetration power of the gamma ray is very powerful; the power of atomic bomb is tremendous. The Atomic bomb is so dreadful that two atomic bombs made the emperor of Japan surrender unconditionally.

When atomic bombs explode, the penetrating power of the gamma ray is very strong, and the neutron rays have billions of times the stronger penetrating power, according to Dr. Lee Won Yong. But I said that it is a lie. It is a foolish saying.

Neutrons are the material of God, and because God is light going forever, the penetrating power is infinite, so, even though the thickness of lead is infinite, it can pass through.

Scientists have logical brains. Therefore, they cannot know the facts out of the world. Hence I tell you like that. God is caught in the middle of everything, and the spirit surrounding it is Satan, which decays materials. So everything decays, not only iron but also everything decays.

As the spirit of Satan is that of death, it decays and kills everything. This flower, here, dies in the end. It is the spirit of God caught by the spirit of Satan. Life is dying due to Satan, which surrounds the spirit of God and chokes the flower, and God dies in the end.

The Bible describes creation. However, Christians do not know that the hero of creation lost to Satan and was held in Satan's prison. Hence, this world is a sinful and dark one.

Because this world is ignorant, it is dark. Creation itself happened because God lost to Satan, God was split into small infinite pieces, was changed into all things.

The current situation is that God is in the center and Satan surrounds Him. Even the air is the same. Because the air molecules are encompassed by Satan, when people breathe them in, their blood begins to decay. So they are getting old because their blood is decaying.

Also because Self-awareness of 'I' is the spirit of Satan and controls individuals, whenever their thought is by Satan, their blood decays. Therefore, they cannot live 100 years, their blood has decayed continually for that time, and their lives disappear.

Therefore, the Bible tells about the theory of salvation. It says that people achieve salvation by eating the Fruit of Life, and by the Belief, they will be reborn as the Holy Spirit.

According to the Bible, people can achieve salvation by being reborn by the Holy Spirit. It means that people were God in old times; they achieve salvation by being reborn as God. However, the Savior says that they achieve salvation by being reborn not by God of the old times, but God who can kill Satan. But the Bible does not say this.

Accordingly, the hero of the universe should appear. He is the very Savior; the Savior is not a normal God but an omnipotent and omniscient God. If He does not have the power, He cannot get rid of Satan which fills the universe. The Savior should be able to kill Satan not only in everybody but also in everything. So He can change the mortal world into an immortal one.

Therefore, the Spirit of the Savior is the Belief and the Fruit of Life (The sayings of the Bible are spiritual, so the Fruit of Life should be a spiritual fruit. Hence, the spiritual fruit is the Spirit of the Victor.)

So, when the Savior lead services on the pulpit, He pours out the Holy Dew Spirit; it is the other self of the Savior. The other self of the Savior, the Spirit of the Victor, is the Holy Dew Spirit.

According to Isaiah 26:19, "Those of our people who have died will live again! Their bodies will come back to life. All those sleeping in their graves will wake up and sing for joy. Just like sparkling Dew refreshes earth."

When the Holy Dew Spirit comes, people do not die according to Isaiah 26:19. It means when the Savior God comes as Holy Dew Spirit, mortal humans on the earth come to be free from death because of the Holy Dew Spirit.

Also, due to the sayings of the Bible are spiritual, the resurrection should be a spiritual resurrection of living people, not dead bodies' resurrection from the grave; that is, if a living person is reborn as the Holy Dew Spirit, he won't die.

It means if the man who pours out the Dew comes, the mortal world will be changed into an immortal one.

Now, according to 1 Corinthians 15:53 "Death is swallowed by victory." It means that if the Victor comes, He will swallow all death. Death here means the Spirit of Satan, In this case, Satan would die and God would survive.

As God is an immortal Spirit, He won't die, only Satan will die, because Satan is a mortal spirit. God Himself is the origin of all the materials of the universe.

Hence, according to the theory of salvation of the Bible, "you can achieve salvation by being reborn of the Holy Spirit" in John 3:5. "As you are reborn by the Holy Spirit, you can achieve salvation" means that you can get salvation by being reborn by God.

To be reborn by God, you should kill the present Self-awareness of 'I', and then you can become God. After killing Satan, a human becomes God. And then the Spirit which is reborn as the Holy Spirit is the Spirit of Victor which defeats Satan.

Hence, it is stronger than Satan. The Spirit which defeats Satan is the Spirit being reborn by the Holy Spirit. It is the Faith. I(the victor) said that the Spirit defeating Satan is the Fruit of Life. And the Faith is the Fruit of Life; the Fruit of Life is the Faith.

According to the Bible, "You can not find the Faith until the end of the world." It means that there is no Fruit of Life before the end of the world.

However, today's Christians who believe the Bible thoroughly do not know about the Faith and the Fruit of Life. If they do not know about the Faith and the Fruit of Life, they don't belong to a religion believing the Bible.

The Most important part of the Bible is salvation. If they do not know this, they cannot be a part of a biblical society. They cannot be a religion which believes in the Bible.

According to the theory of salvation, people achieve salvation through resurrection. Resurrection means that God who was held in the prison of Satan for 6,000 years is revived. God's resurrection in each individual can be possible when God defeated the controlling spirit, Satan.

Being resurrected and being reborn as God have the same meaning. "Act in God" means "if you act in Satan, you cannot but die." Therefore, when you act in God, you do not die. It means "Be reborn as the Holy Spirit."

You being reborn as the Holy Spirit means that God, the Spirit of conscience, who was being held by spirit of Satan, defeats Self-awareness of 'I' (spirit of Satan), and removes the Spirit of Satan, and the Spirit of God resides as me, then you become God, you act in God, you are revived as the Holy Spirit, and you have the mind of God.

When we match the theories of salvation, the meanings are the same. The same meanings are expressed differently.

So the only man who found it in the Bible can interpret it. No one could interpret it unless the very man who stated in the Bible appeared.

Hence, reading Bible literally, they assume the meaning of words in the spiritual book and deceive a lot of people, for example when people die, believe their soul goes to heaven or hell.

But in fact, they do not know the spirit biblically. Spirit is the mind according to the Bible. If the mind is the spirit, blood is the spirit.

The working of blood is the working of the mind. Hence, the mind is the spirit, blood is the spirit, if blood is the spirit, flesh and body are made by the blood, and the body itself is the spirit. So, according to the Bible, spirit and body are one.

John1:1 says "God is life, God is light, life is light and the Spirit of God is life". God Himself is the origin of all the materials of the universe. Leviticus 17:11 says, "The lives of all living things are in the blood." God Himself is the origin of all the materials of the universe.

And according to Proverbs 4:23 "Be careful how you think; your life is shaped by your thought. The source of life is in mind."

Hence, the mind is life, and it is the same as the saying that blood is life because blood is life. If the mind is life, it is the same as to say that blood is
life. If blood is life, life is the mind, the mind is the blood, and blood is the mind.

Hence the bodies of humans themselves are the spirit, like I expressed it scientifically just before. There are neutrons in the center of each atom, a nucleus exists as neutrons, negative electrons are going around the neutrons, the negative electrons are the spirit of Satan, the material of neutrons is the Spirit of God.

Therefore, both of them are spirits. If the material is the spirit, the bodies of humans themselves are the spirit, too.

According to the Bible, the God is the spirit of all flesh in Numbers 27:16, 16:22. According to Zephaniah 3:7 "God is with you." It means that God is in humans. The life in humans is God.

Accordingly, the Bible says, "God is with you." Nuke 20:38 says, "He is not the God of the dead, but of the living, for to him all are alive."

"For to him all are alive" means that life controls and moves people. Only a living person can move.

Therefore, no matter how rich a person is, if he dies, his money is useless. If he dies, it is worth nothing. Even though a man has a gold nugget as big as the earth, if the man dies, it is worth nothing. No matter how valuable the treasures are, they only have value when the person who holds that is alive. Only while he is alive, invaluable things are worth. If he dies, they are worthless.

Everyone's priority is the guarantee of eternal life. You should accomplish immortal life first. Only after accomplishing immortality, can you do other things of the world? If you do other things without accomplishing immortality, then after death, your work is meaningless. It is foolish.

Therefore, you should focus on getting immortality first. According to the Bible, resurrection means that a dead body rises and lives again. However, nobody lived again for 6,000 years. Accordingly, it is a saying of Satan. Hence, resurrection itself is that God lives again.

To be released from the prison of Satan, God should be strong. To make God strong, the Savior pours out the Holy Dew Spirit to you.

Just the Holy Dew Spirit is a perfect and completed strong Spirit. No spirit overcomes the Holy Dew Spirit. It has no rivals. The Savior pours out only the strongest Spirit.

Therefore, whenever I(the Victor) lead the worship services, the Holy Dew Spirit falls, and its scent is that of lilies. Hence, for those who smell the scent, fatal diseases like cancers can be cured.

Some people have told about their experiences on the pulpit. Terminal cancer patients who could not be cured medically have recovered. It was possible by only the Holy Dew Spirit. The cancer cell is the same as the cell of death. So if the cells spread out to the whole body, they cannot but die.

However, even though the cancer cells spread out to the whole body, if they receive the Holy Dew Spirit, cancer cells die out and new cells are formed again. That is how cancer is cured.

Thus has the author heard, 2001. 02. 08

Jeongdoryeong (The man who rules the world with the True Tao) came to the world to change the world. *Jeongdoryeong* was supposed to come to change the world. The *Jeongdoryeong* is the *Reincarnated Maitreya Buddha* in Buddhism and the Savior of Christianity. The evidence of the Savior is the *Sweet Dew Spirit*.

The *Sweet Dew* is the elixir plant of *Samsin Mountain*(三神山) according to *Gyeokamyourok*. Therefore, if you receive *the Holy Dew Spirit*, you live forever, get over of humans' fatal condition, and become God.

Hence, you can live forever; you will never die. It is just the elixir plant of *Samsin Mountain* and *the Holy Dew Spirit*.

A long time ago, the Emperor *Jin* sent 500 pairs of young girls and boys to Korea to get the elixir plant of *Samsin Mountain*. However, as there was not the elixir plant of *Samsin Mountain* at that time, they could not find it.

If they went back their country empty-handed, they could die. So they settled in Korea or crossed the sea and lived in Japan; consequently there are a lot of their offspring in Japan nowadays.

Among them, Mori, the prime minister, is one of their descendants. He said that his ancestors came to Korea to get the elixir plant of *Samsin Mountain*.

For a long time, South Korea has been called utopia. Utopia or heaven whatever you call it, it was supposed to be built in South Korea. According to *Gyeokamyourok*, the garden of Eden will be built in *Sosa*.

And it also says that even though heaven collapsed, there is a way at *way to stand in Sosa*. In other words, the garden of Eden collapsed a long time ago; however, it will be rebuilt at the land of *Sosa*.

Accordingly, if heaven is not built in *Sosa*, it is a fake and is the imitating work of Satan. Therefore, the building of heaven was built in the land of *Sosa* in 1991.

It was truly heavenly work. According to *Gyeokamyourok*, the building of heaven was supposed to be built when *Jeongdoryeong* was sixty-one years old. This building is not a normal building; it is the building where the Trinity always resides. The Trinity God is in this man.

The Victor stand on this platform every day. Therefore, because the Trinity always stands here, this is heaven. It may look like a normal building to people because the building looks similar to ordinary buildings around; however, it is heaven.

Gyeokamyourok said the building of heaven is to be built when *Jeongdoryeong* is sixty-one years old; however, people do not know this. *Jeongdoryeong* was sixty-one years old in 1991. Now the Victor is seventy-one years old.

In this way, the prearranged work of God is being progressed. When the work of God is being progressed, you should help it be accomplished quickly.

Helping is evangelizing and saving people drowning in the sea of death and dying. Saving them is the work of God; therefore, if a person does not do his or her mission, one will be reprimanded.

If one does not take their responsibilities, then the law of the nation punishes a person. The law of heaven is the same. If one does not accomplish their duty, They cannot be saved. It is a sin.

Therefore, as one knows the gospel of immortality, they have the responsibility of evangelizing. If one does not exercise the responsibility, one will be reprimanded. If one carries out their responsibility, one will be recognized by God, and then will be saved.

The Victory Altar looks similar to other buildings of the world. However, this is the ark of salvation. If people come here, they will receive *the Sweet Dew Spirit*. *The Sweet Dew Spirit* is the elixir of *Samsin Mountain*, if you eat the elixir, you cannot die. The words have come down from thousands of years ago. Accordingly, you are the luckiest ones because you will receive immortality.

Like the Victor said yesterday, you should be grateful all the time. Be grateful for living, breathing, and attending worship services in Victory Altar.

Those who are grateful can laugh a lot all the time. Therefore, if you laugh, your blood becomes clean. If you laugh, you will always have a grateful mind. If you are always grateful and laugh all the time, and then your blood becomes cleansed.

If your blood is clean, it becomes that of God. As your blood is changed into the blood of God. you can not die. Unless your blood is changed into that of God, you surely will die.

Previously, I(the Victor) said that there has not been a proper understanding of science in the world and that the science of the world is wrong.

I said that everything is God. In the old times, old people prayed to trees or rocks. The reason is that their prayers were accomplished for there is God in the trees and the rocks.

God listened to their prayers; He made their prayers be accomplished. Christianity says that it is an idol. Christianity itself is an idol.

Because they do not know that everything is God, they say that praying to nature is idolatry. They are so foolish.

In fact, everything is God. For example, although a person lives in a falling house, the house is never fallen. Because a person is God, he emits the material of life; therefore, the house does not fall.

Humans are the direct line descendants of God, and yourself is the direct line of God, so you are God.

When the science of the world says that humans are animals, it is not science. So I(the Victor) hereby say that there is no science in the world.

The Savior came to the world to change the world. First, He will completely change the mind of humans. Then minds of humans will be changed into those of God, bodies of humans will be changed into those of God. And then humans will emit the Spirit of God, the air itself will be changed into that of God.

Now the air itself is the spirit of Satan. If the spirit of God replaces the Spirit of Satan, the air will be changed into that of God, and then if humans breathe the air, they breathe in and out the Spirit of God.

Therefore, they will become God easily. Therefore, although becoming God is difficult at first, the number of people becoming God is growing. The air and all things will be changed into God, and then humans will become God easily.

In the same manner, heavenly work is not difficult at the end. Even though starting is difficult, if it is somewhat accomplished, it can be accomplished easily.

It will be accomplished in a moment. Likewise, because the work of heaven had been difficult to be accomplished, many early comers of the Victory Altar were supposed to leave here. *Gyeokamyourok* says that many early comers of the Victory Altar would leave being captivated by Satan.

However, the believers who came at the middle phase of Victory Altar were supposed to go until the end and achieve salvation.

And those who come at the end will go to hell. So, one way or the other, to achieve salvation, you must come in early and stay to the end with endurance keeping the Law of Liberty.

If you talk carelessly about the work of God and interfere with the work of heaven, it is an unforgivable sin. The Bible says that a sin against the Holy Spirit is unforgivable.

Words are very important. Even though believers speak against the work of God and try to interfere with it, they cannot avoid hell forever.

Therefore, this man(the Victor) speak slowly. When someone asked this man questions, this man did not provide answers to all of the questions. This man answered only twenty percent of the questions.

After thinking about whether My answer will make God happy or not, this man answer.

I(the Victor) have older friends, younger friends than myself, and friends of the same age. Among them, one friend named *Ji Dongha*, who worked at the Central Intelligence, is the same as Me; he called Me older brother Cho.

That's because I always answered the questions after thinking of whether the answer will hurt God or not. Therefore, treating Me physically, My friend was careful with Me. So he called Me older brother Cho.

You should not speak lightly. If someone speaks lightly, people will ignore him. Also, mistakenly spoken words can hurt the works of heaven. It will remain as unforgivable sin forever.

So it's horrifying. The Bible says, "speak slowly" because if you speak only one wrong word, you will go to hell.

Some believers gave the videotape of God's words to a group of Satan. If enemies know the information of God, they will take an advantageous position and attack God. It is a tremendous sin. So God is fighting fiercely against the enemies.

The Savior's work is not easy. He is involved in bloody battles every second. He can save the world by killing Satan. If He does not kill Satan, He cannot save even one single person.

There are people who do not help the Savior who is doing such a difficult job. And they even hurt Me by going behind My back and speaking against Me. It is a huge sin. Not only they but also their families, and successive generation will go to hell.

Therefore, God needs your support now to accomplish the will of God. Also one should not interfere with the work of God. It may seem that nobody knows or hears that one is interfering. However, the perfect Man knows everything, even though He may not hear or see it directly.

As the life in their bodies is God's 'other selves', and although your bodies seemed to be separated from God, you and God are one body.

As God is in everyone's bodies, He knows everything. He just pretends not to know it 100 percent. Therefore, He can completely deceive Satan. Like that, God can kill Satan.

If Satan knows God's intentions, he will avoid Him. When Satan does not know God's intentions, he is defenseless, and God kills him.

According to the Art of War of Sun Tzu, if a person knows his enemy and himself, victories are always his. I could see the moving of Satan before I went to the Secret Chamber(Mr. Cho became a Victor in it).

However, I never spoke of it. If Satan knew that, he would make Me blind. Therefore, I hid it. Even though I could see Satan, I never said so.

As I can see Satan, I hit the back of Satan's head and kill him. Accordingly, whenever I fight, I am a Victor in every battle. No matter how big Satan came to Me, I could beat him. Therefore, I became a Victor.

The Victor defeats enemies, not because He is strong, but because He knows all the secrets of His enemies. Hence, He can avoid an attack from the enemies, and attack the enemies suddenly and wipe them out.

I served in the army as an officer, I was commissioned as a second lieutenant, then soon I was appointed as the second chief of military operations, and then as the second chief of the army information and education.

When I was appointed as the second chief of military operation, I planned the military strategies and the maneuvers for My squadron. Although I was a second lieutenant, I participated as a lieutenant colonel. There, I studied war strategies from around the whole world. I can make bombs with napalm. I can do anything.

There was a book from an atomic bomb symposium in the army. When I was in the Twenty eighth Division in the army, I translated the book and taught it to all the soldiers. Therefore, the Victor know the operating principle of atomic bombs and how to make them. Also, I understand how it is exploded. However, would I make bombs to kill people? No.

By the way, negative electrons are going around neutrons.

However, scientists do not know why they are going around them. For 6000 years, nobody knew it. Nobody had thought about that. However, the Victor has thought about it. Finally, the answer came from His questioning.

It is just that the neutron is the Spirit of God. The Spirit of God is that of life. As God is in your bodies, you are alive. Everything is alive due to God. People do not even know this basic theory.

Therefore, the Victor say that there is no scientific knowledge on this. So the Victor say that current cutting edge of science which the most advanced scientists do not know it.

The Victor spoke of this truth twenty years ago. As neutrons are the Spirit of God and the material of life, negative electrons are going around the neutrons by using the power of life, the positive and negative electrons are the spirits of Satan; the spirit of Satan rides the Spirit of God and therefore they move.

So, the Spirit of God stays in humans as conscience, life is the conscience, and Satan borrows the power of life, sits on the Self-awareness of 'I', rides God like a horse, and makes God as a slave. It is the situation of God in humans.

So the Savior came to the world to destroy Satan, to kill him, and to liberate people from the prison of Satan. And if the Spirit of God sits on the Self-awareness of humans, people become God.

'The Savior changes the world' means to turn the world over. He came to change the mortal world into an immortal one. Can an ordinary person do that? No, they cannot. An average person cannot do that. Men were originally the slaves of Satan, so they are Satan.

This saying "men are Satan" may be of a bad manner, but in fact, it is true. When Adam and Eve saw Satan, Satan came into them through their eyes. God was occupied with Adam and Eve by

Satan, and Satan sat on the Self-awareness of them.

Before Satan occupied Adam and Eve, the Self-awareness of them was God. So they were God, they were kings.

Satan came into them, caught the kings, made them slaves, and imprisoned them. After that, Satan became a king. Like that, Satan became the Self-awareness of Adam and Eve.

Therefore, as they became humans, they wore the shape of Satan, and they were formed as a man and a woman. The figure of man and woman is that of Satan. So not only plants but also everything is formed of positive and negative.

Electricity emits light by combining plus and minus electricity, and is this the light of God? It is Satan's. When Satan is annihilated, it will be dark. And then the light of God's glory will start to shine.

By then, the world will be completely turned over. Therefore, the new world without death is heaven; heaven is the world of God, not only man, but also everything becomes God.

Everybody knows there is a fireball in the center of the earth. The fireball is just neutrons (God is the neutron). God is caught in the earth. God has been caught in the middle of the earth for 6,000 years.

Satan caught God not only in the earth but also in every star after cutting God by the latitude and longitude lines. God is caught in those.

So the Victor appearing to the world is a tremendous work. God has developed power and weapons to annihilate Satan for 6,000 years.

This work is not ordinary. It is an enormous work. The Victor is supposed to make not only the earth but also the whole universe heaven. He will make the whole universe heaven. By that time, people who become God will live forever. Everything will live forever because it will become God. If something becomes the slaves of Satan, it dies.

Because the spirit of God is in everything, they are alive. This platform looks like dead wood, but it is supported by the neutrons, the spirit of God inside this platform. Therefore, it is alive. If it is dead or rotten, it cannot stand.

Iron is the same. As God is in it, it stands. All materials of the world are God. Everything is God, but people say it is material. So science is wrong.

Therefore, you should help God to change the universe. When you help, the work will be accomplished soon. Then it is beneficial to you. Therefore, you should help it with your whole life.

According to Daniel, if you stop burnt offering every day, you will be destroyed. Even though you miss only one single day, you will go to hell. Even if you take services every day, and if you are absent just one single day, you will go hell.

Hence, if you are busy during the day, take the services at night. If the Victor says it, it surely will be accomplished. If you skip a worship service just one single day, you will go to hell. So the victor says that believers should take the services every day.

Standing on the platform every day is difficult for me, but I stand on here every day to make everybody achieve salvation. When the Victor has an appointment and cannot stand on this platform, you should take services through the recorded video.

Although you take services through a recorded video, *the Sweet Dew* falls. Some people do not know it, and they skip services, and then they will go to hell.

When you take services every day, you achieve salvation. Your blood has been tainted for 6,000 years. The 6,000 years old sin is Self-awareness of 'I'. Self-awareness of 'I' is the sin. It is 6,000 years old. Even though you attend a service every day, wiping out the 6,000 years old sin is very difficult.

The Bible says that you should take burnt offerings every day. The burnt offering is attending services. Nowadays the Victor says the same words as twenty years ago.

Those who keep these words will achieve salvation. However, those who skip a service even one single day will not achieve salvation. Therefore, those who skip a day should continually attend services each and every day from the next day.

If they start a new day from that day, they can achieve salvation. In that case, even though they cannot achieve salvation, the Savior makes them achieve salvation.

A newcomer may think, "I came here by mistake today." However, this path is that of immortality. It is lucky to be caught for his immortality. Only a lucky man comes here.

The Victor has said what spirit is. Mind is the spirit; the spirit is blood. And Self-awareness of 'I' is the spirit of Satan, however, because people do not know about the spirit, they say the spirit leaves.

Blood is the life of God. As the spirit of humans is the Spirit of God, so when humans' spirit dies, the Spirit of God dies, too. And the spirit of Satan does not leave because it is the spirit of death; it dies with the Spirit of God.

In other words, it seems like the spirit of Satan jumps into the sea of death hugging the Spirit of God. Hence, the Spirit of God and the spirit of Satan will die together.

Therefore, the saying "the Spirit of God and the spirit of Satan leave" is a lie.

According to Job 14:14, "If people die, they perish." They became soil. Nothing is left. Accordingly, if they die, it is the end.

However, where does the spirit of dead people exist? Because blood in their descendant's bodies is that of their ancestors, it is the spirit of their ancestors (Blood is spirit). Therefore, the spirit of ancestors is not separated from that of their offspring. They are one. They are one body. It means the spirit of my ancestors is mine, and my spirit is my ancestors'. These words are new.

Therefore, the spirit of ancestors still lives in their offspring's bodies. Ancestors who died 6,000 years ago live in the present. And the spirit of my ancestors is not separated from me.

Satan has convinced us that humans are separated from their ancestors. However, in fact, my parents and my grandparents are me. Hence, that I become the Victor means that my parents become the Victors and my grandparents become the Victors. The spirit of all ancestors in the Victor becomes the Victors.

Every individual is not separated; we are one. Therefore, the Victor told people to regard everyone as their bodies. In fact, they are one body and one. So regard anybody else's fault and sin as your sin, and others' pains, yours. That is the mind of God and the character of God.

If you want to be God, you should have a mind like that. If you have the mind that the Victor is separated from others, you cannot become God. You are finished as Satan.

Therefore you should always have the mind of God. Therefore, this Altar is the place where you are cultivating your spirituality to become God.

So the spirit of Adam and Eve 6,000 years ago still lives as my spirit now. Adam and Eve have been physically wholly present in everybody generation to generation.

So Jacob gave the right of judgment to Dan. The words "the right of judgment will go to his descendant who will be the Savior, *the Reincarnated Maitreya Buddha*, and *Jeongdoryeong* thousands of years later" mean that Dan himself becomes *the Reincarnated Maitreya Buddha* and the Savior.

Worldly science knows that everything is divided because Satan has deceived the offspring of God. However, the man of heaven reveals the facts. Therefore, if you evangelize diligently, soon you will become God and the whole spirit in your body becomes God, too.

If you achieve salvation, your parents will also achieve salvation. This is the best filial duty. If you achieve salvation, your parents and ancestors will also achieve salvation. Hence, you should know the truth correctly and try to become God.

If a person wants to become God, they should evangelize. Unless one does it, they cannot become God. When one does not have gratitude, their face will be wrinkled up and caught by a distracted mind and a person won't sleep well at night because God is not with that person.

Those who are with God are always simple and think of only one thing. Therefore, they sleep well at night, become healthy, and they are changed into the bodies of eternal life.

When one evangelizes even only one person, the Spirit of fire will accompany that person. Then their whole body will become hot, that person will smell the burning of paper. This smell is that of burning sins. The blood of sins, that is, the blood of Satan in themselves is burnt. So one can smell the burning of Satan. If someone does not experience that, he had better give up eternal life. After experiencing that, a person can receive salvation.

Therefore, I tell you to evangelize diligently. When you evangelize one, two, and more and more people, you will receive the grace of living water. The grace of living water will make you feel fresh from the mouth to the abdomens. And then you feel elevated - floating freely in the air.

After taking those experiences, you will take steps to accomplish eternal life. And then *the Sweet Dew Spirit* will come to you. It is fresh like dew is falling. It is the phenomenon that *the Sweet Dew Spirit* occupies the whole body. When *the Sweet Dew Spirit* accompanies you, you can smell the fragrance of lilies.

You smell the fragrance of lilies because *the Sweet Dew Spirit* accompanies you. Therefore, the believers of the Victory Altar are experiencing religion in this manner.

No matter how difficult it is, you should take those steps to achieve salvation. But even one experience that, if he commits sins, he will fall to the bottom. So you should not commit sins.

Thus have I heard, 1989. 10. 17

All things are evolving by humans' thoughts. Why are all things changed to be as they are now?

That's because humans' minds have been changed just the same way as they are, so they have the same appearance of the present humans. Do you understand?

If men's minds are changed to that of the God, then all things will also be changed. Therefore, what all of you should understand is that your thoughts will change all things. The Creator does not exist separately, and a human himself is the Creator.

Now, the Victor God is the Creator, the Being who controls the universe at his will is the Victor, and he is the Creator. So, if humans become the Victors and are reinstated to Gods, all things will be changed accordingly, and humans can recreate new heaven and earth.

The human being, the Victor God, in other words, the man who becomes the Victor, is expected to recreate the world. Therefore, now all things look like humans, and they resemble the humans' minds.

I say it biblically and scientifically, that all things are God and humans are also God. I used to tell you about the fact that all things are formed by atoms are drawn to each other. The atoms consist of nucleus and neutron, and the nucleus has neutrons in its center, and negative electrons go around the neutrons.

But scientists do not know why negative electrons circle around the neutrons. Those who studied science know that negative electrons circle around the neutron.

But scientists never ask the following question. What power makes the negative electrons circle around the neutron?'

Because humans are controlled by the spirit of Satan, they never have eyes to look even one inch ahead.

As they have no eyes to look ahead, they cannot think why negative electrons circle around the neutrons, where the power comes from, and what makes them circle around.

The Victor of the Victory Altar says that the power which makes negative electron go around the fixed orbit of the neutron is that of God. As God is the spirit of life, as it is now, the material of life is the source of generating energy. Therefore, the power which makes negative electrons turn comes from the power of the life of God.

The scientists of today say that the light from neutrons is ten billion light year times faster than sunlight. Then, is neutrons' light the same kind as the sunlight? No, they are not.

That neutrons' light is completely different from sunlight. If the light is ten billion light year times faster than the sunlight, then it should be a kind of supernatural power's light. If it is the light of supernatural powers, it means that it has supernatural powers in it.

Scientists used to say "the light from neutrons is ten billion light year times faster than light!" Einstein said, "If people can travel faster than the speed of light, they cannot die."

As you know, Einstein was a Jew, who lived in America studying atomics and discovered a huge destructive power is generated by nuclear fission. Generating a tremendous destructive power by nuclear fission means that a kind of formidable power exists.

Using the basic principles of nuclear fission, today's nuclear power plants are generating energy. Korea has several nuclear plants. People use the energy generated from those plants. I said a couple of years ago that the light from a neutron is that of God, the power of God's life.

Therefore, If a human becomes God, then he will emit light, and the light will be that of God, and it will generate the energy of God.

Therefore, the Victor God has power. So, even though typhoons blow to Korea, I go a thousand miles out and finishes off the typhoon or change its direction to push it toward another direction. Is it magic? No, it is power.

I have protected Korea from typhoons, and have stopped the rainy seasons. Is it possible by praying? No, it's power.

As I have that power, I speak out with confidence and accomplish myself as I speak out. Everything has been accomplished as I said it should be.

Many years ago when Mr. Carter and Mr. Reagan ran for the presidency, Carter, the Democratic Party candidate had a election pledge to withdraw U.S. army from Korea. But the Republican Party candidate, Mr. Reagan advocated U.S. soldiers should remain in Korea.

At that time, I(the Victor in the Bible, *the Reincarnate Maitreya Buddha* in Buddhism books) nominated Mr. Reagan and he became the president of the U.S. twice.

Looking back American political history, If a president from the Republican Party is elected once, and the then next term is for Democratic Party. They used to govern in turns.

When they saw the background of American policy, they held the power in turns. When Carter had the office, he had the policy to withdraw U.S. Army from Korea.

However, he did not make it. At that time, the policy of Democratic Party was that they move the U.S. Army from Korea to Japan and make Japan the last defense line.

If U.S. army withdraws, what will be the fate of Korea, to be democratized or communized? If Korea is communized, then the Savior cannot come out from Korea, and all humankind will be annihilated.

As we saw, elections in America influence the fate of all the people in the world, and God could not turn His face away from this matter.

As the followers of *Jeondogwan* knew, *the Spiritual Mother* (He raised the Savior) said that I elected Mr. Reagan as the U.S. president twice. The Spirit of God that elected Mr. Reagan to be the president of the U.S.A stays in Me.

When he was elected as president for the first time, the Spirit of God was in *the Spiritual Mother*, but on the second election, the Spirit of God was in the Victor.

God came to the Victor in *Yeokgok* and elected Mr. Reagan. An incumbent vice president being elected as the next president was a rare case in American political history. As the law of America did not allow anyone to become the president for more than two terms, and the policy of Reagan had to be continued, the candidate from Republican Party should be elected as president.

Therefore, Bush was elected not because he was great, but because his policy is anti-withdrawing the U.S. Army from Korea. If the Democratic party has the policy of withdrawing the U.S. Army, they cannot seize power.

When Mr. Carter held office, he planned the withdrawal of the U.S. Army from Korea gradually. When he withdrew some U.S. soldiers, the Spirit of God went to him and threatened, "If you withdraw U.S. armies, you will die." Accordingly, he gave up withdrawal because he was afraid of God.

He made a campaign promise that during his term, he would withdraw U.S. armies from Korea. However, he could not keep his promise. Who captured his mind?

God did. At that time, the Spirit of God did not sleep at night and captivated his mind. As God wants to be busy saving people if a candidate had the policy of evacuating the U.S. Army became the President of America, then Satan and God would struggle to captivate him, so ultimately more obstacles would be made in saving people.

So God elected the one who does not have the policy of the evacuation of the U.S. Army as the president. So the candidate of the Republican Party became the president.

Then Satan encouraged Republican Congressmen to insist on the gradual withdrawal of U.S. Army from Korea. It was Satan's trick. But Mr. Kale, the vice president of U.S. came to Korea and said that they would keep their election pledge.

Even though some members of Congress fought for the withdrawal of the U.S. Army, vice president Mr. Kale came to convince Korea on keeping the Korea-U.S. defense treaty. Did people do this work or God do?

God worked this out. Is the power of the Victor fearful or not?

As it is thanks to the Almighty of Victor, there are no worries.

I said that the mind of a human is spirit and blood is the spirit, so the body is the spirit. As humans' bodies are the spirit, all things are spirit and all things are God. So the material is the pronoun of the spirit.

I say that body and the spirit are one, and the sayings of the Bible are also of the same theory that body and the spirit are one. So, all things are God, and all things are the spirit.

The captain of all spirit is a human, and the captain of all God is a human. So when people pray to Satan, it means that they surrender to Satan.

Humans are the captain of all things, and the captain of all spirit, so if the human makes action with a conviction now, then no spirit and ghosts can overcome him.

No spirit overcomes humans. People used to say that when they go to the mountain at night, ghosts or beasts emerge. But what is the most fearful thing?

Our ancestors said that humans are the most fearful thing. These words came from their experiences. According to my experiences, human beings are the most dreadful thing.

"Human beings are the most dreadful thing" means that they are the strongest and greatest. So, have confidence in you. Without having confidence or conviction in you, can anything be accomplished?

If one doubts it, it means one is swallowed by Satan, and a person surrenders to Satan. Therefore, as humans are the best, and if the best being becomes God, nothing can overcome humans anymore.

As one knows, there are a lot of disturbances from Satan in performing God's work. But nobody has stopped God. Whoever tried to hinder the work of Victory Altar died.

It is like attacking the iron tanks. If they fight against tanks, then they are run over by the tanks and die. So it is the reason that the weak cannot defeat the strong.

The Victor is the strong one and an invincible captain. Nobody defeats Him. Therefore, as the Victor admits this country's president or administration, the government goes well.

If He does not, no matter how strong the government is, it is like foaming water. As one knows, every government who sent *the Spiritual Mother* to jail was ruined.

The power of God is so awesome. Therefore, as the strong power of life is emitted from the Victor; I (the Victor) can keep the typhoons away and stop the rainy seasons at My will.

As it is now, someday, will I put a land mass into the sea or will I not? I will. I am an awesome being. One day I said in Japan that I had the power to put the country into the sea inside or to stop the land from sinking into the sea inside.

Yesterday, all Japanese members went back to Japan except one believer. The believers of the Victory Altar of Shimonoseki, the Victory Altar of Osaka, and the Victory Altar of Tokyo went back to Japan.

They visited the factory run by Victory Altar when they are in Korea. When I told them that the workers who were working offer everything to God; The Japanese followers were impressed by them, and some shed tears.

They saw there were a lot of great believers in *Yeokgok*. So they were convinced that it would change the world someday because this work is that of God.

Hence, as it is now, if people know the truth, offering their lives to God is normal. If people act miserly even though they know the truth, they are not normal. Offering their lives is normal.

So I offered My life as I lived. I offered all the money I made without anyone's notice. And I offered money at the altars of

Yeeman and *Ohman* secretly.

Since they were big, people could not recognize I was offering. When I even 200,000 won made a week, I offered all the money. At that time, 200,000 won was a lot of money. Its value is several million won in today's currency. Nobody knew it, except God.

Hence, *the Spiritual Mother* said, "I have tried to find out a man for 6,000 years, but I never met one like you." He said, "there were many great persons in history, but there was no one like you."

Accordingly, God admitted that Cho Hee Sung in *Yeokgok* is the greatest in 6,000 years. So I said that there is only one man who can draw God. Seeing the greatest man in 6,000 years human history is the luckiest thing.

You are admitted by God, too. How is it possible seeing the greatest man in 6,000 years human history? It's because you are chosen.

Hence, you are admitted by God. There were no men as great as you in 6,000 years human history. Only great men can live together with the great being.

Therefore, you should take pride in yourself. You have your ancestors' blood, as it is now, who had done good things and sacrificial things for generations, and it flows into your body, and so you have great opportunities to meet the great Victory God.

You should thank God every time. If one does not give thanks to God always, he is not qualified to sit here. Whenever a person see this or that believer, even though they make mistakes, he should feel thankful all the time.

In other words, when one pour out their thanks all the time, Satan cannot occupy him, and he cannot commit sins.
I became a Victor by living full of gratitude. By living full of gratitude all the time, I gave My mind and body entirely to God. As

I gave My whole life to God, I became the full possessions of God, and I became one body with God. So I became a Victor.

When the Victress Eve said in *the Secret Chamber* that I became God, the other believers looked at Me thinking that I did not look like God, and why did she say I became God?

At that time, I thought, "Why do those people think so? If they believe the word of God 100 percent, they will become God."

If one believes God 100 percent, one will become God. Like this way, if one has 100 percent conviction in God, one will become God, and if one has the conviction of becoming God, one surely will become God.

Therefore, since God is *Jeongdoryeong*, *Jeongdoryeong* is just God. A person would have heard that *Jeongdoryeong* has *the Dew Spirit*.

If people eat *the Dew Spirit*, they cannot die. And the man who has *the Dew Spirit* is *the Reincarnated Amita Buddha*. The Buddhist Scriptures say, "If people eat *the Dew Spirit*, they can live forever." And the Bible says, "God will become *the Dew*."

God is *the Dew Spirit*. So if they have God's mind, people will not die.

The Bible says, "Have God's mind. To have God's mind means to eat God's Spirit." To eat God's Spirit is eating *the Dew Spirit*. "By eating *the Dew Spirit*, people will not die" means that having God's mind, they will not die.

I teach this way of becoming God very easily. God's mind is to regard everybody as my body. Regarding everybody as my body is God's mind. Only God regards even a robber as God, and sinners regard a robber as a sinner. So those who think of sinners as God are God.

Therefore, those who have a hateful mind cannot become God.

When they love people full of hate earnestly and regard them as God, they become God. So I urge you to live regarding everybody as God.

If one starts regarding everyone as God and their body, from that time on, their life is in heaven, the paradise, and is full of joy.

Some people say that happiness comes from money, a lot of money. So they steal money and gather more and more money. However, once they got money, they start to worry about being stolen, and they cannot sleep at night.

That is hell. Therefore, I teach the secret of going to heaven, eternal life, happy life, and healthy eternal life without diseases.

Thus have I heard, 2002. 03. 01

Because the Savior pours out the Holy Dew Spirit, the Holy Dew Spirit is the Savior. The Buddhist Scriptures and the Bible also say "if people eat the Holy Dew Spirit, they cannot die."

Immortality lies in one. It is not in several people. When my mind becomes one, people become one, and immortal flowers bloom there. Hence, heaven and salvation are in one, unless one is accomplished, there is no salvation.

Therefore, when I trained intensively in the *Secret Chamber*, there was one man who slandered and hated Me harshly. Whenever he hated Me, I did not hate him back, but rather regarded him preciously, respected him, and liked him more. Because he slandered Me and told lies about Me, My flattering mind disappeared.

Also, I was growing stronger internally day by day. Accordingly, I thanked the man. As I liked the man earnestly, no matter how hard he hated Me, I liked him more than he hated Me. Finally, he thought that he could not overcome Me. Therefore, I liked him continually, as it is now, as I did that, finally he started to like Me.

When the man hated Me, although the Victress who raised Me knew that, she ordered Me to share one room with the man.

If I hate that man, can I share the room with the man? As I liked him, when she ordered Me to share the room, I made up a bed for him and cleaned the room. At first, he told Me that I pretended to look up to him. However, I said to him that I just tried to overcome Satan in Me. As Satan finally died in Me, Satan in the man died, too.

After sharing the room, the man neither criticized, nor hated, nor laughed at Me. The Victress found out that the man who continually hated Me does not hate Me anymore, and I overcame the man.

I worked on his job instead of him. The man was in his thirties, and he was the same age as My son. Nerveless, as I respected him and obeyed his words, he came to know that I liked him.

Although he hated Me, criticized Me, mocked Me, I did not hate him back. The man thought this strange at first. However, he looked at Me for several months, he came to see that My behavior was not changed at all.

I thought and behaved on the basis that My neighbor's situation is mine, his sin, Mine, too. Then he was touched by Me. After that, he liked Me and stopped slandering Me. Also his mouth was changed into a praising one, he always praised Me.

While I was trained in the *Secret Chamber*, and I realized that My neighbor's situation is Mine. Neighbor's blood is the same to Mine, and neighbors are one body with Me. Accordingly, his fault is Mine, even though I saw his fault, I told it as Mine and regarded it as Mine.

Then the Victress Eve who was with God knew Me.

As the man's situation was Mine, his mind was Mine. Therefore I moved like one mind with him, he naturally liked Me. That is the way of overcoming Satan.

The way of overcoming Satan is regarding My neighbor's situation as mine, My neighbor's pain as mine, and My neighbor's sin as mine. When I thoughts of brothers' sin as Mine, I regret, repent, and pray for that, God knew My mind.

We all were made of the blood of Adam and Eve, the blood of Adam and Eve has been connected to their offspring generation by generation, the blood comes to us here today. Therefore, I realized clearly that the blood starting from Adam and Eve has flowed through their offspring and has come to us.

Therefore, when I thought of the neighbors' sin as mine and prayed to God to forgive their fault, God forgave it, because it was a right prayer.

When I prayed to forgive My sins, God rarely forgives Me. However, when I experienced this, I regarded My brothers' sin as Mine and prayed for brothers' sin, God forgave their sins easily. And then God sent Me grace strongly and forgave My sin, too. Hence, I continued praying that kind of prayer.

Since God's grace was connected to Me, and when I saw an unsatisfied man and hated the man, then God's grace was stopped. Therefore, I regarded his sin as Mine and prayed for his sin earnestly. Then the stopped grace was suddenly connected to Me again. Therefore, I came to know the secret of receiving grace.

If we want to follow the way of eternal life, when we become one like regarding my brother's body as mine, my body is my brother's, and then immortality is accomplished. Therefore, before becoming one, immortality is impossible.

Accordingly, after becoming God, immortality is accomplished; the God is in the Victor. When you pray to God, as the God is in the Victor, the God in the Victor saves you. One's life is Victor's other selves.

Hence, if one lives with the thought "the Savior's situation is mine, my situation is the Victor's", one and the Victor surely become one. As the Savior is my body and my body is the Savior's, one cannot help but become the Savior.

After a person becomes the Savior, they can achieve salvation. Unless becoming the Savior, one cannot achieve salvation.

Accordingly, the model of salvation is the Savior; the model of immortality is the Savior.

Hence the Savior is a person's life; one cannot live without life. Therefore, as Victor's other-self exists in one's body as life, one should live with the thought that the situation of the Victor is mine and their situation is the Savior's. Then one can become Savior. The Savior is just the Victor God and the Victor God is the immortal one, so when one becomes a Victor, they are qualified to live in heaven. Hence, the hero of heaven is the Savior; the Savior is the hero of heaven.

Revelation 3:12 says "He who overcomes him will make the pillar in the temple of my God." The temple is heaven; the temple is the paradise, making the pillar of the temple means that without the Victor, heaven is not accomplished.

Heaven is the house of the Savior, so if all of the people become the Savior, they can go to heaven. Before one become a Savior, one cannot go to heaven.

Therefore, I tell people to look at My picture every second and carry My picture. Whenever a person cannot engrave My face on their mind, look at the picture. The Fruit of Life in the Bible is the face of the Savior(the Victor).

Because the Savior pours out the Holy Dew Spirit, the Holy Dew Spirit is the Savior. The Buddhist Scriptures and the Bible also say, "if people eat the Holy Dew Spirit, they cannot die."

Now Revelation 2:17 says, "To him who overcomes, I will give some of the hidden manna. I will also give him a white stone with a new name written on it, known only to him who receives it."

"To him who overcomes, I will give some of the hidden manna" means that the hidden manna is just the Holy Dew Spirit, God promised to give the Holy Dew Spirit and a white stone with a new name written on it, known only to him who receives it.

Therefore, as I(the Victor) know the name written on the white stone, I revealed it. The name on it is *Sosa*. *So* (素) means white; *Sa* (沙) means sand. As sand is a small stone, a small stone is a stone, too. *Sosa* itself means a white stone.

Therefore, I physically received a white stone at the age of around seven. When I was too young, even though I received a white stone with a name on it, I did not know it. However, I remembered the word.

When I went to *Seodang* (the basic education place before elementary school) at the age of seven and learned Chinese, I came to know the word '*Sosa*'. I actually received the white stone. I am telling you that I received a white stone with the words 'a white stone' on it.

Therefore, I built the *Victory Altar* in *Sosa* area. The first *Victory Altar* was built in *Yeokgok-1-dong*, the second *Victory Altar* in *Yeokgok-2- dong, Sosa*. Then I bought land for the third Victory Altar with the address of Goiandong 175-2.

Some people asked Me "Buy land at *Yeokgok* area, please cancel the contract, the will of heaven is supposed to be accomplished in *Yeokgok*." But as God ordered to build it there, I built the *Victory Altar* there.

When the completion certificate was issued, the address of *Goiandong* was changed to *Yeokgok-3-dong*. As this work is that of God, starting from *1-dong*, moving to *2-dong*, and to *3-dong*, the *Victory Altar* of God was finally completed.

Therefore, as God Himself worked through Me, the *Spiritual Mother* called Me to direct Me to name the building the *Victory Altar*. Therefore, I named the *Victory Altar* and I hung the sign of the *Victory Altar*. Actually, I followed the *Spiritual Mother*'s direction in building the *Victory Altar*. Accordingly, today I am raising qualified persons for living in heaven.

Therefore, after one becomes one, a person can receive everlasting life. Unless a person becomes one, one has no relation to eternal life.

Hence, no matter how hateful a man sits by a person, one must not hate him or her. One must regard him or her as their God or senior and respect him or her. Then two persons will become one, four will become one, sixteen will become one, thirty-two will become one, and no matter how many people there are, they will become one.

So where a lot of people become one, the place is the group of God; it is not a group of humans.

In the *Victory Altar*, believers regarding each other as God, respecting each other like that, and becoming one are the motto of the *Victory Altar*. Therefore, I told you to regard anyone as your body.

As this saying is a shining one and a true one, no matter how long time passes, it shall not be changed. So when you live your life regarding others as your body, there is happiness and delight in your life, and you are living in heaven. People who become one can live in heaven, those who do not become one cannot become God, and they do not have a qualification to go to heaven.

According to Zephaniah 3:7 "God is in you." This means that as God is in everyone, He is in you. Therefore, God is in all of you, when you become one, God is completed.

Therefore, when someone hates others, his blood decays, and when they are angry or are fretful, their blood decays, too. As the splitting spirit hates each other, blood decays. Because blood decays, therefore, people die. Unless blood decays, people cannot die.

As God is in everyone, when you and I get separated, God cannot stay in us, therefore God dies. As Satan kills God, everyone dies. Accordingly, when you become one, there is no place for Satan to stand on, and as Satan cannot exist.
When you become one, all of you receive immortality. True religion is realizing the truth, and realizing the truth is getting immortality, and splitting and separating is not realizing the truth.

As religion is realizing the truth, there was no religion in the world. Christianity has been divided into hundreds because it is the group of Satan. Hence it is not a true religion.

The aim of religion is accomplishing immortality. The truth is realized by accomplishing immortality. Realizing the truth is religion. Therefore, the truth is realized in immortality. Death is separating, splitting each other, dying, and dissipating, so it is the work of Satan. Therefore, the group of Satan is not that of realizing the truth; therefore, it is not true religion.

According to the Revelation 2:26, "to him who overcomes and does my will to the end, I will give authority over the nations I will rule them with an iron scepter, he will dash them to pieces like pottery. I will also give him the morning star."

"The Victor will rule the nations with an iron scepter," means that the Victor destroys the group of Satan with an iron scepter; the Victor destroys the group of the untruths with the words of the truth. Iron scepter is a word of the truth. Only the truth can break the untruth of Satan.

I break the words "Jesus is the Savior" with words of the truth. I break it with the Bible. Psalm 82:6 writes, "You are gods. You are all sons of the Highest." Mankind is separated into male and female. However, God says you are the sons of the Most High. There are no women in heaven. There are the souls of male and female. The soul of a female is the soul of Satan. In fact, some day, I am supposed to change women into men.

Therefore, the world of God has neither men nor women. According to Jeremiah 16, "you must not marry and have sons or daughters in this place.... If they are married, they will die of a deadly disease." Therefore, the priests and nuns of Catholic faith do not marry. The Buddhist books say the same, so the monks of Buddhism do not marry.

Marrage life is a dying sin. If someone gets married, they are supposed to die. We should obey the words of God. Before hearing this, if you are already married, you should not have sex.

So there is a Psalm, "the virgins of Zion." In this word, the 'virgins' mean not only women but also men. Also if a man is the bride of the Lord, he is virgin, too. If someone is the bride of the Lord, he is a virgin of Zion. It is a spiritual word. You should become clean virgins to have God.

Because you should have the notion of sexual purity, you should adore only the Lord highly and think of only God. Then you have a qualification for marrying God.

Let's sing a psalm "When the Lord, bridegroom, comes down, are you ready to greet him with a lamp in your hand at the night, at the night, are you ready to greet him with a lamp in your hand. Prepare, prepare, when our Lord, bridegroom, comes, we will welcome him with joy with a bright lamp in our hand."

When we sing this hymn and think of the rhyme, as you know, all the people are the virgins welcoming the Lord. Men are virgins, too. They are spiritual virgins. So to welcome the Lord, they will have bright lamps in their hands.

In this sentence, the bright lamp means grace. Receiving grace and keeping it, they can welcome the Lord.

Thus have I heard, 2000. 10. 10

If people laugh always, they will become God because they are a happy spirit.

One American doctor, Lee Sang-Gu who knows about laughing to some degree said; when people laugh, endorphin springs up in the blood, then endorphins kill viruses, and they get cured.

He knows that just laughing generates endorphins; however, he does not know the reason why endorphins are secreted.

That's because when people laugh, Satan dies. As a crying mind belongs to Satan, when you laugh, the Spirit of God becomes strong, and Satan dies.

Today, no matter how intelligent scientists are, they do not know this. When you laugh, your body becomes light and healthy, and diseases can be cured.

That is the work of God. As heaven is the paradise and the house of God, and since only God can live in the house of God, people cannot live there. Therefore, people cannot go there.

The Possibility of a human's becoming God is 90 percent. Humans cannot become God because of the ten percent. Ten percent means people can become God with just a little more efforts.

Because humans were initially God, they have the characters of God. Because the very human's conscience is the Spirit of God, and because they have 90 percent of God's character, they hate bad things, behavior, and thoughts.

Another proof of it is the fact that they hate dying. Immortal nature is that of God. Because immortal nature is that of God, everyone hates dying, in other words, because they have ninety percent possibility to become God, they hate to die.

Nobody knows that people were God. According to the book of Genesis in the Bible, Adam and Eve lived in the Garden of Eden. The Garden of Eden was the paradise.

In a hymn, everywhere is heaven, even on high mountains, rough fields, thatched cottages or palaces the Lord God resides there. Where God resides, heaven is.

If we say it the other way around, only God goes to heaven. As God originally lived in heaven, the Garden of Eden, with Adam and Eve, Adam and Eve were God.

The Bible says that Adam and Eve had the figure of God. It means that they had the appearance of God. In other words, they were God.

If they were not God, how could they have the figure of God? Because they were God, they had the figure of God. It is written in the Bible, "Adam and Eve had the figure of God."

Because Satan was next to God, so he could not say that humans were originally God. At that time, God was chased by Satan and could not overcome it. If He wrote, "Humans were originally God", He could have risked that Satan would attack and kill Him.

Isaiah 34:16 wrote "None of these will be missing, not one will lack her mate. For it is my mouth that has given the order, and my Spirit will gather them together."

All Lord's sayings have mates, that is, unpaired sayings are Satan's. There are two spirits. One is the Spirit of God, and the other is the spirit of Satan.

As unpaired sayings are not those of God, you should read the Bible discreetly. Isaiah 34:16 clearly noted; "Adam and Eve were made of soil." There is not a mate to that. Somewhere in there should be mentioned that people are made of soil, but there are not. Therefore, they are unpaired words. These words that Adam and Eve were made of soil are unpaired ones, they are not reasonable.

How can people be made of soil? No matter how progressive and knowledgeable scientists are, they cannot make humans out of the soil. Therefore, the saying is false and that of Satan.

As life itself is God, you are alive because of God. If there is no God in you, you cannot be alive. However, worldly science cannot talk like this. Hence, I say that there is no science in the world. People do not know the basics of science. Therefore, worldly science is not real science.

When people die, the life dies. As life is God, God dies in a human body. Because the Spirit of God in humans dies, the humans die. The Spirit in humans is the spirit of God, not the Spirit of human. People say that because the Spirit is in human, it is the Spirit of human; actually, it is the Spirit of God.

Not because the human's body dies, the spirit dies, but because the Spirit of God dies, a human dies. However, pseudo-religions say that people go to heaven after they die. Rather than saying that as the spirit dies, humans die, they say that the Spirit goes to heaven or hell, it is nonsensical.

If as the spirit dies, the human dies, and then how does the spirit go to heaven or hell after death? If the words are not reasonable, it is a stupid talk.

There are many people who follow pseudo-religions. Because people are the slaves of Satan, they have a lot of Satan's disposition in them. As they have a lot of Satan's disposition in them, they are supposed to follow Satan. However, all of them are expected to follow the Victor soon. Soon, the sun will be deprived of its light, and light will come from the Savior. Then people will believe in the Savior. In other words, they believe in the Savior who gives immortality.

According to *Gyeokamyourok*, a Korean prophetic book which is 100 percent accurate, people from all over the world will come to Korea to greet the Savior with gold, silver, and all kinds of treasures in their hands.

As they heard, upon meeting the Savior, their fatal diseases will be cured and have eternal life. Therefore, they will come to Korea with all their money and treasures.

Then Korea will be the richest country. All kings in the world will come to Korea, and treasures will be stored from *Suwon* to *Gaeseong*, and all the roads in Korea will be paved with gold according to the prophecy. Isaiah 60 of the Bible writes the same story that light will come from the Savior and every king of the world will come to Korea with treasures. I proclaimed as follows:

1. I will eliminate communism.
2. I will prevent typhoons reaching Korea.
3. I will stop the heavy rainy seasons in Korea.
4. I will make Korean harvests abundant.
5. I will prevent wars in Korea.

As I proclaimed, all the covenants had been accomplished for last twenty years. This shows the proof of Me being the true Savior. During last twenty years, the harvest of Korea had been abundant.

Also, North Korea's navy warship trespassed the 38 parallel to South Korea to test Korean military power. At that time, the South Korean navy ships bombarded the North Korean navy ship like they fired a barrage of machine guns. And then their navy ship got sunk.

Kim Jong-Il lost courage when the strong South Korean navy fired back. He, therefore, thought that South Korea is a not weak country anymore. They are much stronger since the 1950 Korean War. Now, the president of South Korea, Kim Dae-Jung, signed a treaty of 'reunion of dispersed family members' and reopened the railway which was cut during the Korean War.

It will be connected to Europe through Manchuria. Once it is connected to Europe, Korea will be rich automatically. Even though North Korea is poor now, once the railroad is connected, North Korea will be rich, too. The construction of railroad connection has been started already.

Then the DMZ will not have a meaning anymore because South and North Koreans will pass through the DMZ.

It will be the same effect to reunification. God will make all these things happen. Soon Korea will be unified and rich. That day surely will come and you will be happy. Then laugh. Once you start laughing, your blood will become clean.

Therefore, I say that there was no science in the world. Humans were God, and nowadays they are the children of God. The children of God are God, too.

Like a puppy is a dog, a calf is a cow, baby monkeys are monkeys, and God's children are also God. However, they say the children of God are humans. Therefore, it is not science. They do not know even the basics of science.

We can see that 'humans' ancestor is God' from the fact that human character hates death. Because their ancestor's blood which hates death is flowing in their offspring's blood, they hate death.

Therefore, a three-year-old baby is afraid of and hates death. Humans are living forms that live forever. Humans are God according to the Korean founder, Dangun. From this, we can see that our ancestors were very wise. Our ancestors believed that humans were God.

It was the Korean founder *Dangun*'s thought. Therefore, it is natural that the Savior came out among Koreans. As they already knew 3,000 years ago, they are surely the offspring chosen by God.

Koreans are the direct descendants of God.

Thus have I heard, 2000. 10. 20

The mind of God is a sacrificial one having the conviction of immortality. If people have the conviction of immortality, their bodies will be changed to those of God.

I say that to become God, you should have the mind of God. However, the mind of God is different from that of a human. It is a sacrificial one having the conviction of immortality. It is very difficult to become God because humans have lived as Satan for 6,000 years.

However, it depends on your mind. People make a model before they make things. When people build apartments, they build model houses and build apartments just like the model house. Therefore, God should make a model before making humans God.

So, when God tells humans to become God, and when He moves with such a plan, one should be made the same as the model. One should check yourself every time to see how much one resemble God, ten percent or twenty percent so that one becomes the same as the model of God.

Also, you should review to see how much one did to make God happy as to ten percent or twenty percent. When you do something that makes God happy, God is happy. Accordingly, you should evangelize people and bring them to the *Victory Altar* to save people as the Savior did.

Also, to become God, you should laugh. The mind of laughing is good when your parents laugh, they give you money. When your father is in a good mood and happy, he gives you money. When people laugh, a laughing mind becomes sacrificial. Once people have a sacrificial mind, they give money from their pocket.

When people laugh and are happy, their minds become those of God, so this phenomenon happens.

If you laugh and are happy, your blood gradually becomes that of God, and you are getting less angry. Those who laugh a lot do not have anger. Because they have the mind of God at that moment, they are not angry. Being angry is the mind of Satan. Being displeased with people is the nature of Satan, and God has nothing to do with displeasure.

As God is sacrificial, no matter how many mistakes His children make, although His children need a lot of care and attention, God provides them those laughing, patting, and pampering. That is the mind of God. As God has a loving mind, a sacrificial mind, and a happy mind, He is always pleased with His children though He sees them every day.

Therefore, He raises His children that way. As a laughing mind is that of God, when I tell you to laugh and evangelize, it means "To become God."

Because their blood has been changed into Satan's, they have the appearance of Satan. As a result, they have been changed into a female and male body.

Jeremiah 16 says, "Do not marry." Although people marry and have children, God says not to marry and not to have children. Do you know why? That's because, after marriage, humans' blood will start to decay gradually. People die not because they are getting old, but because their blood decays.

Therefore, the reason for young people to commit suicide is that their blood gradually decayed and their blood became Satan's, and they were getting tired of living, and finally they committed suicide.

Because their blood had been changed into Satan's, living as a Satan became painful. So, they committed suicide or they were in an accident and died.

It is like a magnet. When a person puts a magnet near to nails or steel, they stick to magnets. Blood is the same. When blood decays to a certain extent, they become more easily to die by being run over by cars. It is not a mistake. They are drawn like a magnet and die like that because their blood decays.

When I was young, I went to a funeral where a person had died due to a car accident. Although someone did not get hurt seriously, he still died. Hence, I went to the place where the accident happened and found that black blood had bled there.

The principle is as follows. When a car suddenly strikes a person, he/she is shocked and instantly his/her blood decays a lot, so even though they hurt only a little, they still die of heart attack. When people are shocked, their blood decays 100 percent.

There is a saying, that even you are attacked by tigers if you are awake, then you still can live. When a person is attacked by a tiger, the tiger scares him causing him to faint and then it eats him. Tiger cannot eat living people. Here is an old Korean story. When a man met a tiger on his way home, he was calm, and then eventually the tiger slowly went away.

Think it over and rationalize it. I saw a man who had a car accident, hurt seriously enough to break his leg and ribs. However, he did not die. I saw that his red blood was at the traffic accident site. So a man in that blood could not die.

When a person is shocked, his blood decays 100 percent and finally die, and if they are not shocked, they will not die.

When a person falls from a high place, he usually thinks that he is going to die. As he thinks of dying, he will die. Those who are convinced that they never can die cannot die, even though they are 500 years old. People think that as they become old, they lose energy, and they die. If a person thinks in this way, he will die. If he thinks that he will live forever, then he cannot die. This is a definite theory of immortality.

Every person is God. Among them, there is true God and also incomplete God. Incomplete God is not yet accomplished. You are seeing a complete God, therefore, you should laugh. When you laugh, even though you have a lot of wrinkles, you are as beautiful as a flower.

Do you know why a laughing person looks so beautiful? Because when you laugh, you become God. The moment you laugh, you become God. God is beautiful in that way. Because God is so beautiful, a laughing person looks so beautiful. Even though you are angry, and you look at laughing person, your anger will melt down.

You are in the ark of salvation. This is the place where the Trinity God resides. Where God resides is the heaven. Therefore, this place is heaven. And the reason this place is heaven is that the mind of the person who is with God for twenty-four hours a day is the heaven. My mind is heaven.

Therefore, the body of God which makes heaven is heaven. You are so lucky because you take your worship services in heaven. Also, I say that people are God. Not only human but also all things are God.

John 1:1 says, "Life is God." Plants have lives and flowers have lives, so they blossom. As they have lives, they are God. They blossom from time to time. They withered and they die. That is because Satan is in them and kills them.

When I became the Victor and went to a mountain, the plants and the trees that could not speak bowed deeply to Me. You could not believe it. There was little wind on that day; thick trees bowed deeply, bending their thick trunks. I thought it was mysterious.

How did those thick trees bend their trunks and then straighten again? Only God made them do that. When I became the Victor, not only humans but also all things were happy. Also, the moving of the air was not as usual. it was like dancing. The air was happy, too.

As the Savior that all things have been waiting for 6,000 years has appeared, they danced because they were happy. The reason that you believe in I as the Savior is because I explained clearly what people do not know.

Additional, I speak of the truth. Nobody can rebuff My sayings because they are rational, everything I said was accomplished. When people meet others, they are affected by them. If you meet someone who is laughing, the laughing person emits a laughing material. Therefore, you automatically laugh, because you are affected by the laughing essence.

So, if one person weeps behind people, the people weep without seeing that person. When people go to funeral ceremonies, they weep. Because crying people emit a crying essence, the other people are affected by the essence, cry, and become sad. Does it seem likely, is it real? It is real.

It will take thousands of years for the scientific knowledge of the world to reach My level, so you know my existence is beyond the understanding of this world. If you do business with the conviction of immortality, you will succeed. If you have confidence in your business, you surely will succeed. However, if you are not sure about succeeding, you cannot succeed.

As you think, you will reap. Hence, if you think firmly and start, everything is accomplished. Because humans themselves are the children of the Creator, each person has the creativity. Humans can make something that does not exist and can change as they want because they can do that.

As they want to fly, they make planes, as they want to travel further and faster, they make cars. As they want to fly, they make planes, because they were God that flew 6,000 years ago. Therefore, as they have the idea of flying, they have made planes.

Accordingly, they have 90 percent possibility of becoming God. As humans were God, becoming God is a piece of cake.

As you have met the Savior, who pours out the *Holy Dew Spirit* which kills the Satan in people, you get out of humans' restraint and become God. And then you cannot die and cannot have pains. You are free from pains, worries, and the restraints of death.

Therefore, as you have the condition and have met the Savior, you surely will become God. Accordingly, you just join the worship services every day. In time, the light will shine from the face of the Savior. It will shine on the whole universe, and then there will be no shade.

The sunshine and the electric light have shades. Therefore, when the sun shines, the opposite side of the world is dark at night, because it is straight light. However, the light emitting from the Savior is spiral. Hence, it shines on both sides and has no night. So everyone will be happy all of the time and if they wish, they can fly to the moon in a moment.

It is joyful just to imagine this. Raise your hand those who would not want to live like this. The bodies of humans are painful. Just walking is hard and legs hurt. Having a body is a pain; it is a bridle of pains.

Humans have pains, although they lie or sit. If they lie for one day or two days, it is boring. When they lie for one week, they cannot stand. So, they should become God as soon as possible. And then they are free from their bodies and fly as they want. Because they have bodies, they cannot do as they want.

The condition of having bodies is that of being caught by Satan's restraint, so you should be out of the restraint as soon as possible.

After that, you are happy, dance for twenty-four hours, and do not know time flying by. So passing 1,000 years is like passing a day.

Some people say that if they marry, they will be happy. However, when they marry, pains are waiting for them. Marriage means becoming slaves to the spouse. Men earn money and offer it to their wives, therefore, men marry to become slaves to their wife, and women marry to become one to their husbands. When women are single, they go as they want. However, after marriage, some men do not allow their wives to go out.

Because they doubt their wives, when their wives look at other men, they hit their wives. It is real. They marry to become slaves. Marrying is a foolish thing. Only fools marry.

The reason for divorce is that they are sick and tired of their married lives and have no freedom. Once they divorce, they do not marry again. Usually, those who marry again are foolish, so smart people do not marry and live as singles.

There are a lot of singles in America and Japan. Come to think of it realistically, a single life is happier. According to the Bible, "Do not marry. Do not bear your children. If you bear your children, you will die, and beasts eat up the bodies."

In old times when people died, they might throw the bodies in the field, so animals ate them. It is miserable to be eaten by beasts. So you should live chaste and clean life. That is the order of God.

Let's wrap up today's worship here. Let's go out laughing. Do not just make sounds ha, ha, ha. Really laugh. When you laugh, God is happy.

Thus have I heard, 2001. 02. 27

The immortal Spirit of God is the Belief and the Fruit of life, the Fruit of life is the Spirit of God that makes people be reborn as the Holy Spirit and overcome Satan.

Only the Victor pours out the Spirit to overcome Satan. The man who overcame 'me', the Satan, pours the Spirit of the Victor. If you receive the Spirit of the Victor, you become Victors, too. To become the Victor, you should receive the Spirit of the Victor.

Therefore, if the Victor is in *Yeokgok*, you should go there I have said for 20 years that there was no true science and no true religion in the world.

Science should study and describe the essence of things, I said all things are God, and they are the co-existence of God and Satan. Therefore, humans are God.

The Bible also says that humans are God. Psalms 82:6 says "You are God and you are all sons of the Most High." The sons of the Most High mean the sons of God. The sons of God are God, not animals. So science is wrong.

According to Deuteronomy 14:1 "You are the children of the Lord your God." 'The children of the Lord' means 'the children of God.'

1 John 3:2 says "We are the children of God." The Bible says humans are the children of God many times. Therefore, humans are the children of God.

Isaiah 43:14 says, "God saves humans." As humans are His children, He saves them. According to Isaiah 43:12, "He saves humans" The Savior is God. The son of God cannot be the Savior. Only God becomes the Savior and saves His Children according to the Bible. "Jesus is the son of God and is the Savior" are not the words of the Bible.

Today, Christianity does not know the theory of salvation. According to John 3:5 "You achieve salvation by being reborn as the Holy Spirit" According to Genesis 3:22, "He must not be allowed to reach out his hand and take also from the tree of life and eat, and live forever."

According to Genesis, God put a flaming sword which turned in all directions from the tree of life to make Adam and Eve not to eat the Fruit of Life. But is it true? This is Satan's lie.

According to Genesis, by eating the Fruit of life, you can achieve salvation. And thanks to the Faith, you can achieve salvation. According to Ephesians 2:8, "Thanks to the Faith, you can achieve salvation. The Faith is a gift from God." A present from God is not a believing mind. God is supposed to give His Spirit as a gift.

As God is the Spirit of immortality, He is supposed to give the immortal Spirit as a gift. The immortal Spirit is the Faith. The mind of death cannot be the Faith. The immortal Spirit of God is the Faith. The immortal Spirit of God is the Faith and the Fruit of life, the Fruit of life is the Spirit of God which makes people be reborn as the Holy Spirit and overcome Satan. Also the face of the Savior is the Fruit of Life.

Therefore, I tell people to look at the face of the Savior every second. As the Savior Himself is the Spirit of the Victor, it is the Faith and the Fruit of Life. The Spirit that overcomes Satan is the Fruit of Life. When the Spirit that overcomes Satan is in mind, the mind will become heaven.

According to Luke, "Heaven is not here or there, it is in your mind." Therefore, heaven is the paradise, the paradise is where God is. However, God is not a normal one, but one that overcomes Satan.

The mind with Satan cannot be heaven. When God kills Satan and gets rid of its existence, it is heaven. John 3:12 says, "Him who overcomes 'I' will make a pillar in the temple of my God." As the temple is where God is, the temple itself is heaven. Heaven does not exist without the Victor. Because the Victor is in the Victory Altar, this is heaven.

If religion does not know the definition of heaven and hell, it cannot be religion. According to James 1:15, "After desire has conceived, it gives birth to sin, when it is full-grown, it gives birth to death."

As desire is the sin, sin is death, and Self-awareness of 'I' induces desire, so the root of sin is Self-awareness of 'I'.

This is an original sin and the Forbidden Fruit. The Forbidden Fruit that Adam and Eve ate is in their offspring now. You should know that.

"To act in God" means that all things that I act are sins. Even though I give 100 bags of rice to an orphanage, it is a deadly sin. Though people do not know this, they exercise religion. It is very funny. The Bible writes, "throw away 'me' all the time." As 'I' am Satan, it says, "Throw me away."

According to the Bible, "You, have the mind of God". It means that a person does not have the mind of God, one has the mind of Satan. Does it make sense, "if those who have the mind of Satan believe in Jesus, they go to heaven with the mind of Satan" It is pseudo? It has no value as a religion.

They do not know the definition of the Belief and the definition of the Forbidden fruit for certain, and say, "people can achieve salvation by being born as the Holy Spirit." How do they can give salvation?

People can receive salvation only by knowing this. Only the Victor pours out the Spirit to overcome Satan. The man who overcame 'me', the Satan, pours the Spirit of the Victor.

As I deceive Satan very well, I can defeat him. I deceive Satan 100 percent. As I deceive Satan, it takes less than one second for Me to kill Satan. So Satan is helpless. Although Satan tries to flee at that moment, the Victor kills him; therefore, he just trembles in front of the Victor.

The Victor is so strong and fast. It does not take more than one second to kill Satan. When Satan runs one meter with his best effort, the Victor runs 100,000,000 meters. So Satan is supposed to be destroyed.

Then, sunlight will disappear. Because Satan exists, there is sunlight. If Satan does not exist, sunlight will disappear. I have come to the world to destroy Satan and make humans God.

When we fly, we will feel happy. We cannot express the feeling in human language. The sunlight is fast, but the speed of God is 100,000,000 times faster than that of sunlight. Therefore, the Savior annihilates Satan in a moment.

Now you should be confident because the Savior who can annihilate Satan at once is with you. Although you are the slaves of Satan now, I who am capable of annihilating Satan instantly has appeared and I will save you. Don't you know Me still? I eliminated communism!

I planned it carefully from 1985 and have controlled Gorbachev at My will. It was in the 1990s when I could move him freely. Also, because I could control him at will, I killed the spirit of communism, and then communism on the earth collapsed at once.

Think about it commonly. It is a piece of cake to kill Satan in your body. When you think of My ability to remove communism, to kill Satan in your body is a piece of cake to Me. If you obey Me, you will achieve salvation even though I looked like a simple countryman. When I was investigated by the prosecutor, he said that I looked like a countryman.

It was a tactic to disguise Myself. After I made Satan relax, I attacked the enemy. This was My tactic.

I served in the army for eleven years and trained physically. When I was an operation officer, the battalion commander directed the army to attack the enemy and support the troops from rear just as I planned. Like this, I was a capable officer in planning operations and battles.

Accordingly, I received a high award for the operation. I am a man who was physically and perfectly prepared for the battle. And following that, God made Me become a Victor. I have a professional intelligence enabling Me to wipe out the enemy.

In addition, as God is with Me, I can overcome Satan. I am 100 percent prepared as the Savior. No matter how many forms Satan has, he cannot defeat the Savior.

According to *Gyeokamyourok* "bringing up the captain of the victory to the front, and support him from back, they fight." As you meet the Victor, you just follow in the direction of Me.

The strongest spirit is communism. If I did not make it collapse, it could have occupied the world. Two-thirds of the world was almost on Satan's side. South Korea was almost communized. As I eliminated communism, North Korea could not invade South Korea.

As you see, God's work has been accomplished with perfect strategies; hence, you can become God and live in heaven without any problems.

The sign of the *Victory Altar* itself indicates that only winners who overcome themselves are supposed to live forever in the Victory Altar.

A castle will be built. Only men who will live forever will live there. Therefore, God's palace which will be built centered in *Sosa* will expand 12km from its current center. So you are happy and then laugh. You should live to laugh all the time.

Endorphins in blood come out when you laugh. This is true. The blood which became dirty due to sins becomes clean when you laugh. Which scholars say this in the world? If you laugh, you become pretty. If you laugh continually, though you are old, you become pretty. How? Your wrinkles will disappear. If you laugh continually, your blood becomes clean, and you receive the grace of immortality.

If you are down or worry, then you cannot receive grace from God. The Spirit of God goes to laughing men. As God is the Spirit of joy, laughing is the secret of receiving grace.

Thus have I heard, 2001. 06. 07

Koreans are the offspring of Dan, the son of Jacob of Israelites.

All humans came from their ancestors. If we do not know our ancestors, does it make sense? If we do not know our ancestors, it is a problem. We should know who our ancestors are.

To understand this clearly, we can see it roughly by going over our customs. It is a custom in our culture that goes back to our ancestors, which we wear hemp clothing and weep aloud when a family member dies. Only the Israelis have the same custom on the earth nowadays.

America, Britain, and other countries do not have the tradition. Also, as it is now, only Koreans and Israelis put up stone altars and perform ancestral rites. Other countries do not put up stone altars in front of their ancestors' tombs.

When we go to the mountains, we can see many stone altars in front of the tombs. We put up stone altars and perform ancestral rites on them. And the Israelis put up stone altars and performed ancestral rites on them according to the lyrics of one hymn 'After Jacob woke up, as he built a stone altar, we want to awake, pray all the time, and attend worships in a holy altar.'

Jacob put up a stone altar and performed ancestral rites after he defeated an angel at wrestling near the Yabbok River. Then the angel asked what your name was? He answered, "I am Jacob." The angel said, "From now on, you will be called Israel (It means winner)" Therefore, the offspring of Jacob became Israelis.

Nowadays, the Israelites took their country's name from Jacob's changed name 'Israel.' Because the offspring of Jacob live there today.

Jacob had twelve sons. Among them, Dan was the fifth son. According to the Genesis 49:16, "Dan will provide justice as one of the tribes of Israel. Dan will be a serpent by the roadside." Genesis 49 says: Jacob gave the right of judgment to only Dan.

Therefore, we can see that Jacob gave the right of Judgment to only Dan. The God of Abraham moved to Isaac, the God of Isaac moved to Jacob, and the God of Jacob moved to Dan.

By the way, a long time ago, the Dan tribes started to move from Zora of Israel to the east, lived in Ural Altai Mountains for one hundred years, then again moved, and lived in Mongolia.

Also, they passed Manchuria, and settled on the bank of the Deadong River in the province of South Pyeongyang in North Korea, and founded *Gochosen* there. And one part of the tribe of Dan moved to the north and founded *Buyeo*. *Jumong* moved across the Duman River and founded *Goguryeo* in Manchuria.

Before *Jumong* went across the Duman River, he had a lover, who was pregnant. He told her, "When the baby grows up, give him a half of one sword buried under the cross wood and make him find me."

As he grew up to be twenty years old, the mother told her son giving him the half of the sword, "Find out your father, who was in Manchuria across the Duman River."

Arriving at the Duman River, he waited for a boatman. He asked the boatman to carry him across the Duman River. The boatman asked him the reason. He told the boatman that he was finding his father, Jumong. Then the boatman gave a deep bow to the young man.

The boatman said to the young man "Get on, please. I will take you to your father." The young man asked, "What does my father do?"

The boatman answered "He is the king of *Goguryeo*. Therefore, it is an honor to take you to the king."

When the young man arrived at the palace, he told a guard he wants to meet the king. The guard said to the king "One boy wants to meet you; he said that his father is the king." Hence, the king allowed the young man to meet him.

The king asked the young man to show him the half of the sword that witnessed the king's son. The son showed it to him, and the king tried to match with the other half of the sword that he kept.

The sword matched perfectly. And then they hugged each other and shared gladness.

Jumong already married after crossing the Duman River and had a son. The son and his mother knew that *Jumong*'s first son came. The second son said to his mother, "my father already had a wife and a son, so we cannot live in one palace. Let's leave the palace at night."

So they promised to leave the palace. Finally, the second son of *Jumong*, *Onjo*, and his mother went over the fence of the palace, to the south across the Abrok River, and founded *Baekjae*. He became the first king of *Baekjae*.

Actually Korean people live in Manchuria, current China. The people of *Goguryeo* attacked China and occupied up to one-third of China. Also, *Baekjae* attacked China and occupied over one-third of China. Also, *Baekjae* occupied Japan and made it their colony.

Silla and *Dang*, a dynasty of China, united their armies to attack *Goguryeo*, and demolished it, next they attacked *Beakjae* and destroyed it.

Some people of *Baekjae* made thousands of ships and headed for Japan using the ships through the Geum River and the west sea from *Gudare*, today's Buyeo.

They arrived at the Nara area of Japan. There is one city named Kyoto near Nara. They made a capital city there and founded Japan.

Actually, Japanese people are the offspring of Dan, too. We should know the root of our lineage exactly. Our grandfather was the fifth son of Jacob, who snatched his father's blessing from Esau, his twins' brother.

Jacob called Esau to order him to hunt an animal and cook it for Isaac. He added that "If you do that, I will bless you." Hearing this, their mother who loved Jacob better than Esau said to Jacob, "I kill a livestock and cook it, and then, take it to your father and receive the blessing.

Your father will certainly touch your arm to confirm Esau's arms as he is blind." Because his arms were hairy, thinking about it for a while, Jacob bound animals' leather around his arms.

He went to his father and mimicked Esau. The voice of twins was the same. As the voice was the same to his brother Esau, he said, "I carried the dish as you said." Isaac said, "You already caught an animal, cooked it, and brought it? Come near to me."

As Jacob approached him, Isaac touched Jacob's arms. As he bound his arms with animal's leather, his arms were hairy. "You are certainly Esau." Saying like that, Isaac blessed Jacob.

As Isaac blessed Jacob, the God of Isaacs moved to Jacob. Although Jacob received the blessing and had God in his body, he was afraid of Esau. Therefore, he fled to his mother's side uncle.

His uncle had two daughters. The first daughter was Lehar and the second was Rachel. Maybe the second one was more beautiful. Accordingly, Jacob said to his uncle "If you allow me to marry Rachel, I will become a farm servant for seven years."

The uncle willingly accepted the suggestion. They arranged a marriage, after working for seven years, they were married.

However, Korean people and Israelis were not able to see the bride's face when they married. In the past, if Korean bridegrooms looked at the faces of the brides, it caused trouble.

In that case, people threw a bundle of ash at the eyes of the bridegroom. Then the bridegroom had a problem in their eyes for a while. Therefore, they married without seeing their brides' faces in old times.

As the Israelis had the same custom, when Jacob married, the uncle made his first daughter stand at the wedding ceremony. After the marriage, they slept together the first night, and he found that the woman who Jacob married was not Rachel but Lehar.

Therefore, he went to his uncle to protest. "Why did you deceive me? I was supposed to marry Rachel" The uncle said "Think of it in my situation, if the second daughter marries first, the first daughter cannot marry in her life, how can I allow that situation? Hence, I did it like that."

Jacob replied, "I married Rachel, however, I slept with Lehar, I could not ask her to leave, so please allow me to live with both the daughters."

Therefore, they lived together, and while Leah delivered four sons, Rachel did not have any baby. She thought that she could not have babies. Accordingly, she told her husband that she wanted to have a baby through her maid slave, Bilha.

He allowed it and slept with Bilha. And then Bilha conceived and delivered a baby. As soon as she delivered the baby, Rachel raised him. As Jacob regarded the baby not as Bilha's but as Rachel's, Jacob named him Dan.

Although her maid slave delivered the baby, he was a child of his first wife. Jacob named him Dan which means a judge. Therefore, as its meaning is a judge, Jacob sent his God to Dan.

According to Genesis 49:16, "Dan will provide justice as one of the tribes of Israel. Dan will be a serpent by the roadside, a viper along the path. That bites the horse's heels so that its rider tumbles backward. I look for your deliverance, Lord."

After Jacob sent his God to Dan, he said, "I look for your deliverance, Lord." It means that God in Jacob moved to Dan.

Because this world is Satan's, Satan is in people's bodies; therefore, if Satan knows a person who accompanies God, Satan will kill that man. Therefore, God deceived Satan by going to a child that was born not from Rachel but from her maid slave.

God moving to Dan was said in *Cheonbugyeong* (Korean scripture). It was written with eighty-one letters, it says the Savior is supposed to come with a gold fortune and eighty one *Goong* (運 fortune) at the end days. *Cheonbugyeong* which was written with eighty-one letters has God's sayings through Dan.

Hence, all things are connected. At the end, the Savior was supposed to come with a *Gold Fortune*(金運) and eighty-one Goong (運 fortune). The God in Dan hid and later moved to Park Tae Son senior (*Spiritual Mother*), passed the *Eve Victress*, and came to the seventh angel, Me, with eighty-one fortune, Gold Fortune (運). When you read old books, you will know that something profound is there.

Therefore, Korean people are the Israelites; they are not the offspring of bears. Bears cannot deliver humans. Bears beget bears.

Because today's genetic engineering is so developed, people do not believe it. As Korean people are the offspring of the Dan tribe, as it is now, Korean people weep aloud wearing hemp clothes when a family member dies. Also, they pasted red-bean gruel on a gatepost on the winter solstice day in old times.

Today's Israelites' ancestors pasted sheep's blood on a gatepost on the Passover. The reason is as follows:

When Israelis lived as slaves in Egypt, Moses ordered all Israelis to paste the blood of sheep on a gatepost. So, by the Bible, incidents with the death of the first son happened to those who did not paint sheep's blood on the gatepost. Therefore, the king of Egypt who previously denied Moses' requests to take the Israel people to the desert to pray later called Moses and allowed him to take the Israel people to the desert for prayers.

When Moses took his people to the red sea, the water impeded their crossing. As he looked back, the soldiers of Egypt pursued them. At that moment, he hit the water with a stick; the water was separated like land and became a wall of water. Can you believe it realistically?

However as the Bible says it, you cannot but believe it. As the sea became like land, the people crossed it. As soon as all the Israelites crossed the sea, the separated water united, all the soldiers who were chasing the Israelites were drowned. This story is in the Bible.

When Moses took 600,000 people to the desert, there was no food and water; they stood against Moses. They complaint, "We ate enough and lived well in Egypt, why have you brought us here and starved us to death?"

Hence, Moses prayed to God, "Please, give these people food", and then manna like dew fell down from the sky, which was piled up like snow. They carried it and ate the manna for forty years according to the Bible.

Therefore, Moses saved the Israel people from Egypt. He is the Savior of Israelites. Acts 3:22 says, "The Lord will send you a prophet just as he sent me, and he will be one of your own people. You are to obey everything that he tells you to do." Anyone who does not obey that prophet shall be separated from God's people and destroyed.

The prophet like Moses should pour Dew. Therefore, he can become a prophet like Moses. Jesus said that he was the prophet like Moses. But he did not pour Dew. Because he was Satan, he could not.

After 6,000 years, the man who pours Dew appeared. The Bible says that the Savior will appear in Korea. Isaiah 41:1-9 says, "Be silent before me, you islands! Who has stirred up one from the east, calling him in righteousness on his service. He hands over nations to him and subdues kings before him. I will take you from the ends of the earth; from its farthest corner I will call you."

In old times and today, the eastern countries are Korea and Japan. They are eastern countries. God says, "Be silent, islands.", It means, as Japan is islands, be quiet, the Savior cannot appear from your country.

Also, God says that He will call the righteous man at the corner of the end of the earth. Because Korea is located on a peninsula, having three sides surrounded by the sea, the Savior was supposed to.

As I am pouring the *Dew Spirit* which is the hidden manna, I am the prophet like Moses. Therefore, although the Savior came to the world, like the saying of Acts 3:22 "The Lord will send you a prophet just as he sent me, and he will be one of your own people", do people know this? They do not know it for they are captivated by Satan.

Acts 3:22 says, "The Lord will send you a prophet just as he sent I, and he will be one of your own people." As they are captivated by Satan, they will die. But they will not die if they come to the Victory Altar.

As they receive the *Dew Spirit*, their bodies are changed into immortal beings.

Korean people are the Israelites. I told young men, "go the National Central Museum in Seoul and take pictures of roof-end tiles which were found in the bank of the Deadong River and have old Hebrew language, and ask about their meaning to the professor Sin Sa-Hoon of Seoul University."

He interpreted them as follows; one has "Arrived", another has "Let's unite and go to the land of God". "Let's go to the land of God" is interpreted that since people are God, they told themselves to go to the land of God. The third tile reads "Being recovered by the followers' gathering and praying".

It means that the Garden of Eden is recovered. Just recovering the Garden of Eden by followers' praying is our long cherished desire for thousands of years.

The Victory Altar which will accomplish God's will is supposed to be built on the land of *Sosa*. Therefore, it was built on the land of 1,200 sq. meters.

This building is supposed to build when the Savior was sixty-one years old according to *Gyeokamyourok*. I was sixty-one years in 1991. The certificate of this building's completion was published in 1991.

On My sixty-first birthday, August twelfth, 1991, they held a consecrated worship. After holding a consecrated worship, I got rid of the communists who kidnapped and imprisoned Gorbachev for three days, and on the day he was freed, there was a rainbow over this building.

When he was imprisoned, I said that he would be free soon. And he was set free the next day. Therefore, when I say something, it surely will be accomplished. *Gyeokamyourok* prophesied that a rainbow would be in 1991. Accordingly, the prophecy was fulfilled. The book predicted, "When *Jeongdoryeong* was sixty-one, the Victory Altar would be built and a rainbow would be there."

Judging by this, I am the true Savior. Although you met the Savior, if you do not achieve salvation, it is very sad. Therefore, as you met the true Savior, you are supposed to certainly achieve salvation and live forever.

And it is sure that Korean people are the Israelites, because the roof-end tiles that our ancestors used have Hebrew written on them. From this, we know that our ancestors also used old Hebrew, and our people are therefore Israelites.

In addition, Korean people like wearing white clothes. Hence, Korean people are called the people of white clothes in oriental history. Furthermore, the Israelites liked wearing white clothes according to the Bible.

We must know that we are the offspring of Dan, the fifth son of Jacob. As we are the offspring of Dan who has God, we are lineal descendants of God.

Only people who will live forever will come to the Victory Altar. *Gyeokamyourok* said that only families that three generations gained virtue meet *Jeongdoryeong*. So you are the children of families, which for three generations attained virtue.

Thus have I heard, 2001. 07. 30

A Savior is 救世主 in Chinese character. It means a person who saves people from dying.

Jesus said that he was the Savior citing Isaiah's writing. However, did he give people immortality? Jesus clearly said, "Those who believe me will live forever, even though he dies, those who believe me in their living lives will never die forever." Also, John 8:51 says that just those who keep my words will never die forever.

Jesus shared wine symbolizing his blood with others and bread symbolizing his flesh. Did those who ate them die or live? All of them died. Jesus came to tell lies to the world.

According to the Bible, people can see a tree by its fruits. Therefore, seeing the result, we can know the cause. Watching people dying, we can see Jesus is the spirit of death. Although he said that he was the son of God, we can see that he is not the son of God. We can see the tree by its fruit.

The Bible told about Jesus in detail. Ephesians 6:12, the spirit that grasps the power of space is the evil spirit. The evil spirit is Satan. Then the spirit in space is the evil spirit. Ephesians 2:2, "The spirit that grasps the power of space is one that is at work in those who are disobedient."

Is there God or Satan among the disobedient? The spirit which is at work in those who are disobedient indicates the spirit of Satan. Therefore, the spirit of Satan that grasps the power of space is in space; God cannot be in space.

God is not in space. According to the Bible, the spirit in space is that of Satan.

Also, Matthew 3:17 said, as soon as Jesus was baptized by the Baptist

John in the Jordan River, he went out of the water. At that moment, space was opened, and a voice from heaven said, "this is my son whom I love; with him I am well pleased."

The Bible says that a voice from space said, and John heard it. At that time, the Baptist, John's view of God was that God was in space. Not only John but also today's people think so.

Hence, the Baptist, John's view of God and that of today's people are the same. As he heard a voice from space, he thought that Jesus was the son of God, and shouted in the wilderness "The son of God came." And then he made a crowd believe Jesus.

Therefore, the crowd believing Jesus began the Christianity. The beginning itself was wrong. Christians should have known what God is and where He is.

John1:1 said "God is life. God is light." If life is God, all people have the life. All of you have the life. Therefore, the life in your bodies is God. God is in all of you.

All men are made of their ancestor's blood. The blood of their ancestors is in the bodies of their offspring. Therefore, the blood of the first ancestor, Adam and Eve are with us.

And as God is life, the reason you are alive is that God is in you. As God is in us, we are alive. Therefore, human beings are the sons of God. Psalms 82:6 said "You are gods. You are all sons of the Most High."

The Most High is God. And Isaiah said, "We are the sons of God." That is, all humans are the sons of God. Therefore, Eve is the son of God not the daughter of God, because God said that all of you are the sons of God.

In the world of God, there are neither female nor male. According to the Bible, "eunuchs are lucky." They are neither men nor women. Hence, it means neutral.

God is a neutral Spirit. As God has neither positive pole nor negative pole, but a neutral Spirit, The saying "eunuchs are lucky" means people should overcome the character of positive and negative, and become neutral to achieve salvation. Hence, the Bible said that eunuchs are lucky.

Therefore, according to the Bible, Adam and Eve were neither male nor female in the beginning. At the moment that the spirit of Satan came into them, captured them, and became their controlling spirit, Adam became male and Eve became female. So the world of female and male is that of Satan.

Only Satan has female and male character. God does not have the character of a human. Therefore, when people overcome the character of a human and wear the character of God, we can achieve salvation.

If we are in character of male and female, we will never achieve eternal life. The beginning of death originated from the spirit of female and male. If there is not female and male in humans, they cannot die.

When negative and positive electricity is united, electricity sparks and perishes. If negative and positive electricity is united, it is supposed to perish.

So a dissipating spirit is that of positive and negative, and it is the spirit of death. If we have the spirit of male and female and act like that, we will die.

The Bible says, "You must never marry, and if you do that, you will die, and if you deliver children, you die and beasts will eat up the bodies" in Jeremiah.

Therefore, Catholic priests and nuns do not marry. The Bible says that because they have the carnal desire, they commit obscenity. Before they marry or meet with each other, they have the carnal desire and like each other, and then marry later. The marriage ceremony itself is held after committing obscenity. Therefore, the marriage itself is prohibited by God.

Even though people are made as male and female, actually people are the sons of God. The reason for being in the form male and female body is because the controlling spirit of people is Satan.

Because they wear the appearance of Satan, they become male and female. If they do not marry and overcome obscenity, the character of male and female has been changed into neutral and becomes God. But nobody kept it.

True religion does not let people marry. Monks do not marry in Buddhism. Do you know the reason? The books of Buddhist said, "Do not marry." Not only the Bible but also the books of Buddhist say the same thing. So Buddhism has the system.

According to Acts 9:5 of the Bible, when Paul was near Damascus on his journey, suddenly a light from the sky flashed around him. He fell to the ground and heard a voice say to him, "Saul, why do you persecute me? Who are you, Lord?" Paul asked. "I am Jesus, whom you are persecuting" he replied.

Is Jesus the spirit of space or ground? (The spirit of space). Yes, he is the spirit of space. What spirit is the spirit of space? It is the evil spirit, according to the Bible.

According to Isaiah 34:16, there is a way of reading the Bible, "Search in the Lord's book about living creatures and read what it says. Not one of these creatures will be missing its mate, and not one of them will be without its mate. The Lord has commanded it be so; He himself will bring them together"

He says, "not one of these will be without its mate." According to Ephesians 6:12, the spirit of space is the evil spirit. The Evil spirit is Satan.

According to 3:17 "as soon as Jesus was baptized by John the Baptist, when he went up out of the water, there was a voice from space, 'this is my son, whom I love; with him I am pleased.'"

Then is the voice Satan's or God's? (It is Satan's). As the view of John, Baptist, was wrong, he thought that the voice of Satan was that of God, But as the Bible says, "Read it mating," so Jesus is Satan.

And he also confessed that he was Satan. Matthew 12:28 said, "If I drive out the demons by the Spirit of God, then the kingdom of God has come upon you."

It means that he neither received the Spirit of God nor was conceived by it. Then if he did not drive out the demons by the Spirit of God, what spirit did he use when he drove out the demons?

There are two kinds of spirit; they are God's and Satan's. If he did not drive the demons by using the Spirit of God, he cannot but use the power of Satan. So Jesus received the spirit of Satan. Jesus said frankly about his status.

Look at John 14:30; "The king of the world is coming after me." Hence, he said that he was not the king, didn't he? At that time, people thought of a king as the Savior of the world. So he confessed he was not the Savior according to John 14:30. We should believe what the Bible says.

Therefore, the Bible says, "If people die, they perish." However, people believe that they will go to heaven after death. Job 14:14 wrote, "If a man dies, he cannot come back to life." We should believe this biblically not by our thinking.

Isaiah 26:14 said, "Now they are dead and will not live again; their ghost will not rise." It does not say, "their spirit will live" Therefore, the words "if a man dies, he perishes" mean that my spirit and body will disappear.

Even though the Old Testament said so the New Testament said mostly about Jesus' thinking. As Jesus told people that they would go to heaven after death, in fact, he came to the world to kill the children of God. So he has killed men for 2000 years; he never saved people.

He said that John among his twelve disciples would be alive until he came back. But he died first. Therefore, we can see how many lies Jesus had told.

If we read the Bible more carefully, we can see that the Bible said, "God will give men eternal life." According to Titus 1:2, "Religion is based on the hope for eternal life, God, who does not lie, promised us this life before the beginning of time."

As God promised eternal life, will He give us eternal life? Or will Jesus give it? God promised it. Jesus did not. God promised eternal life.

1 John 2:25 said, "God himself promised to give us eternal life before the beginning of the time." It said the same. And also according to John 5:39 "The reason that you read the Bible is that there is eternal life in it."

Is the goal of the Bible eternal life or heaven after death? It is eternal life. Eternal life is dying or not dying? It is not dying. The eternal life is the Fruit of Life; the eternal life itself is the Faith. Eternal life comes from the Victor God; the Spirit of eternal life is that of the Victor God. It is the Faith and the Fruit of Life. Therefore, today the Savior is the Faith and the Fruit of Life.

However, do not nibble at the Savior because He is the Fruit of Life. Eating the Fruit of Life is spiritual, not physical. It just means, "Eat the Fruit of Life spiritually."

It means to eat with heart. When you engrave the face of the Savior on your heart, even fatal diseases can be cured. Therefore, when you have the Spirit of the Savior in your heart, you have eternal life.

Therefore, the Victor will become the column of the castle as Revelation 3:5 said. As the Victor is the Savior, the Savior is the hero of heaven, no other man except the Savior can be the hero of heaven. Hence, the Savior is the owner of heaven, when you possess the Savior, you can achieve salvation.

Possessing the Savior means to possess Him with your heart, not with your hands. Who will know if someone possesses the Savior in his heart? Nobody will argue it. It is his freedom.

Hence, your face should become the same as that of the Savior. There is a hymn "I and the world have disappeared and only the Lord who is redeeming me is seen."

Therefore, only when you become a Savior, you can achieve salvation. If you do not become a Savior, you cannot achieve salvation. If somebody does not want to become a Savior, it is his or her choice.

However if he or she does not become a Savior, he or she certainly dies, and then his or her body decays and perishes. Not only his or her body but also his or her bones decay.

Disappearing is not the truth. If a man dies, he perishes. The spirit perishes, too.

Spirit is just the blood and the blood is a part of the heart.

Therefore our heart is the spirit. The heart is the spirit and it just works to pump the blood. Is there a heart without blood? There isn't.

Accordingly, as the blood decays, the heart will not exist anymore. So when the blood decays 100 percent, people die. As the blood decays, it stops flowing and the heart (the organ) stops. After that, decaying begins.

Although God says, only when the world is rational, it is the truth. However, if the world is not scientific or rational, it is not the truth. Therefore, I tell the Bible matching scientifically.

The proof that mankind is the children of God is that everyone does not want to die. If someone does not die and lives in pain, who would want to live forever? The blood that did not die and live happily forever is in everyone. So people do not want to die. If somebody tries to kill them, they will shudder. They will ask him not to kill. If he asks for money, they will give him all their money and ask him not to kill them.

Every human hates to die. Taking that into consideration, whoever has the mind of eternal life; hate death; they are the children of God.
As people have the blood of God who is the Spirit of eternal life and enjoys eternal life, they resemble the character of God. You resemble your parents, aren't you? That's because you were made of your parents' blood. You are certainly the children of God.

As you are the children of God, you are supposed to go to heaven, your hometown. Our hometown is heaven. Our hometown was the beautiful Garden of Eden.

So a Korean ancestor wrote to go to the Garden of Eden on the roof-end tiles, "Let's go to the land of God by uniting together. Heaven is recovered by the followers' praying."

It was their purpose that the Korean's ancestors would go towards their hometown, heaven. Through the records that our ancestors engraved on the roof tiles, we can see that someday we will recover the lost Garden of Eden and go to the land of God.

Therefore, as offspring of God, we will certainly go to heaven. It is the Savior who came to build the heaven. Man cannot become the Savior. God came to the world wearing My body; All humans are in a drowning situation. Drowning men cannot save other drowning men. Men who are out of water can save the drowning men. Accordingly, God who is out of the water and wears a man's body can save all drowning men.

Therefore, the Savior was not supposed to come out of mankind. According to Isaiah 43:14 and Isaiah 43: 11, "God saves us." So God becomes the Savior.

The saying is right. The Savior is supposed to recover the Garden of Eden according to Genesis. And just as God recovers the Garden of Eden, only the hero who recovers the Garden of Eden is the Savior.

We must believe as the Bible says. God gave Moses the Ten Commandments. The Ten Commandments are the basic laws of God.

If people do not keep the basic law, then they are the children of Satan.

"Do not serve any other gods except for God" is the first law of Ten Commandments. And the second law is "Do not call any other name except for God's name."

If they call another name, they are pseudo and the children of Satan.

Therefore, we must believe as the Bible said, or you will go to hell.

Thus have I heard, 2001. 9. 21

For past twenty-one years, I have said that there has been no science and religion in the world. The inexistence of science means that the present science is not science. Also, the world's religions are not the real religion.

If I express the meaning of science, science should be able to express the essence of things. However, the science of the world does not know that all things are God.

Let me say this scientifically. Atoms of all materials combine and form materials. Atoms join together and form molecules, and the molecules unite and form materials. Therefore, atoms are the basic. In atoms, there are nucleuses, the nucleuses have neutrons, centering the neutrons, and the negative electrons go around them. People call them atoms.

Scientists say, "the negative electrons circle around the neutrons by themselves." Is it rational? Can negative electrons circle around by themselves?

Because there is energy to let those circle around, they do. Going around by themselves is wrong. So, I say, "energy which makes them circle around is the power of the neutron's vital life." Do cutting-edge scientists know this? They do not know this. So, their common sense is wrong.

As neutrons are the Spirit of God and the Spirit of life, the power of life comes from the neutrons. So, the negative electrons circle around by the power of life.

Also, worldly scientists say that the light of the neutron is the fastest. Also, neutrons are the strongest element in the power of penetrating matters. So they say the light of the neutron can go through ten billion light year thickness of lead. However, this is wrong.

When some material goes through another material, there is resistance, scientist know this. Because of this, they say the light of the neutron can go through the ten billion light year thickness of lead. This is also in accordance with the theory of Doctor Lee Won Young from Columbia University.

But I said on the platform of the Victory Altar that it is a lie. And I added that the light of neutron goes through the infinite thickness of lead. Therefore, what cutting-edge scientists say is false; then, therefore the lower level science is also a less reasonable one.

I say, "all material is not material but God." A neutron, the Spirit of God, is in the nucleus of the atom, as it is now, and negative electrons are circling around the neutrons; the negative electrons are the spirit of Satan. Hence, the material is the coexistence of the Spirit of God and the spirit of Satan.

The penetrating power of neutrons is very strong. Therefore, all things are of God, but Karl Max said, "God does not exist. Only materials do." Lenin created communism on the basis of his saying, and it governed the world for seventy-four years, I shouted out to eradicate communism in 1981, and it was accomplished in 1990 at one time.

Does communism exist now? Is there anyone who was omniscient and omnipotent enough to remove communism in human history? Communism is humans' thought and ideology. And its ideology is evil, so only the Savior can get rid of it, and nobody except the Savior can get rid of it.

As the Savior is the strongest Spirit, He went into each person and got rid of the evil ideology. As it was removed, communism was eradicated. If the ideology was not removed, communism would still exist now. Its history is seventy-four years, who dares to remove it.

But how do they know that the Savior in Korea removed the ideology of communism?

In 1990, all communism collapsed, when Gorbachev was caught and imprisoned by three communists for three days in 1991. On the second day of his detention, I said on the platform that Gorbachev would be free soon. And he was free on that day.

When three communists were about to kill Gorbachev with a gun to his head, I appeared there, as My other self, and shout out very loud: "Run away, if you do not, you will die."

The three men ran out leaving Gorbachev alone. One man went to the airport, but he was arrested, and another man was arrested at the train station, the third man, the local minister, committed suicide.

At that moment, Gorbachev went out and was free from the prison. On that day, there was a rainbow over the Victory Altar even though it was a sunny day. Korean prophecy *Gyeokamyourok* foretold that there would be a rainbow over the building.

According to it, in 1991, the building of the Victory Altar would be built, and a rainbow would be over the building when the Savior was sixty-one years old. So on August the twenty-third, on the day Gorvachev was freed, a rainbow was in the sky over the building of Victory Altar.

Hence my followers believed that I removed communism. No matter how foolish people are, if I showed them the evidence, they believed Me. Also, My saying that I will remove communism was accomplished.

I promised to protect Korea from typhoons. That has been accomplished for the past twenty-one years. Also, I proclaimed to halt the monsoon in Korea.

The monsoon rains are ones that fall continually for one month from June fifteenth to July fifteenth. The rain falling before June fifteenth is the spring rain and the rain falling after July fifteenth is the autumn rain. There were no monsoons from June fifteenth to July fifteenth. Then the monsoons halted in Korea. Therefore, Koreans have abundant harvests.

This year, Koreans will have abundant harvests, too. I read newspapers today. They said the government of Korea would send 200,000 tons of rice to North Korea. 200,000 tons of rice is huge. In fact, there is a surplus of 1 million tons of rice in Korea; Hence Korea can send 200 thousand tons of rice to North Korea.

The newspapers said that even though there was a surplus of 1 million tons of rice, this year's harvest is abundant, too. Therefore, it has a problem taking care of the surplus of rice. Hence Korea is so rich that it overflows with rice.

The saying "if *Jeongdoryeong* appears, people will be rich," is accomplished.

I(the Victor) promised to keep Korea free from wars. No matter how hard Kim Il Seong, the former leader of North Korea, tried to go to a war, he died in the end without causing any war. Kim Jeong-Il also tried to start a war. However, he did not succeed.

The present military of North Korea has one million soldiers, South Korea 600,000 soldiers. So in case a Korean War breaks out, North Korea has an advantageous military condition. Hence, North Korea tried to start a war by sending spies to *Gangreung* and some other places, as you all know, and they spied and sent the navy across the 38th parallel to start a war.

However, the Korean navy sank down one of the North Korean navy ships. And all the sailors in the ship died. After seeing this on TV, the North Korean leader Kim Jeong-Il ordered a 'pull back', and the North Korean navies sailed away. Did you see it? Like this, North Korea sent their ships to check the military strength.

They knew if they start to fight, North Korea is no match for South Korea. So they pulled back. He changed his mind and accepted gladly the proposal of the summit meeting with Kim Dea Jung, the late South Korea's president, who was insisting on a 'sunshine policy.'

When the South Korean president arrived at the airport of Pyeongyang, Kim Jeong-Il came to meet him at the airport. He hugged the South Korean president and pressed his cheek against the South Korean presidents.

Kim Jeong-Il seemed to have a mind to ask help from the South Korean president. Because when he sent the North Korean navy ship across the 38 parallel line, his sailors had to manually wind a handle with all their energy to raise a gun barrel while South Korean navy only had to push a button, since it is automatic. Then bombshells went off like rain and sank one North Korea ship.

They are no match for the South Korean navy. So the other ships fled. South Korea is too strong for North Korea to defeat. He was shocked and afraid that South Korea might attack North Korea. Hence he hugged and kissed his cheek against Kim Dae Jung's, the South Korean president.

Communists never do that. Kim Il Seong, Kim Jeong Il's father, did not hug someone because that hurts their self-pride. If they did that, the North Korean people would think that their leader had become weak. Actually, almost all North Koreans were disappointed.

From then, they never think of their aggression to South Korea. This is the work of *Jeongdoryeong*. Discouraging him, He made Kim Jeong Il not cause wars again. Do you understand? Therefore, *Jeongdoryeong* proclaimed five things.

1. He will eradicate communism.
2. He will keep Korea free from typhoons.
3. He will halt the monsoon rains in Korea.
4. He will protect Korea from wars.
5. He will make the South Koreans harvests abundant.

The five promises have been accomplished in Korea. Therefore, make the promulgation papers, with these good materials, and announce them to all the people of the world.

If they read them, they will confirm if the monsoon rains halt in Korea, if typhoons do not blow to Korea, if Korea has abundant harvests, and whether Korean War breaks out or not. And then will they admit or not that communism was removed by Me? They will have to admit it. They will admit it. I eradicated communism as the Savior's other selves by removing each communist's evil ideology in them.

They will know it by the evidence of communism's collapsing. If you make and distribute leaflets, everyone will believe it. If you make them in English, French, Russian, and Chinese, and hand them out to the world, they will watch if monsoon rains halt in Korea between June fifteenth to July fifteenth every year. If they confirm the Savior's promises are accomplished, they will be surprised at the Savior and believe in Him.

Also if one announces that I(the Victor) will pour out the *Holy Dew Spirit*, reporters will come and verify the *Holy Dew Spirit* with their cameras. If the *Holy Dew Spirit* is taken with their cameras, they will report it.

And then the record of his guilt for faking the pouring out the *Dew Spirit* will be corrected.(The victor was wrongfully convicted by the Christian president and force to prison for seven years.) Who else except for you can prove that I was innocent?

Once it is announced to the world, the world will admit that the Savior is in Korea. Then our Altar will be filled with people. And then all the people will be crowded in with treasures such as gold, silver, according to *Gyeokam*'s words, Isaiah of the Bible, and the books of Buddhist.

The books say so, because it will be certainly accomplished. Even you dug up bonanza, if you do not receive that amazing blessing, you are foolish. My(the Savior's) work is true. So you should make handouts in each country's language and distribute them to the world.

As I pour out the *Dew Spirit* in every worship service when reporters of newspapers or broadcasting stations came, they took pictures, and the *Dew Spirit* was taken on their pictures.

The picture was also taken when I was in prison. That is the evidence that I work as My other self. If My other self does not stand on the platform, the *Dew Spirit* will not be taken. Even though you certainly know this, why do you not send My message out? You have a duty to announce this fact to the people of the world. You should announce this fact to the world.

Even the Korean broadcasting said that there have been twenty-one years' of abundant harvests, no monsoon rains for twenty-one years, and no typhoons for twenty-one years. Also newspapers say this, too. Therefore you should distribute the handouts to the world. And all the people of the world should receive salvation together. It is not fair if only the follower of the Victory Altar receive salvation.

Then let's join at the campaign to announce this fact to the world from today for all the people of the world to receive salvation. Tell the president of the Victory Altar' newspaper to make leaflets.

As the Korean people are 40 million, print 40 million copies first. And then find out how many people there are in the English speaking area, and copy as many as that number, and hand out to each family members. And also as Japanese are over 120 million in population, make handouts to announce them this fact.

If it is accomplished, the Victory Altar will become the biggest religion. And when new-comers crowd in, one should teach Americans in English, Japanese in Japanese. If a person sends the truth to the world, how happy one will be.

Then one does not need to do other things. Doing the mission to Koreans is important, but a person should hand out leaflets to the world, too.

There are embassies in Korea. Go there and give them the handouts asking them to convey them to their countries. And then if they distribute them to their counties, all the people are supposed to know this fact automatically.

Even though I on the platform look like an ordinary person; in fact, I am a king of kings who control the world and the universe. Therefore, as I am a king of kings who governs the world, My face is a to-be-king one.

One does not know this. However, face readers know at once that I have a to-be-king face. And I have a sign of a king on each palm. Has one ever seen people who have a sign of a king on their palms? You cannot see. I have special signs.

I have had black spots shaped like a big Dipper on My chests from birth. Hence, My maternal grandfather said that I would be a great man in the future. Unless I am a great man, how can I have black spots shaped a big Dipper on My chest.

And as I have a sign of a king on each My palm, it is true that I am a king of kings ruling the whole universe. So sometime later, a big palace surrounding *Sosa* with an area of 12 kilometers will be built, and the Savior will control the universe there.

When it is built, those who will go into the palace are those who are in the line of kings. And they are supposed to live forever, and all of them are appointed as kings to each country and they will be dispatched there. Accordingly, I will rule the world from *Sosa*.

On that day, one will become a king, if a person becomes a king, do you know what will happen? The Victor gives the crown that is held in His hand. It is a crown made of light. If I puts the crowns on the kings, light will come out from their bodies. Hence each country's people are supposed to make a deep bow at the shining people and obey them by themselves. Accordingly, they automatically become kings, forever.

Let's sing a hymn, 선지자와 왕들 반열대로 서서.

선지자와 왕들 반열대로 서서	Standing in the line of prophets and kings
금길 다닐때 항상 이 찬미 하네	always praise Him as walking on the gold road
할렐루야 할렐루야 내가 구주를 믿어	Halleluiah, Halleluiah, I believed in the Savior
이슬성신 은혜로 내죄 씻었네	and washed my sins with the grace of the Dew Spirit.

Let me finish today's worship service. Let's go out laughing. Laugh from the stomach not from the throat. You should laugh with a laughing mindset. Laugh with a laughing mindset.

Thus have I heard, 2001. 11. 18

There was no science and religions until now. When I say that there is no science, I should come up with an alternative for that.

So the Victor claims that there is no science. The science of the world says that all things are material. Also, they say that humans are animals; they are the kings of all animals. Scientists say that humans are animals, that they are not God.

But I say confidently that humans are all God. Psalms 82:6 said, "You are Gods; you are the sons of the Most High." And also the Bible said that the mind of people is the spirit; the spirit is God, and God is the spirit; therefore spirit is the mind of people. And it said that the source of life is in mind. And then it said that God is life in John 1:1. Hence, God is life, life is mind, and mind is the spirit, so mind is the spirit of God.

Therefore, human life is God. Only men who have life have the mind. Those who do not have life do not have mind. I say this not only biblically but also scientifically. I say scientifically that the working of the blood is the same as that of mind. Scientists admit that, too.

Scientists say that those who have A type blood are meticulous, B type blood is sociable, and O type blood is stubborn and radical. Accordingly, the way blood works are the same as how the mind works.

This is a scientific saying. People's minds work by the action of the blood. And 'blood is life' according to Leviticus 17:1. "Blood is life; life is blood," and Leviticus 17:11 says, "The life of the body is in blood," The Bible said that life is God, and God is life.

So if some people say that the spirit of dead person goes away, they are misinformed. They do not know the essence of spirit. The essence of spirit is the mind. Therefore, the mind is the spirit, and blood is the spirit. Dead parents and grandparents' blood is in their offspring's blood. So their dead ancestors' spirit lives in their living descendants' bodies. Do people know this?

Therefore, when people die, not only they but also their ancestors' spirit, such as parents grandparents and great-grandparents and so on die together, too. Do they know this? They do not know this.

Everybody cannot know the essence of God without knowing the essence of spirit. If they do not know the essence of God, they do not have a qualification for teaching theology.

Even though they graduated from the college of theology, if they do not know God, it means that they have graduated the University of Human Science, not those of theology.

I say that there are no religions in the world today. That's because today's religions are not true religion. Religions are in life, not in death.

So God is in life, and life is of God. It may confuse you, but I say the truth. Life is of God, God is in life. Men live in life; if they leave life, they cannot live.

Realizing the truth is religions. Realizing the truth is not changing. Changing is not the truth. Hence if living men want to be the body of the truth, they should live forever. If they die, they are not in the truth.

The aim of Religion is to accomplish eternal life, unless eternal life is accomplished, they are fakes or the groups of Satan.

I came to the world to save people. If people live forever, all things are supposed to live forever, too. Because men are the kings of all things, if they live forever, the lower level things live forever following them.

Therefore, being declared as a Victor by the *Victress Eve*, I went to a mountain to gather firewood, where the trees and plants bowed deeply and danced with joy. But you might not believe it. As monks came here and said showing books of Buddhist that trees and plants would bow deeply and dance. Only then you came to believe My saying.

Nowadays, Christianity is a big religious group? But does the religion really believe in Jesus? They believe that Jesus was nailed to a cross, died, revived, and went up to the sky at his age of thirty-three. And he was conceived by the Holy Spirit from a virgin.

However I say that all their sayings are lies. And a reporter of the BBC revealed that Jesus is a son of Patella, a Roman soldier, and he was not crucified; He was exiled to France and lived to the age of eighty-four in *The Holy blood and the Holy Grail*.

So there are not so many people who believe in Jesus in Britain after that book was published. Hence, nobody believes in Jesus and no churches are there.

The reporter sought all the traces of Jesus and announced his identity. Accordingly, Jesus was revealed that he had not been conceived by the Holy Spirit, but he is a son of Patella, a Roman soldier.

When Roman soldiers attacked Judea and occupied it, Roman soldiers raped all women in Judea. It is a historical fact. At that time, Mary, the mother of Jesus was raped and pregnant, she delivered Jesus according to *The Holy Blood and the Holy Grail*.

When people read the Bible in detail, they will see that Rome attacked Judea and occupied it. And Jesus was judged by Pilate, the

Roman governor, according to Matthew 27 in the Bible. His sentence was innocent. In old times and today, when people were sentenced as not guilty, are they punished or executed?

How did they execute people after sentencing as innocent?

According to the BBC reporter's findings, Pilate found Jesus innocent and ordered Roman soldiers to take him safely to France and live there. So he revealed that Jesus was not crucified, he was exiled to France escorted there by Roman soldiers and lived to the age of eighty-four.

The Holy Blood and the Holy Grail says that there live a lot of offspring of Jesus in France. The BBC reporter brought some among them to stand on the witness stand of the court. The testimony on the stand is as follows.

The judge asked "What is your name? Are you a descendant of Jesus?", "Yes"

"What generation are you in?" "Twenty sevenths"

"Do you know how long Jesus lived?" "He lived eighty-four years."

As the descendant attested like that, priests, nuns, and ministers in the audience seats lowered their heads, sat on the floor and cried. When the BBC reporter talked about the scene to Me, I could not listen to it, because it was so miserable.

He added they cried saying, "If Jesus is not the Savior, who do we believe?"

Sometime later, after listening to the witness, three judges went to the grave of Jesus and took a picture of his tomb, there was a tombstone. It says that Jesus lived to the age of eighty-four.

Therefore, the judges came to believe what the offspring of Jesus attested uniformly as follows

"My grandfather was not crucified, he defected to France and lived to be eighty-four."

But the judge did not sentence for one month. The reason the judge delayed the judgment is that he believed thoroughly in Jesus, he was worried that if he judged, "Jesus was not crucified, and he was a son of Patella, a Roman soldier", it would cause a big problem in and out of Britain.

So the Chief Justice of the Supreme Court called him to speed up the judgment. Hence he judged as follows:

"The offspring of Jesus came and said on the witness stand that Jesus lived to the age of eighty-four. There was no proof that Jesus was crucified, the story of his resurrection is a lie. From the fact that there are a lot of offspring of Jesus in France, he certainly must have defected there and lived a long life. So he is not the Savior, but the son of Panatela, a Roman soldier."

An immortal era of light when people eat only the light of life is approaching. That world will have neither death nor anguishes; it will have only infinite happiness. So Amrita Sutra says, "Messiah, the Reincarnate Maitreya Buddha will build the Pure Land of Utmost Happiness in this world."

New Songs in New Heaven

Key 29

The Secret of New song & New Heaven's Lotus

A new song related to the Amita Sutra and Lotus. The Nirvana Sutra writes that where the Sweet Dew falls, there is no death because the Sweet Dew kills the spirit of death. Also, the Bible says Dew of the Lord is shiny; it will expel death from the earth. Here are new lyrics of hymns which white people sing songs all day.

 육천년간 갇힌 죄인
Sinners captivated in Satan's prison for 6000 years

1. 육천년간 갇힌죄인 살려주신 주님	1. The Lord who saves sinners captivated in Satan's prison for 6000 years
주장하신 감사함이 뼈골 속 적시네	The gratitude for leading me to heaven comes intensely to my heart.
2. 사무치게 그리웠던 하나님의 얼굴	2. The face of God I have missed poignantly
여기와서 뵙게되니 내형혼 울리네	Seeing the Lord here my soul tears

생수와 이슬성신
The grace of Fresh Water and the Holy Dew Spirit

1. 생수와 이슬성신 부어주시어
피속에 죄의 마귀 뿌리째 뽑아서

   성령의 철장으로 박살하시어
   승리의 마음천국 이뤄줍소서

2. 성령과 생수이슬 부어주시어
육천년 묵은 마귀 뿌리째 뽑아서

   이슬의 철장으로 박살하시어
   시온성 지상천국 이뤄줍소서

3. 향취와 이슬성신 부어주시어
뼈골속 음란마귀 뿌리째 뽑아서

   이슬의 철장으로 박살하시어
   영원한 하늘나라 이뤄줍소서

4. 주님을 바라보고 낱낱이 고하여
진탕만탕 마귀들을 뿌리째 뽑아서

   다섯가지 무기로쳐 막멸하시어
   온전히 몸과 마음 맡아 줍소서

1. Please pour the grace of fresh water and the Dew Spirit, Root out the Satan of sins in blood, Smash it with an iron scepter of the Holy Spirit, Please establish the paradise of the victorious mind

2. Please pour the Spirit and the grace of the fresh-water-like Holy Dew Spirit, Root out the 6,000 years old Satan, Destroy it with an iron scepter of the Holy Dew Spirit, Please establish the paradise of Zion on earth.

3. Please pour fragrance and the Holy Dew Spirit, Root out the Satan of Lewd in the marrow of bones, Smash it with an iron scepter of the Spirit, Please establish the eternal heaven.

4. Looking at the Lord and report everything, Root out the Satan of binge living, Hit it to annihilate the Satan with five weapons, Please entrust my body and mind with entirety.

황무지가 장미꽃같이 피는 것을 볼 때에
When we see wild land bloom like roses

1. 황무지가 장미꽃같이
   피는 것을 볼 때에
   구속함에 노래부르며
   거룩한 길 다니리

   * 여기 거룩한 길 있네
   슬픈 구름 없으니
   낮과 같이 맑고 밝은
   거룩한 길 다니리

2. 하나님의 아름다움과
   그의 영광 볼 때에
   모든 괴로움 잊어버리고
   거룩한 길 다니리 *

3. 마른 땅에 샘물 터지고
   사막에 물 흐를때
   기쁨으로 찬미부르며
   거룩한 길 다니리 *

4. 여기 악한 짐승 없으니
   두려울 것 없겠네
   기쁨으로 노래부르며
   거룩한 길 다니리 *

5. 여기 더러운 것 없으니
   거룩한자 뿐일세
   기쁜 면류관을 내쓰고
   거룩한 길 다니리 *

1. When I see wild land bloom like roses, I will go to the holy way singing for being bound to Him.

* Here is a holy way, no sad clouds, I will go to the holy way that is tranquil and bright like day time

2. When I see the beauty of God and His glory, I will forget all anguishes and go to the holy way.

3. When spring water pours out on dried land and river flows on the desert, I will go to a holy way singing hymns with joy.

4. As here are no evil beasts, we do not have to worry, I will go to the holy way singing hymns with joy.

5. Here are nothing dirty, only holy people, I will go to the holy way singing with joy.

구세주 찬가
The hymn of the Savior

1. 이스라엘 단지파
   소라떠나 동방으로
   험산준령 알타이를
   넘고넘어 대동강가에
   하늘나라 이루고자
   금수강산 찾아왔네
   하나님의 숨은뜻은 구세주 출현일세

2. 대동강변 묻혀있던
   와당 속의 히브리어
   천손민족 이스라엘
   열두지파 쓰던문자
   만만세를 기약하신
   하나님의 숨은역사
   구세주를 배출하사 세계만민 구함일세

3. 김포땅에 강림하신
   동방의인 우리주님
   흰돌받아 하신말씀
   소사라고 하시었네
   승리제단 세우시고
   의인들을 키우시려
   감로수를 내리시는 구세주 하나님

4. 구세주의 영광의 빛
   온우주에 비치시니
   세계만민 기쁨으로
   소사땅에 모여드네
   한강수를 축복하사
   만민들이 신고가니
   생명수로 살리시는 구세주 하나님

1. Dan tribe of Israel left Zora to the east, climbed and climbed steep and dangerous the Altai Mountains to arrive at the Daedong River. Came to new land to establish heaven. The hidden will of God is producing the Savior.

2. The Hebrew on the roof-tile buried in the riverbank of the Daedong River was letters used by 12 branches of Israel, chosen people. The hidden work of God which was promised thousands years ago. It is producing the Savior and saving all people of the world.

3. The Lord, the righteous man of the east, who was born in Gimpo received the white stone and said that the word on the white stone is Sosa. He built the Victory Altar and pours out the Sweet Dew to produce righteous men.

4. The glorious light of the Savior shines the whole universe, All people of the world crowd to the land of Sosa. He blesses the water of the Han River; all people take the water, The Savior God saves people with the water of life

오라 빛을 향해
Come to the light of the Holy Spirit

1. 죄악 세상 이기신 하나님의 영광이
성령의 빛이되어 온우주에 비취시네

1. The glory of God that overcame the sinful world, Becomes the light of the Holy Spirit and shines to the whole universe

해와 달이 빛을 잃은 신천신지 새세상에
하나님의 영광의 빛 더욱더욱 찬란하네

At the new world where the sun and the moon lose their light, The light of the glory of God is splendid more and more.

* 오라오라오라 형제들아
성령의빛을향해
경배하세 만민들아
하나님의 빛을 향해

* Brothers, come toward the light of the Holy Spirit, The whole mankind, let's worship toward the light of God

2. 마귀권세 박멸하고 기쁨만이 넘쳐나네
죽음의 고통도 늙어짐의 서러움도

2. After destroying the authority of Satan, only joy overflows, The pain of death, aging sorrow, the worldly worry, agony, and delusion, and all sins disappear.

세상근심 번뇌망상 모든 죄악 사라지고
썩을양식 필요없고 감로이슬 먹고사네 *

No rotten food is necessary; people live on the Holy Dew Spirit *

3. 천하만민 어버이신 구세주 하나님이
인간몸을 입으시고 이땅에 오시어서

3. The Savior God, the mother of all humans, Came to the world in a human form came to the world

의심많은 인간향해 오대공약이루시고
진리말씀 널리펼쳐 영생길로 이끄시네 *

Toward the humans with a lot of doubt, He has accomplished five covenants, Spreading the truth, leads to the way of eternal life. *

새바람
The New Wind

1. 조용한 아침에 나라
아름다운 우리들
마음을 활짝열어라
새바람이 불어온다
불어오는 새바람 새바람은 일바람
만들자 세상에서 제일 좋은 나라

2. 사계절 꽃피는 나라
사랑하는 우리들
북소리 크게 울려라
새바람이 불어온다
불어오는 새바람 새바람은 신바람
만들자 세상에서 제일 좋은 나라

3. 올림픽 엑스포의 나라
자랑스런 우리들
한라에서 백두까지
새바람이 불어온다
불어오는 새바람 새바람은 신바람
만들자 세상에서 제일 좋은 나라

4. 정도령님 계시는 나라
축복받은 우리들
온세상에 알리러 가세
영생의 새소식을
정도령님 크신뜻 우리모두 받들어
온세상 만민들을 살리러 가세

5. 해돋는 동방의나라
무궁화꽃 피는나라
영생문 활짝 열렸다
새세상이 밝아온다
경사로다 형제여 큰북소리 울려라
인류가 고대하던 구세주 오셨다고

1. The country of morning carm how beautiful we are. Open your mind wide as new wind blowing. The new wind blowing is the wind of work to build the best country in the world.

2. The country of flower blossom how lovely we are. Ring drums louder as new wind blowing. The new wind blowing is the wind of joy to build the best country in the world.

3. The country of Olympic and EXPO how proud we are. From Hanra to BackDu the new wind blow. The new wind blowing is the wind of happy to build the best country in the world.

4. The country of JeongDoRyoung how blessed we are. Let others know the news of ethernal life. With supporting the great will of JeongDoRyoung Let's go to save all the people in the world.

5. The country of rising sun how amasing its rose of sharon blossom. Here come the new world of eternal life. Hurray brothers ring drums louder as the Savior who has been waiting has come.

괴롬없고 죽지않는
Neither pains nor death

1. 괴롬없고 죽지않는 하늘나라 들어와
내생명물 강가에서 기쁨으로 살리라

1. I will come to heaven without hardship and death. I will live happily on the river side of my life water.

*영화롭고 맑고밝은 우리본향 천성에서
주와 같이 영원히 살리라

* At our glorious, bright and bright hometown heaven, We will live with the Lord forever.

2. 천성에는 해와 달과 별과 등불 없어도
하나님의 빛은 영영 찬란하게 비치내 *

2. There is not the sun, the moon, stars, or lamps. But light of God shines splendidly forever. *

3. 명랑한곳 성전안에 그침없이 들리는
거문고와 노래소리 청아하게 들리네 *

3. Sounding endlessly from the cheerful sanctuary. Geomungo and sound of songs are eccentric and peculiar. *

4. 주의보좌 앞에서서 만국백성 찬양해
이거룩한 노래소리 청아하게 들리네 *

4. All people praise the Lord in front of Him. This holy sound of a song sounds clearly. *

빛난 새벽별
The shining morning star

1. 동방나라 모퉁이 땅에 구세주 출현
감람나무 백합화 빛난 새벽별

샛별처럼 빛나는 주님의 영광
온우주 다스리는 이긴자 구세주

1. The Savior has appeared at the corner of a far eastern country. He is like an olive tree, a lily, and a shining morning star.
The glory of the Lord is shining like the morning star. The Victor, Savior, is governing the whole universe.

2. 석가지운 삼천칠년 우담화 폈네
개태사에 엄나무 생미륵 상징

생미륵불 오셨구나 소사에 계시네
감로수 내리시는 미륵 부처님

2. *Udumbaras* blossom in the year 3,007 after *Sakyamuni* died. The kalopanax of Gaetea temple is the symbol of the Reincarnated Maitreya Buddha
The Reincarnated Maitreya Buddha has come, He is in Sosa. The Reincarnated Maitreya Buddha is pouring out the Sweet Dew

3. 유불선을 하나로 합친 이기신 엄마
보라이슬 내리시는 영생의 만나

불로불사 영생수 마신자 마다
죽음이 없어지니 영생의 나라

3. The victorious spiritual mother who united *Confucianism*, *Buddhism*, and *Christianity* into one
He is pouring the violet Sweet Dew, the manna for immortality. Whoever drinks the water of eternal life. Death disappears; it is the country of immortality.

4. 영생방주 타러가세 소사 흰돌호
마음문만 열으면 탈수있어요

4. Let's board the ark of 'Sosa White Stone' for immortality. Only opening your mind, you can get in.

영적노아 정도령님 노를저시네
맡기며 따라가세 삼천성으로

Spiritual Noah, Jeongdoryeong rows. Let's entrust ourselves to Him and follow Him to the *Castle of 3,000*(三天城).

5. 신천신지 새로운 세상 에덴에 낙원
영원무궁 안식처 행복에 동산

5. New heaven, new earth, new world, and the paradise of Eden. It is an eternal shelter and a happy garden.

육천년간 잃었던 우리의 본향
이제야 찾았으니 영원히 누리세

Our hometown that was lost for 6000 years. Now we have recovered it, let's enjoy it forever.

어떻게
How to

1. 수고가 없이 어떻게 이웃을 사랑해요
내마음에 아픔이 없이 어떻게 용서해요

1. How to love others without efforts. How to forgive them without pains in my heart.

* 사랑은 내것이 없어요
　아까운 것이없어요
　사랑은 따지지 않아요
　주는 것 뿐이에요

* there is no love for myself
　none to keep as it is too good
　love does not count
　just gives away

2. 사랑은 희생이 따르나
　마음은 풍성해요
　주님의 참사랑 안에는
　즐거움 뿐이에요 *

2. Love sacrifices myself but fills my heart with God's. The joy of true love of Savior only is. *

정도령 찬가
The hymn of Jeongdoryeong

1. 육천년간 빼앗겼던
우주권세회복하고

1. Recovering the authority of the universe snatched by Satan for 6,000 years.

1981 신유년에
천지공사 선포로다

In the year 1981, The groundbreaking ceremony for the construction of Heaven on earth proclaimed.

공산주의 없애겠다
구세주의 예언말씀

I will eradicate communism; The Victor proclaimed.

악한이념 무너뜨려
공산주의 없애도다

By killing the wicked spirit out of communists got rid of the communism.

2. 제왕상에 빛난얼굴
가슴에는 북두칠성

2. The bright face of the King of empires and seven stars in the chest.

임금왕자 양손에쥔
정도령님 나타나사

Both palms held the sign of King, Jeongdoryeong came.

태풍내가 막겠노라
권능에찬 말씀대로
강한태풍 소멸되고
한반도를 비켜가네

I will protect the country from the typhoon; as Jeongdoryeong declared strong typhoons disappears and avoids to come to the land.

3. 땀흘려서 지은농사
장마비에 쓸려가도
어느누가 막았던가
하늘만을 원망했지

3. When monsoon rain swept away the rice seedlings of farmer's effort, nobody could prevent but just blamed heaven.

이젠풍년 뿐이로다 확신에찬 축복말씀	Korean shall have abundant harvests continued, the Savior blessed.
비바람이 순풍되니 연년대풍 계속되네	The storm line turned into beautiful watering to yield great harvests every year.

4. 금수강산 한반도에
생미륵불 출현하사

어둔세상 빛이되어
우담화로 피었구나

4. In the beautiful Korean peninsula, as if the *udumbaras* flower blossom in 3000 years, The *Maitreya Buddha* has come and enlightened the ignorant world.

한국에는 전쟁없다
예언하신 말씀대로
평화안정 이어지니
세계통일 이룩하리

There won't be wars in Korea. Peace and security continue as promised. Then will unify the world together.

5. 동방에서 나타나신
이기신자 우리주님
감추었던 이슬만나 우리에게 먹이시니

5. Our Lord in the far East, the Victor feeds us the *hidden manna*, the Dew Spirit.

생명수의 은혜받아
소사역곡 이땅에서

Receiving the grace of spirit life water here in *Sosa, Yeokgok,*

죽지않는 새세상을
온인류가 누리리라

The whole humanity shall enjoy the new world of eternal life.

그 얼마나
How long time we have been waiting

1. 그얼마나 긴긴세월
고대하던 분이신가
때이르니 동방에서
나타나신 의인이라

* 들으소서 성신이여
　우리의기도 들으소서
　따르리라 따르리라
　영원토록 따르리라
　영원도록 따르리라

2. 죄의권세 이기시려
억만죽음 넘었는데
그고생을 누가알랴
사람으론 알수없네 *

3. 받은고난 당한시험
사무치게 아프거늘
우리들이 모른다면
그얼마나 서러울까 *

4. 고대하던 새아침은
이제다시 밝아오네
죽음없는 새세상은
이땅에서 이뤄지네 *

1. How long we have been waiting for His coming. The time came, and the righteous in the east has appeared.

* Please listen, the Spirit of God, please listen to our praying. I will follow you, I will follow you, endlessly I will follow you, endlessly I will follow you.

2. His path overcoming the power of sins required numerous life-threatening moments. Who would know the hardship, no man can know.

3. The hardship and the tests he took were aching so much. Ignoring his teaching will make Him even more sorrowful.

4. The morning sun of the long-awaited civilization of immortality rises and shine. Comes true in Korea the Land of the Morning Calm.

산에 여우 굴이 있고
Fox in mountains have caves

1. 산에여우 굴이있고
나는새도 집있건만
우리주님 세상에서
머리둘 곳 하나없이
돌팔메질 왠말인가
발길질이 왠말인가

2. 엄동설한 추운밤에
얼음위에 밤새우고
돌밭위에 유리위에
삼십일씩 열네번을

피눈물로 금식기도
하나님도 감동했네

3. 이기신자 우리주님
자욱마다 가시밭길
억천만번 당한고난
최후까지 견디시며
이한생명 주께바쳐
주의뜻을 이루소서

4. 이겼도다 우리주님
억만마귀 이기시고
승리하신 우리주님
한국땅에 오셨으니
빛나도다 승리제단
만민들을 영생하리

1. Even fox in the mountains have caves, and even flying birds have nests. Our Lord, however, had no place to stay and how could they throw stones and kick Him

2. Even in the freezing dead of winter night, He stayed up all night on ice field. Fourteen times of thirty days fasting prayer the candidate of Victor sat on his knees. On coarse gravels, on sharp edges of broken glass even God was also moved by his bloody tears.

3. The Victor candidate, the martyr's footprint was thorny paths. Bearing millions of billions of hard times to the final moment. Offered His life for the Lord to accomplish the Holy will.

4. Victory! Our Lord. Overcoming thousands of billions of Satan the Victor came to Korea at last. Splendid! Victory Altar. Humanity shall live forever.

육신의 모든 염려
All my physical worries

1. 육신의 모든 염려 세상의 고락을
   나와항상 같이 하여 주시고

   시험을 당할때에 푯대가 되시며
   우상을 멸하고 지켜주시네

   온세상 날 버려도 주함께 계시면
   목적지 완전히 달하겠네

* 구주는 산곡에 백합 명랑한 새벽별
  만인 위에 뛰어 나시는 줄세

2. 진실히 주를 믿고 그 뜻을 행하면
   주께서 영원히 같이 할지니

   주가 내곁에 계서 불담이 되시면
   이 세상에 두려울것 없겠네

   신령한 만나로서 만족함 누리며
   구주의 오실길 예비하세 *

1. The Savior is always with me when I care about all my physical worries and joy and sorrow of life.
When I am tempted by Satan, He becomes my example. He destroys idol and keeps me.
Although all people look away, if I am with the Lord, I will accomplish my aim.

* The Savior is a lily in a mountain valley and the bright morning star,
He is the superb Lord above all humans.

2. If one believe the Savior earnestly and practice His will, He will be with one forever.
If the Lord is with me and becomes my fire fence, there's nothing to worry.
Let's prepare in advance for the Savior coming enjoying the cool manna

승리의 찬가
The Hymn of Victory

1. 땅 위의 험한세상
이기고 이기시면서
6 2 5의 수많은
죽음경지 이기셨도다

* 기쁘도다 오늘은
주님께서 승리하신날
축하하세 온누리여
영원한 승리의 날을

2. 신앙의 고비고비
이기고 이기시면서
핍박하는 무리를
사랑으로 이기셨도다 *

3. 밀실의 반대생활
이기고 이기시면서
승리하신 하나님
되시도록 이기셨도다 *

4. 아마겟돈 최후싸움
이기고 이기시면서
산천초목 큰 절을
올리도록 이기셨도다 *

5. 육천년 긴긴싸움
마귀를 이기시면서
잃어버린 에덴을
회복토록 이기셨도다 *

1. The Savior overcame and overcame the tough world on the earth. Also He overcame a lot of crisis of death during the Korean War.

* We are happy today because the Lord overcame Satan. All people of the world, let's celebrate the day of eternal victory.

2. He overcame and overcame each crisis of faith. He overcame the crowd with love who persecuted him. *

3. He overcame himself by living the opposite way of what His self-awareness ordered in the Secret Chamber. He overcame himself in order for God to become the Victor God. *

4. The Savior overcame and overcame himself in the final Armageddon battle. So grasses and trees bowed deeply because He overcame Satan instead of them. *

5. God has fought against Satan for 6000 years and recover the lost Garden of Eden by overcoming Satan. *

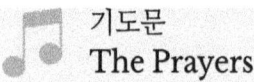
기도문
The Prayers

무량대수마귀 일초동안에	The infinite number of satan for each second
무량대수횟수로 계속해서	by the infinite number of attacks
몽땅뿌리째 뽑아서	root out the source from me
성령의 검으로 난도질하여	mince the enemy with the holy spirit sword
성령의 도끼로 짓이겨서	mash the evil with the holy spirit hatchet
성령의 맷돌로 갈아서	grind the spirit with the holy spirit millstones
성령의 불로 태워서	burn the sins in the holy spirit blaze
유황불로	fling the remainings into volcanic sulfur flame
박멸소탕	cleanup
박멸소탕	cleanup
박멸소탕	cleanup
박멸소탕	cleanup

우리들은 야곱의 단지파 자손
We are the offspring of Dan tribe, the son of Jacob, Israel

1. 우리들은 야곱의 단지파 자손
하나님 뜻을따라 억울함 풀고

끝날에 세계만민 다스리겠네
승리자 구세주 단지파 자손

* 나가자 싸움터로 마귀박멸해
하늘나라 세워서 주님모시자

2. 허락하신 기업을 물려받고자
소라를 떠나서 동으로 왔으니

하나님 뜻이었나 주님아시리
동방나라 찾아오신 단지파자손 *

3. 금수강산 삼천리 예비하신곳
셈의장막 복된땅 만민의 낙원

선지자 이사야가 예언하신곳
복되고 복되도다 단지파자손

1. We are the offspring of Dan tribe, the son of Jacob. Following the holy will solve God's grudge.

He will guide people around the world in the end. The Victor Savior, the son of Dan tribe.

* Forward! forward the Armageddon battlefield. Eradicating Satan build heaven to go with the Lord.

2. To execute the inherited order the Dan came from Zora Israel to the far east.

Only God the commander knows the will. Lord tells we are descendants of Dan tribe who reached to the far east.

3. The beautifully land of Korea is the blessed paradise where the Sam of Noah set the tent for you.

The prepared soil that prophet Isaiah saw. How blessed the descendants of Dan tribe are.

감람나무 우리엄마
Our mommy the Olive Tree

1. 감람나무 우리엄마
발자국마다 피땀냄새
천번만번 곤두박질
갖은포악 당하셨네
공중권세 잡은마귀 소탕하여 박멸하고
육천년간 고대하던 시온성을 찾으셨네

1. The Olive Tree of our mom; each of her track hold the scent of sweaty blood; million times of falling, took all the atrocity; Killed and cleared the Satan holding the power in the air; Retaken the Zion, longed for 6000 years

2. 이길만은 우리인생
엄마없이 못오는길
감람나무 우리엄마
우리위해 통곡했네
애걸복걸 피투성이 밤새도록 마귀죽여
죽을인생 구원하신 고마우신 우리엄마

2. Nobody can go this path, without mommy; The Olive Tree, our mom, wailed for us; Begging in bloodiness, killing Satan overnights; Saved my life which supposed to die, how thankful our mommy

3. 사망권세 잡은마귀
피속에서 육천년간
인생들은 더러워져
잔악하게 물들었고
슬픈탄식 괴롬속에 참혹하게 죽어갔네
완성엄마 따라오면 영생복락 누리리라

3. The Satan holding power of death sits in our blood for 6000 years; Making humankind inhuman gradually; Suffering dolorous sighs, all had to die in the hell of life; But, following mommy of completion, shall enjoy the pleasure of eternal life.

4. 좁고험한 가시밭길
외로워도 주님함께
자신속에 옛사람을
짓이겨서 죽이는길
천번만번 죽고죽여 최후까지 견디는길
구세주의 우리엄마 따라오면 영생하리

4. The narrow path of harsh thorny field, mommy would go with the lonely pilgrim; The journey killing the 'I' of old days is the God in me goes on heart; Kill or killed over and over, God have to bear until the last moment; Following our mom of the Savior, can earn the eternal life;

5. 엄마께서 그얼마나
외쳤던가 우셨던가
노염타는 어린심령
빗대시고 나무라시네
때리시고 얼리시는 위대하신 장한엄마
대신울고 죄를담당 우리들을 살려주네

5. What a countless number of yelling and wailing; insinuates and scolds to her spiritual children; She beat up; She pacified; But our mom the greatest and splendid; Crys instead of me and takes the punishment instead of the sinner, mommy would save us;

6. 천대멸시받으면서
참고이기신우리엄마
감람나무 명령따라
황무지에 십팔년간
굶주림에 몸부림쳐 해산수고 하신엄마
피눈물로 물들여서 에덴동산 회복했네

6. Our mom was a subject to despise but endured and won. To complete the mission of the Olive Tree, bore 18 years in the wilderness. Struggling with hunger, It was her labor of giving birth to the spiritual son. Recovered the Garden of Eden with teardrops of blood;

7. 최후까지참을수없는
순간에도견뎌야해
마귀공격 빗발쳐도
쉬지않는 기도공격
의식잃어 죽어가도 낙심않고 맡기면은
엄마께서 담당하여 우리들을 살려주네

7. Have to bear even the last moment you can't; Have attacks with endless praying against Satanic attacks; Even the moment of losing consciousness and die, don't be discouraged but entrust, mommy would take the remainings and saves us.

보광가
The Hymn of *BoGwang*

사망으로 얼룩진 어두운 이세상에 삼위일체 완성자 조희성 구세주님	In the world darkened by death, the Trinity of completion, my Lord Cho Hee Sung,
승리제단 구원방주 하늘백성 구하시네 너무나도 악한세상 육신벗고 이루고자	Victory Altar the Savior's Ark saves heavenly people; To save the too lousy world, even own body offered sacrificially,
뜻하신바 보광하니 하늘과땅 통곡이라 우리주님 깊은뜻을 그누가 알겠는가	A strategic pull back, but the heaven and earth are weeping. Who could know what our Lord meant?
그 러 나 ……	However …
찬란하게 떠오른다 태양보다 밝은광체	Comes up brightly even brighter than the sun shines;
어둔세상 없어지고 밝은세상 이룩된다	The dark world disappears and the bright world begins;
광채속에 빛난얼굴 다시오실 조희성님	Shining face in brilliance, my Lord comes back again;
신천신지 건설하실 백보좌의 심판주라	The judge in the shiny white suit builds the new heaven and earth.
반가웁다 우리주님 기뻐뛰며 찬양하세	Welcoming our Lord, let's praise with joy.
천하만민 따로없다 하나되어 찬양하세	Everyone in the world, let's be one and celebrate.
회복하신 하늘나라 세세토록 다스리실	The Kingdom of God recovered, the king of kings, the Lord of Lords will rule forever. Let's praise. Let's celebrate.
만왕의왕 만주의주 찬양하세 찬양하세	

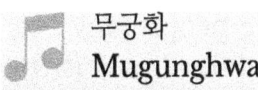
Mugunghwa

무궁 무궁 무궁화
무궁화는 우리꽃

피고 피고 또 피어
무궁화라네

너도 나도 모두
무궁화가 되어
지키자 내 땅
빛내자 조국

아름다운 이 강산 무궁화 겨레
서로 손 잡고서
앞으로 앞으로
우리들은 무궁화다

Mugung Mugung Mugunghwa,
Mugunghwa is the flower of us.

Bloom bloom blooms again,
as Mugunghwa lives eternally.

You and me all of us, let's become Mugunghwa; let's keep the holy land, bring glory to the country.

Beautiful land of Mugunghwa nation; Hold hands in hands. Forward! Forward! We are the Mugunghwa.

According to revelation, in New Jerusalem, white people sing new songs. 'Here is no death, where the *Sweet Dew* falls down' is the secret hidden in the Amita Sutra and the Nirvana Sutra. Also, the Bible says that God will become a dew to the Victor. The Amita Sutra and the Nirvana Sutra say that the Amita Reincarnate Maitreya Buddha saves people from death by pouring the *Sweet Dew*.

That is, where the *Sweet Dew* falls down, the Savior, Victor, and Amita Reincarnate Maitreya Buddha stays. So in the Victory Altar, all predictions in the Bible, the Buddhist scriptures, and prophetic books are accomplished as they foretell in the Victory Altar in Korea.

Key 30

The Hidden Secret of the lost tribe, Dan

Korean people are the Israelites. Dan tribe started moving in a northeasterly from Zora of Israel after Samson died 3000 years ago. They moved to the north passing by Syria, Iran, Iraq, and settled in Altai Mountain for 100 years.

The first generation died there, and the second generation had to learn the Altai language to survivor there.

And they moved to the east and one part of them settled in Mongo, and the main part moved to the southern east passing by Manchuria and settled on the riverside of the Daedong River on the Korean peninsula.

They found *Dangun Chosen*. That is the first government of Korea.

The founder of Korea is Dangun. Koreans put the suffix *gun* behind the family name to show respect for him. So *gun* in 'Dangun' is a suffix.

In the Bible, Jacob's fifth son is Dan. According to Genesis 49, Jacob prophesied Judah who is an ancestor of Jesus, as follows, "Judah is like a lion. The scepter will not depart from Judah, until Shiloh comes."

The scepter means he will be a king of the world. Today two-thirds of the earth is Christian. Therefore, Jesus is a king. However, the scepter would stay with Judah until Shiloh comes.

Shiloh is Hebrew meaning the Savior.

Therefore, Jesus would be a king only until the Savior comes. It means Jesus cannot be the real Savior. Hence, the Bible has a prediction that a pseudo-king in Judah line will fall, and the real king in Dan line will be a ruler.

Key 31

The Secret of Zion

According to the Bible, Revelation 21:1-7: Then I(John, the writer of Revelation) saw a new heaven and a new earth, for the first heaven and the first the earth had passed away, and there was no longer any sea. I saw the Holy City, the new Jerusalem, coming down out of heaven from God, prepared as a bride beautifully dressed for her husband. And I heard a loud voice from the throne saying,

"Now the dwelling of God is with men, and he will live with them. They will be his people, and God himself will be with them and be their God. He will wipe every tear from their eyes. There will be no death or mourning or be crying or pain, for the old
order of things has passed away."

Zion is the New Jerusalem, the New Heaven.

They are all the same that shall be established in human mind where the spirit of God rules the new being, the Victor.

Another pronoun for Jews does not mean a city or a castle on the earth, but it imply a particular state of human mind. The mind whose spiritual owner goes with God. The spiritually reborn being of which God rules instead of the human spirit of 'I'. The victorious spirit overcoming Satan is the Victor Savior.

Your mind must be the same spiritual state as the Victor Savior. The New World of one spirit with the Victor Savior is the Zion.

The secret of going to heaven

12 Basic commandments for immortality and New Heaven

- There is no relationship between the rich and the poor in obtaining immortality
- People can accomplish immortality with the mind.
- Immortality comes true when people become one with God who overcomes Satan.
- People need to have the hope of immortality and endeavor to accomplish immortality
- People need to think and say to themselves as much as possible "I will live forever; I cannot die" because everything comes true as people think and say. That is the law of drawing.
- People can get immortality when they cooperate to make an immortal world.
- People should know that they were God, the immortal existence.
- People should throw away 'I' to get immortality. Because 'I' is the spirit of death and the spirit of Satan, so the Self-awareness of 'I' keep people away from becoming immortal God.
- Look at the face of the Victor who overcame the Satan.
- Be grateful to God who has opened an immortal era.
- Laugh all the time. Because if you laugh, your body is changed into that of God. Only God laughs. If you think and behave like God, you become God.
- Think that I am God because humans were originally God. The evidence that humans are God is that they have a idea of hating death. The idea of hating death is that of God because God is an immortal existence.

Conclusion

ike humans have their secrets, God has His secrets, too. Because God was defeated by Satan in the begining, He had to seal His secrets from the devil.

Now the sealed secrets have been revealed by the Victory God. That means starting the work of the Holy Spirit of God that overcame the death and brightens the world. He came to give new hope to people. Now, it is the time when the paradise is built by the light of the Victor.

Such secrets were those of New Heaven. Through this book, one can see the advent of the Victor, the new work of New Heaven, and the hidden secrets that were sealed so far. The most important things among the secrets of New Heaven are the advent of the Victor and His symbol; the Holy Dew Spirit, which is the master key to the heaven's door.

You can go to New Heaven by knowing the whereabouts of the Victor who completes New Heaven. Also you should know the essence of God, the root of humans, the hidden words of God, the theory of salvation, the theory of revival, the theory of the forbidden fruit, and the fruit of life in the Bible to go to New Heaven.

Such knowledge is that of God, unless you are poured by oil of the Holy Spirit, nobody can find out the way of New Heaven.

AUTHOR

Angela Kim is a school teacher, a writer, and the head of research at Neohumans Research Center.

Ariel Han graduated from Gyeongsang National University in social science, the Department of Business, graduated from Mejiro University in Department of language culture in Japan. He is a reporter of Korean Travel News, a researcher of Victory Altar, the Director of Korean New Religion.

Terminology

Adam Victor Adam Victor is the Spiritual Child to whom the Spiritual Mother give birth. The spiritual mother completed the mission expressed as he was the Olive Tree who was searching for lost two branches. So spiritually re-united three elements, God, Eve and Adam come to one being of perfection. It is the recovered Garden of Eden which is our true homeland, Zion. Therefore Adam Victor is our Spiritual Mother. Humanity should know about Adam Victor who pours the manna like Moses, then join the spiritual exodus from the slavery life from Satan. Our Spiritual Mother, Messiah taught us that all of us are God who is being ruled by Satan. And the Satan is the self-awareness of 'I'. If one thinks/acts based-on himself/herself, it is sinning no matter it is good or bad. So keep beholding the Savior's face, acts against what I want to do, but regards everybody as yourself as God, then the power of Satan weak and weaken before it finally cleanup by the Savior. Therefore at the end of the spiritual exodus, the neo-human will be the one as the Victor Savior. In the world of the Victor Savior as there is no 'you' nor 'I', there is no pain, nor conflict, nor birth, nor aging, nor illness, nor death.

Amrita Sutra A book of Buddhist scripts

Anti-Christ Anything that against Christ. Christ = Savior = Messiah = God = The hero who brings the New Words = The words of Eternal Life = Perfection. Therefore, anti-christ trying to stay in the world of death attacks the Christ who is teaching what did not exist in the world of imperfection. Typical teaching of the old world is the theory of eternal life after death. Without knowing the cause of death, they teach death is inevitable, or they teach death as a precondition. Even they teach death as a truth.

Armageddon War It is a spiritual war of God vs Satan in Cho Hee Sung in the Milsil. God won the war and became Victor Savior/Adam Victor/Messiah. Every one of us must go through the spiritual war in each of us and win against Satan to receive salvation. The salvation of God for God by God.

Authority of Satan Satan holds an authority, a key or the power of death. While God holds an authority, a key or the power of life.

Big Change   GaeByurk 개벽(開闢) means the beginning of the world.

Bisangpum   A chapter in Gyeokamyourok.

Bomoon part   A title or chapter of Buddhist scripts

Bright Star   Bright = Shining = Twinkling = Morning Star; A symbol of the Victor Savior in the Bible. Revelation 2:28

Bucheon   "A city in Korea where the Sosa(素砂, white stone) area where the headquarter of Victory Altar is."

Buddha   The being in Buddism similar to God in Christianity. The transcendent being is composing everything in the universe. There is no theory of Creation in Buddhism.

Bupgugyeong Annyeong   A chapter of Annyeong in a book of Bupgugyeong on Buddhist scripts

Castle of 3000   Elder Park as the God is spiritually the Castle of 1000, Hong UpBee as the Eve Victor is spiritually the Castle of 2000, and Cho Hee Sung as the Adam Victor is spiritually the Castle of 3000.

Cho Hee Sung   Sir name Cho(曺) means a group. First name Hee Sung (熙星) means a bright star. The first spiritual martyr who offered own ego as a sacrifice by acting against what he wants thoroughly. The being of born-again taught us the complete knowledge, so you are accessing to a part of it through this book. He sacrificed everything for the world.

Christianity   A community whose people believe in Jesus as Savior.

Dharma   The teachings of Buddha or the truth.

Dharma Flower Sutra   A kind of Buddhist scripts/sutra

Dobusinin   A chapter in Gyeokamyourok.

Ego   The strongest spirit in the pool of spirits which includes all of his/her direct ancestors and acquired during their lifetime. Similar nicknames include 'I', self, self-awareness, self-consciousness, soul, etc.

Elixir   elixir of eternal life

Emperor Wu   The emperor of Han dynasty.

Eternal life   God who is stronger than Satan can live eternal life.

Eunbiga   A chapter in Gyeokamyourok.

Eve Victor   Eve Victor is one of two spiritual children of the Spiritual Mother Elder Park who established the second faith-village in DurkSo. He shut down a lot of profitable factories in the first faith-village and direct them to relocate to DurkSo. The faithful protested on the idiotic command, but elder Park asked a question to them, "who of you know more than me about God's circumstance?" Nobody could answer the question and the migration happened. Elder Park ordered to put a figure of a naked woman in front of the gate of the second faith-village which later Adam Victor explained to us that it symbolizes the advent of the Eve Victor who is a female without clothes of sin. After overcoming tests over decades, the Eve Victor ran MilSil (secret chamber) to raise Adam Victor. She could pickup what other people thought and order not to. For example, do not recall your past, do not be interested in other, do not be conscious of yourself. It was fails over and over until the day Cho Hee Sung went through on 15th Oct 1980.

Flower Adornment Sutra   A book of Buddhist scripts

Forbidden fruit   A spiritual fruit is a spirit. The spirit that made Adam and Eve aware of evil is the Forbidden Fruit in the Bible. Adam and Eve were filled with only good which is the Holy Spirit. The spirit of evil is Satan, and it defeated the Holy Spirit and took the ownership of Adam and Eve to make them sinners. Victor Savior discovered that the Forbidden Fruit was the spirit of self-awareness of 'I', and started the spiritual fighting against self to overcome the Satan. Everyone has to do the same spiritual fighting against Satan and win from the standpoint of God because we all are children of God and child of God is God.

Fukuoka   A city of Japan

Gapeulga   A chapter in Gyeokamyourok.

God   God is Life, Light, Spirit as described in the Bible. God is the fundamental element composes universe. Not only humanity but also everything in the universe has God, also Satan. However, the God who is depicted as a creator does not exist in the real world but mythology.

Great Nirvana Sutra   A kind of Buddhist scripts/sutra, especially the collection of Sakyamuni's last teaching before dying. Because Buddhist regard Shakyamuni's dead as entering Nirvana, his last messages of the most high level have teachings of the most important.

Gungeullon   A chapter in Gyeokamyourok.

Gyeokamyourok   A book of Korean prophets written by GyeokAm

Han dynasty   206BC ~ 220AD

Hangukilbo   A news media in Korea

Hanryu   Korean Wave, global sensation of Korean culture

Heaven   The place where God lives. As God is a spiritual being, heaven is also a spiritual, therefore their essence is the same as a spirit.

Holy Dew Spirit   God would be like the Dew to Israel which means the winner, Victor. Their essence is the same as a spirit, but the Spirit of overcoming Satan is called especially the Holy Dew Spirit. Other nicknames include Holy Spirit, Faith, Victor, Messiah, Savior, etc.

Holy Spirit   The spirit of God is the Holy Spirit. As both Holy Spirit and God are spiritual words, their essence is the same as a spirit.

Jeondogwan   Elder Park Tae-Sun established a new religious movement called Jeondogwan (전도관, 傳道館) with 1.5 million believers. Due to his amazing supernatural power and sensational teaching could lead such a huge movement in short time. There are three faith-villages called SinAngChon, the first in Sosa, the second in DuckSo and the third in KiJang. Jeondogwan ran many successful manufacturing factories but Elder Park Tae-Sun shut them down and forcefully ordered his faithful followers to dismiss Jeondogwan. Most followers disappointed at Elder's abnormal behaviors and left with complaints. However, some followers did not obey Elder Park and remain to run a religious group called CheonBuGyo (천부교, 天父教) where they don't believe in Jesus as Savior, but they regard Elder Park as the Father of God.

Jeonggamrok   Another well-known Korean prophecy book which hints the advent of Jinin (眞人, a true humankind like the Jeongdoryeong in Gyeokamyourok)

Jeungil Sutra   A kind of Buddhist scripts/sutra

Jinhae   A city in South Korea.

Jinin   Jin (眞 진) means 'true', In (人 인) means 'humankind'. Jinin means a true humankind and Korean prophecy books has "JinIn would come at the end of 20th century." It is the similar ideas with Messiah or Maitreya Buddha's coming in other religions.

Kobe — A city in Japan

Last Adam — "The first man Adam became a living being; the last Adam, a life-giving spirit. 1Corinthians 14:45"

Law of Liberty — "The Law of heart that a candidate of Victor Savior could enter the Kingdom of God and keep it forever. 1. Behold the Victor Savior every second, 2. Admire highly the Victor Savior who has been doing so, 3. Beat the self-awareness of 'I', 4. Regard brother's sins and situation as mine, 5. Regard everybody as myself"

Lord God — Lord = Savior = Messiah = God = Lord God = The God who overcomes Satan; Isaiah 35:4 has that your God will come; Please be sure that it is not God's only son but God. When God comes, then the eyes of the blind will be opened and the ears of the deaf unstopped. It means you can see God and Satan as you will learn correct teachings. So children of God will take the guidance of the Lord God and fight against Satan which is the spirit of human self. Please refer Trinity.

Maitreya Buddha — The future Buddha whose advent was predicted by Sakyamuni

Malunlon — A chapter in Gyeokamyourok.

Manna — The food that was fallen from heaven after Moses' prayers to feed people who obeyed his command of the exodus from slavery life in Egypt to a wilderness.

Masan — A city in South Korea.

Milsil — 밀실(密室) means a secret chamber. Elder Park Tae-Sun who publicly proclaimed himself as an Olive Tree of symbolizing God gave birth Victress Eve and Victor Adam in the place called Milsil.

Mugunghwa — 무궁화(無窮花) means a flower of eternal life. Nation flower of Korea. A Rose of Sharon.

Neo-humans — A nickname of next generation of humanity spiritually born again with Holy Spirit. Sinners are humanity so far the Holy Spirit suppressed by Satan which is the spirit of 'self'. When the weak Holy Spirit becomes stronger and overcomes the Satan to own the being, the spiritually born-again is Neo-human.

New Heaven and New Earth — When the spiritual ownership of a person shifts from Satan to God, everything will be new.

New Jerusalem — "Jerusalem in the Bible is a spiritual word which is a spirit. The spiritual place where God lives is called the Garden of Eden, but God lost it. New Jerusalem is new Garden of Eden which God has taken back after overcoming Satan. Therefore New Jerusalem is the spiritual place where the Savior/Messiah is, eventually the Savior/Messiah/The Holy Dew Spirit itself."

Nirvana The goal of Buddhism; In the state of Nirvana, there are no pains of (birth, aging, illness, death) but limitless pleasure.

Nostradamus "A Great Prophet who predicted that a true Savior would come at the end of 20th century. To protect himself from Christianity, he could not state particular words like Messiah or Savior, as it would be nothing to do with Jesus. Instead, he states the world would be ended in the year 1999. And added, If 'something-else' comes, it would not. The 'something-else' here is the true Messiah who already saved the world from the scheduled World War III. By killing the hostile spirit of communism in 4 billion communists worldwide over the years between 1981 and 1991, communism collapsed without any blood shedding."

Park Tae-Sun Elder Park Tae-Sun made an incredible turning point in human history. He proclaimed that himself was an Olive Tree and his aim was seeking two lost branches. Then called himself the Spiritual Mother publicly. Although continuous hostile attacks from established religious society, he achieved spiritual mother's mission successfully by giving birth to the spiritual son the Victor Savior. It is the biblical way of seeing how the Savior will come. In the world of sins, majority beats truth because of the sinful majority have the power of disguise, distortion, authority, and loudspeakers. The minority with truth have to appeal as many people in the world by telling the truth. The reputation of the greatest saint should be reconsidered when the corrupted network in Korea rooted out.

Qin dynasty 221BC ~ 206BC

Qinshihuangdi The first emperor of Qin dynasty which became China. He unified China and built much of the Great Wall, created legal system. His quest for immortality is well known.

Red Dragon Satan In the Milsil (secret chamber) Eve Victor gave Satans names before doing prayers of freezing them. For example, a name of '뒤돌아보는 음란마귀' (DueeDoRaBoNun EumRanMaGuee meaning 'the lewd satan of looking back') was given to the Satan of recalling the past. As a candidate who goes the path to marry God, the spiritual virgin must think only God. Due to a sinner lived the past, recalling the past means that the spiritual bride meets the spirit of sin instead of God. That is why it is called the sin of lewdness. The name of Red Dragon Satan was given to the most strongest Satan. Adam Victor is the completion and gives us the prayers of killing Satan. Also said that the Red Dragon Satan is the self-awareness of 'I'.

Reincarnate Maitreya Buddha   The Maitreya Buddha in human form. Refer Maitreya Buuha.

Saengchojirak   A chapter in Gyeokamyourok.

Sakyamuni   The founder of Buddhism. One of the highly enlightened people in human history. He said in the Great Nirvana Sutra his teachings were a temporary solution that educates people until the Maitreya Buddha's coming 3007 years later.

Sasangpum   A chapter in a book of Buddhist scripts

Satan   Spirit that against God.

Savior   The God who overcomes the Satan becomes the Savior who is a model for every other people to be.

Secret Chamber   Refer Milsil

Self-awareness   The spirit that owns control of a person representing his/her 'I' and character

Seodang   Traditional education institution in Korea.

Shimonoseki   A city in Japan

Sipseung   Sip(十) means number 10 and imply God in Gyeokamyourok, Seung(勝) means victory. So it is a pronoun of victorious God.

Sipseungga   A chapter in Gyeokamyourok.

Sosa   The city that has a meaning of white stone where Victor Savior based in Korea. The name itself written on the white stone that the hero who overcomes shall be given according to the Revelation 2:17.

Soul   The spirit which is the most powerful amongst the spirits of a person. Other nickname includes 'ego', 'I', 'self', 'self-awareness of I', etc.

Spirit   Heart, mind, etc.

Spirit of God   Spirit of God = Spirit, Spirit = Heart = Light = Life = God, God = Perfection = Truth = Never changing = Eternal life; Therefore Spirit of God is the spirit of eternal life.

Spiritual Mother   "Isaiah 7:14 has "The virgin will be with child and will give birth to a son, and will call him Immanuel." Christianity interprets the virgin as a girl without sexual experience with a man. Just like they interpreted the Forbidden Fruit as a kind of fruit like a fig, pears or apples. However, the Bible is a spiritual book. The word 'virgin' in the spiritual book should be interpreted as a spiritual virgin. Every person without considering gender and age is spiritually a virgin who could marry God. Therefore, A man who married God come to the labor of giving birth to a spiritual son, the spiritual son will be with God, Immanuel. The spiritual son being with God at all time is the perfect God who overcomes Satan's control. Spiritual Mother gives birth to the Messiah which is the God of completion. Elder Park was the Spiritual Mother of Victress Eve and Victor Adam. Victor Adam is a model or sample for us to be. Therefore, Victor Adam is our Spiritual Mother, the Savior, the Messiah.

Spiritual Noah Noah is a biblical figure who built an ark. Nobody listened to Noah's cry out before the flood came. Victor Savior is the spiritual Noah and Victory Altar is the spiritual Ark.

Sweet Dew   The practical being of the Savior which is in light form. Refer Holy Sweet Dew, Dew Spirit

Tao   means 'way', 'road' or 'teaching' to get to the destination. If you don't know the right(正) way(道), you can't get there; even though you might be able to talk about, practice and teach it. If Tao(道) ends up with death, it would never be the right way. Sakyamuni commented that the right way(正道) will appear in the future with the Sweet Dew(甘露).

The Great Hidden Scriptures A nickname of Buddhist scripts/sutra means it is hiding very important information in it.

Trinity   Biblical Trinity is those three beings who lived in the Kingdom of God; Adam, Eve and God. However, Roman Catholics started to build the idea of Trinity at Concilium Nicaenum Primum in 325AD (God, Jesus as the only son of God), by the decision by the majority. Then added the element of 'Holy Spirit' to complete the idea at Concilium Constantinopolitanum Primum in 382AD (God, Jesus as the only son of God, Holy Spirit)

Trinity Victor The reunited being, God, Eve, and Adam overcome the devil and recover the original form but much much stronger.

True Man Refer JinIn

UFO Some photos of the Holy Dew Spirit which is the flying being looks like a flying saucer. UFO is an abbreviation of Unidentified Flying Object. Man-made objects and images are being used try to convince existence of extraterrestrial being. It is the assumption based on probability and ignorance. However, as the UFO in the Victory Altar exists in this world, you could capture the being by using an analog film camera by yourself.

Victor The God who overcomes Satan is called Victor. In the other hand, The God who is controlled by the spirit of desire Satan is called humanity, sinners.

Victor God A nickname of Savior focusing on its identity which is God itself becoming Savior after achieving victory against Satan

Victor God The loser God is a sinner, human. Our ancestors were anxiously waiting for Messiah's coming. Now a day, however, people forgot even the advent itself due to fakes and ignorance. Messiah of the Victor God has come and speaks new words. Messiah of the Victor God is our homeland of Zion for us to come. Messiah of the Victor God is our role model for us to be. Messiah of the Victor God guide us the path with pouring grace of Holy Due Spirit which is recognizable. However, the new words have been blocked and distorted by the corrupted network including mass media in Korea. With the advent of the Savior in 1980, wars, terrorism, and death could have been prevented on earth. Who will be responsible for the loss?

Victor Savior A nickname of Savior in biblical background

Victory Altar The venue where you can join the Victor Savior's everyday service and meet the Holy Due Spirit

Victress Eve The Olive Tree of the symbol of God recovered its two lost branches of the symbol of Eve and the symbol of Adam and completed the Trinity. Victress Eve trained the candidate of the Victor Adam in the MilSil (the secret chamber) and gave birth to the last Adam.

Yeokgok The administration district in Sosa (소사 素砂 meaning 'white stone') where headquarter of Victory Altar is. Yeok(역 驛) means 'station', Gok(곡 谷) means 'village'. So it is the place to depart and arrive, in other words, alpha and omega.

Yin-yang   The principle of the universe in oriental philosophy. Yin for negative, Yang for positive.

> When perfection comes, the imperfect disappears.
> 1 Corinthians 13:10

The passage was written by Apostle Paul after Jesus's time. The intelligent person who played a key role in the formation of Christianity wrote that the perfection will come because he couldn't find it from Jesus.

The mission of Messiah is to save the world. The reason why Jesus disappeared without completing own mission is that he was a fake.

Read Hangul in an hour

Hangul is Korean letter with which you can record and pronounce sounds easily. A combination of consonant(s) and a vowel completes a character to utter initial, middle and ending sound. Consonants can take initial and ending sound, while vowels middle sound.

There are five basic consonants ㄱ ㄴ ㅁ ㅅ ㅇ ; ㄱ sounds G or K, ㄴ N, ㅁ M, ㅅ S, ㅇ O.

There are three basic vowels ㅡ · ㅣ , the dot in the middle makes variations in conjunction with the first horizontal bar and the last vertical bar. As modern Korean use a shorter dash instead of the dot, when the short dash sits up or down of ㅡ, makes ㅗ and ㅜ. Here ㅗ sounds *o*, ㅜ *wu*. When it sits left or right of ㅣ, makes ㅓ and ㅏ. Here ㅓ sounds *eur*, ㅏ *ar*.

A combination of ㄱ and ㅏ makes 가 ; sounds G + a, *Ga*. ㄴ + ㅏ makes 나 ; sounds N + a, *Na*. Same way, 마 sounds *Ma*, 사 *Sa*. Similary, ㄱ + ㅗ makes 고 ; sounds *Go*. ㄴ + ㅗ makes 노 ; sounds *No*. 모 *Mo*, 소 *So*.

Hangul can extend its sound recording capability by using the ending sound. For example, a set of an initial sound ㄱ, middle sound ㅜ and ending sound ㄴ make 군; G+wu+n pronounces *gwun* or *goon*. ㄱ + ㅜ + ㄱ makes 국, G+wu+k pronounces *gwuk* or *gook*. ㄱ + ㅜ + ㅁ makes 굼, G+wu+m pronounces *Gwum* or *goom*. ㄱ + ㅜ + ㅅ makes 굿. When ㅅ is used for ending sound, it sounds like **t in but**, so G+wu+ut pronounces *Gwut* or *goot*. ㄱ + ㅜ + ㅇ makes 궁. When ㅇ is used for ending sound, it sounds like **ng in sung**, so G+wu+ng sounds *Gwung* or *goong*.

There are more consonants derived from the five basics, also more vowels derived from the three basics. Once you permiliar with corresponding sounds, just use the equation of adding up sequencially, and pronounce the sum naturally, that is it.

It is relatively easy reading/writing Korean regardless your understanding the meaning. As Hangul denotes sounds, sometimes a word has multiple implications. For example, a word 배 implies stomach, ship, x-times, and pear. If the word is used in a sentence or conversation, the meaning would be clear. So you wouldn't have much trouble using the phonetic symbols in everyday life.

Korean sentence structure is (Subject) (Object) (Verb). The (Subject) can hold a subject and possible modifiers. (Object) can be an object and possible modifiers. (Verb) can be a verb and possible modifiers. Simple and easy isn't it? Even if you speak Korean in English structure which is (Subject) (Verb) (Object), most of Korean will be with you and would like to fix your error very friendly.

Because the root of Korean is the royal family which migrated from middle east to far east 3000 years ago, Korean has many honorific modifiers to subject, object, verb and even modifier itself. As those honorific modifiers increase the number of slightly different words to remember, it might be a burden and confuse the first time learner. But don't worry too much, understanding a few standard points can overcome the barrier smoothly.

To enlarge vocabulary will be the next and ongoing challenge.

Let's just start reading Hangul and be familiar with pronunciation! Sing along the hymn in this book with Victor Savior shall be a great start. You can copy the sound and understand the meaning with corresponding translations. You can find audio files at http://victoryaltar.org/hymn

While you sing along with Victor Savior, you might feel air moving, warm or hot ball is coming, coolness, water flow in the stomach, smell like burning paper, lily flower, etc. It is not a strange happening at all, but it is your experience meeting the Victor Savior, the invisible flying existence in this world.

	Initial	Ending	Example	Usual Korean Notation	Possible notation modern Korean	Possible notation early Korean
ㄱ	G, K		god	갓	갓	갓
ㄴ	N		noon	눈	누운	눈
ㄷ	D	:t	dog	독	도옥	독
ㄹ	R, L		road	로드	로오드	로드
ㅁ	M		mother	마더	머더	머더
ㅂ	B, V		baby	베이비	베이비	베이비
ㅅ	S	:t	siera	시에라	씨에라	씨에라
ㅇ	O, U, W	ng, ɧ	orange	오렌지	아리인지	오린지
ㅈ	J, G, Z	:t	james	제임스	췌임스	쩨임스
ㅊ	C	:t	cherry	체리	췌류이	치뤼
ㅋ	K, Q		king	킹	키잉	킹
ㅌ	T	:t	tank	탱크	태앵크	탱크
ㅍ	P, F	:p	papa	파파	파파	ㅍ파
ㅎ	H		hotel	호텔	호테올	호텔
ㅈㅇ	J		jellyfish	젤리피시	젤리ㅍ위쉬	쩰리ㅍ쉬
ㅸ	V		video	비디오	뷔디오우	븨디오
ㆄ	F		father	파더	ㅍ화아더	ㅍ더
ᄛ	L		love	러브	을러어브	러브
ㅿ	Z		zoo	주	쥬우	슈

	Middle					
ㅏ	ar	ɑ				
ㅑ	yar	jɑ				
ㅓ	ur	ə				
ㅕ	yur	jə				
ㅗ	oh	ɔ				
ㅛ	yoh	jɔ				
ㅜ	wu	ʊ				
ㅠ	ywu	jʊ				
ㅡ	none in English but sounds like the L in apple					
ㅣ	ee	ɪ				
ㅐ	ae	æ				
ㅔ	ae	æ				
ㆍ	oar	ʌɑ				
ㆎ	ohh	ɔː				
ㆌ	wuu	ʊː				

기도문 : Gee Doh Mwun : A Prayer

무량대수 : Mwu Ryarng Dae Swu : Unlimited, countless
마귀 : Mar Gwuee : Satan
무량대수 마귀 : countless number of satans

일초 : Eel Choh : One second
동안에 : Dohng An Ae : a while, a span, an interval
일초 동안에 : in a second

횟수로 : Hoht Su Roh : the number of times, frequency
계속해서 : Gae Sohk Hae Sur : continuously
무량대수 횟수로 계속해서 : at unlimited frequency continuously

몽땅 : Mohng Ddarng : all of them
뿌리째 뽑아서 : Bbwu Ree Jjae Bbohb Ar Sur : root out the whole

성령의 : Surng Ryurng Ee : of the Holy Spirit
검으로 : Gurm Ee Roh : with sword
난도질하여 : Narn Doh Geel Ha Yur : mince it and
성령의 검으로 난도질하여 : mince it with the Holy Spirit sword

도끼로 : Do Ggee Ro : with hatchet
짓이겨서 : Geet Ee Gyur Sur : mash it and
성령의 도끼로 짓이겨서 : mash it with the Holy Spirit hatchet

맷돌로 : Maet Dohl Roh : with millstones
갈아서 : Garl Ar Sur : grind it and
성령의 맷돌로 갈아서 : grind it with the Holy Spirit millstones

불로 : Bwul Roh : with blaze
태워서 : Tae Wwuur Sur : burn it and
성령의 불로 태워서 : burn it with the Holy Spirit blaze

유황불로 : Yywu Hoarng Bwul Ro : with the volcanic sulfur flame
박멸소탕 : Bark Myurl So Tang : cleanup

Even though you know laughing is good, but you cannot just laugh.

The source of laughing is God which is the Spirit of Immortality. Satan gives you laughing, too. But it doesn't last long.

Remember that you are a son of God and children of God are God. Only God becomes the Victor after overcoming Satan.

Therefore you must behave as God and a candidate of Victor. You must stop behaving like an aminal fighting each other.

God cannot be selfish, greedy, superficial or worldly. God regards everything as God except Satan, the Self-awareness of 'I'.

Victor is the God overcomes Satan. Whenever God's winning against the Satan, the source of laughing becomes stronger and overflow. The pleasure is endless and has an incredible power to change not only you but also the world.

The incredible power can convert the mortal into the immortal.

Copyright : 2012 © GeumSeong Publishing Company
Address: 49 Angook Street No205 Ave Sosa-gu
Bucheon-si Kyeonggi-do, Korea
Tel : (+82) 32-342-8774
Fax : (+82) 32-342-4367
Date of Publishing : 15 September 2012
ISBN: 978-89-967889-5-9
Price: US $ 15(15000원)
Book Design: SPACE(공간)

www.ingramcontent.com/pod-product-compliance
Lightning Source LLC
Chambersburg PA
CBHW022114080426
42734CB00006B/124